The Barnstaple Staghounds

Richard Lethbridge
MBE

Richard Lethbridge MBE

Edward Gaskell publishers
6 Grenville Street
Bideford
Devon
EX39 2EA

First published 2004

isbn: 1-898546-66-5

The Barnstaple Staghounds

Richard Lethbridge
MBE

Printed and bound by
Lazarus Press
Unit 7 Caddsdown Business Park
Bideford
Devon
EX39 3DX

I dedicate this book to the followers of
the Devon and Somerset, the Tiverton,
and the Quantock Staghounds.

Prosperity to Staghunting.
Long may it continue.

Acknowledgements

I would like to thank everyone who has given me help with this book, especially Sheila Gear, Glenda Tucker, John Parker and the late Arthur Parker all of whom were valuable resources for this project, coming up with photos, hunt buttons and memorabilia relating to their ancestor William Lawrence Ashton, who was an important part of the history of the Barnstaple Staghounds and Barnstaple and North Devon Harriers as huntsman and secretary.

Thanks also go to Pearson Publishing (Baily's Hunting Directory), Michael Sagar (Editor, Hounds Magazine), the staff of the local studies department of Barnstaple Library for copying back-dated *Journal* articles for me, the *North Devon Journal*, *Tiverton Gazette*, Lazarus Press, Hazel Down, Mary-Ann Knill, Andrew May, Mr & Mrs Morgan (Kingdon Gardens), Mark Amory, Edward Holroyd, Terry Gable for her wonderful sketches which enhance this book, Johnny Kingdom, Terry Moule, Steve Knight, Simon Eggleton, John Smith, George and Ann Douglas, S A Hesman (Scenic Prints), Mrs Dallyn (Parracombe), Henry Barrett, Alan Stapleton, Rodney & Shirley Grant, Stuart Brocklehurst. June Bailey. My apologies to anyone I've missed.

Contents

INTRODUCTION

The articles in this book are used courtesy of
The North Devon Journal

Barnstaple seems an unlikely place to have a pack of staghounds, but 100 years ago Barnstaple did indeed have its own hunt. The pack only had a short existence (from 1901-1905, and then reinstated from 1908-1910), and for this reason many people, including some keen staghunters and residents of Barnstaple, know very little, if anything, of this pack.

Through this book I hope to draw people's attention to the Barnstaple Staghounds so their name doesn't fade away, and to relive some of their notable runs for the sake of the heritage of Barnstaple and the hunters in the town and country alike. Due to the obvious lack of first-hand memories, much of my research has been centered on looking through back dated copies of the *North Devon Journal*. The paper's correspondents of the time have left a wealth of information, providing a graphic history of the hunt. We are also lucky that the family of Mr W L Ashton (one-time huntsman of the Barnstaple Staghounds), have still retained his hunt trophies.

The need for a pack of staghounds in the Barnstaple district was apparent in 1897 when numbers of deer were increasing in the valley between Barnstaple and Arlington and, in consequence, doing a considerable amount of damage to crops adjoining the large covers on Sir Arthur Chichester's property. For seasons past the Devon and Somerset Staghounds had put in an occasional day and some fine runs had been experienced from the neighbourhood. But the deer were now so numerous that it was thought desirable for more hunting to take place along the valley. Mr C H Basset made a representation to this effect to the Master of the Devon and Somerset, and the latter kindly permitted Mr Basset to invite Sir John Amory's Staghounds (now known as the Tiverton Staghounds), to come down to the district. They arrived with Sir John's son, Ian Amory, who was hunting his fathers hounds at the time. Accommodation was provided for horses, hounds and servants at Pilton stables, while Ian Amory and the whips (Messrs De las Casas) were entertained at Westaway by Mr Basset.

Mr Ian Amory of Sir John Amory's Staghounds, who brought his father's hounds down to hunt the Barnstaple district from 1897-1900 and was the guest of Mr C H Basset of Westaway

Mr Charles H Basset was a former Master of the Devon and Somerset Staghounds (1887-1893), and played a prominent role in establishing the Barnstaple Staghounds. He became an MP for a short period, representing Barnstaple in Parliament. Mr Basset married the eldest daughter of the late Mr Arthur Davie-Basset, of Watermouth Castle (Miss Harriet Mary Bassett), and when his wife succeeded to the property at Watermouth and Umberleigh estates on the death of her brother, the Rev Arthur Davie-Basset in 1880, he assumed the name of Basset in lieu of his original patronyme, Williams. He became a very practical Master of Staghounds, and on more than one occasion he harboured the stags himself. Mr Basset only had one arm, having lost the other in an accident whilst working a steam engine at Barnstaple in 1873. As a cattle and horse breeder, he was looked upon as owning some of the best blood to be found in the West of England, he kept what has often been described as a model farm at Westaway, with a splendid herd of pedigree cattle, which contained some fine class beasts.

Mr C H Basset, former Master of the Devon and Somerset Staghounds (1887-1893).

Photograph taken from *British Hunts and Huntsmen of the South West*, printed 1908.

Westaway House, Mr Basset's home at Barnstaple, where Ian Amory and the Messrs De las Casas were entertained while hunting in the Barnstaple district. In 1901 the Barnstaple Staghounds killed a stag in the pool close to the house.

On the wall at Westaway, Mr Basset's coat of arms and a 'fine beast' from his model farm.

Photographs © Richard Lethbridge with thanks to Andrew May and Stuart Brocklehurst

8

Mr Ian Amory continued hunting hounds in the Barnstaple district until 1900 when he withdrew. This was partly because Miss Chichester of Arlington Court, who was against hunting at the time, made it very uncomfortable for him when she applied for an injunction to stop hounds from entering her property.

A need now arose for a permanent pack of staghounds. In response Peter Ormrod, who had a pack of hounds in Lancashire known as Peter Ormrod's Staghounds, came forward and agreed to bring down 30 couple of hounds to hunt the district. Mr Ormrod had been in the habit of hunting carted deer in and around Wyresdale, and his long cherished desire was to hunt the red deer in its natural state. At his first opening meet at Old Youlston Park, Shirwell, around 600-700 people attended. While Mr Ormrod was hunting in the district Mr C H Basset, with his usual kindness, placed the kennels and stables at Pilton House at his disposal. The newspapers of the time sometimes referred to the pack as Peter Ormrod's Staghounds and sometimes as the Barnstaple Staghounds. The kennels at this stage were in the grounds of Pilton House and are thought by many to be where the row of cottages called River View are situated in Higher Raleigh Road today. The kennel-man's cottage was the one on the end, nearest the Pilton Causeway. There is a long low building adjoining the left hand side of the end cottage, now incorporated as part of the living accommodation, which was probably the kennel building.

Pilton House where Sir John Amory's Staghounds and Peter Ormrod's Staghounds were kenneled while hunting the Barnstaple district. Later, the Cheriton Otter Hounds were also kenneled here. Today this is a residential home.

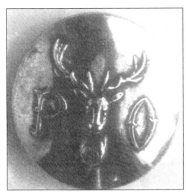
Peter Ormrod's hunt button

This set up continued until 1901 when the parting of the waves became apparent; newspaper reports give Peter Ormord's last season as being inglorious with no desire to resume connections upon either side. From 1904-1905 Peter Ormrod became Master of the Exmoor Foxhounds and at the same time brought his staghounds down to hunt the deer on Exmoor.

In the second part of 1901 a new regime took over with hounds being procured at considerable expense from different parts of the United Kingdom. This was the year the Barnstaple Staghounds were officially established and was constituted under the Joint Mastership of Capt Ewing Paterson (Adjutant of the Royal North Devon Imperial Yeomanry) from Bickington Lodge, and Mr Arundell Clarke of Fremington. The Bailys hunting directory tells us the kennels were at Sowden. Another pack, known as the Barnstaple and North Devon Harriers (who mostly hunted the hare but occasionally hunted the fox and deer), were situated at the same kennels; paper reports of the time suggest it was more desirable and cost effective for both packs to share, and this seemed to be the case with the Masters hunting both packs. In 1902 the Barnstaple Staghounds moved into new kennels at Brynsworthy.

In 1903 news came that Capt Paterson was to give up the Mastership as he was leaving the district, as his period of service as Adjutant of the

Peter Ormrod

10

Royal North Devon Imperial Yeomanry was then expiring. Mr Arundell Clarke felt bound to retire also as no one came forward to join him in the Mastership. The pack was sold, causing great regret in sporting circles, and was secured by Mr E A V Stanley, Master of the Quantock Staghounds, although some of the hounds went to the New Forest in Hampshire. It was suggested at the time that Mr A L Christie might take on the Mastership, but with various difficulties in his way, he declined the offer. It was thought that staghunting might continue with the Barnstaple and North Devon Harriers, and it seemed to do so for a time.

Within a short period newspaper reports of the Barnstaple Staghounds were appearing again, suggesting the pack had reformed. Lieut E G Chichester RN, (son of Sir Edward Chichester, Bart), became temporary Master, and during his absence on His Majesty's Service, his father took on as deputy Master with Major Penn Curzon as field Master and, on occasions, Mr C H Basset as Master. In 1904 writing, from sea, Lieut E G Chichester now placed his resignation in the hands of the committee owing to his prolonged absence in the King's Service. Major Penn-Curzon was unanimously elected as the new Master.

Major Ernest Charles Penn-Curzon was holder of a distinguished military record. Son of the late Colonel, the hon Ernest George Curzon, Major Curzon was born in 1856, was educated privately, and joined the army in 1877. He secured his first commission in the old 34th Regiment, being transferred shortly afterwards to the staff of the late Sir Ashley Eden, Lieut General of Bengal, as ADC. In 1882 he was transferred to the Hussars and five years later to the 18th Hussars. He served in the South African war as Chief Regiment Officer to Sir Fred Carrington's column in Rhodesia, and later became head of the Remounts at Blomfontein. For five years he was Adjutant to the Leicestershire Yeomanry. Major Penn-Curzon was a keen huntsman, and hunted in India and Africa and became Master of the Shorncliff Draghounds. In 1882 he married Edith Basset, daughter of Mr Charles Henry Basset, former Master of the Devon and Somerset Staghounds and instigator of the Barnstaple Staghounds. Major and Mrs Penn-Curzon were married in the Curzon chapel, Mayfair, London, the chapel being specially loaned by the Archbishop of Canterbury.

Sir William Williams, Bart
From *Hunts and Huntsman of the South West*, published 1908

In 1905 the Barnstaple Staghounds were sold because the country was so confined and due to the hindrance to hunting caused by certain estates that were closed to all packs, but the Barnstaple and North Devon Harriers remained. From 1905-1908 the Bailys hunting directory reports no hunting, although a few reports were given of the Barnstaple Staghounds during that period. In 1908 the Barnstaple Staghounds were started up again on a smaller scale with Mr B Chester appointed as the new Master. This continued until 1910, and this is the last we hear of the hounds.

In 1910 a public meeting was held in Barnstaple to consider the question of hunting the deer in the Barnstaple country in the forthcoming season. This was when the Minehead Staghounds came on the scene. They were a draft pack from the Devon and Somerset Staghounds and were established to counter the damage being done by the enormous herds of deer in their district. While coping with their own deer, they were now appointed to also hunt the Barnstaple dis-

These derelict buildings at Springfield near Ashford are thought to have been the kennels of the Barnstaple Staghounds.
© Richard Lethbridge

12

trict with their Master, Mr J W Ridler. This continued until March 1911 when they seemed to suddenly disappear. With no further reports, we can safely say that this was now the end of staghunting in the Barnstaple district.

My research on the Barnstaple Staghounds has revealed much more than I expected and has revealed a host of additional sporting activities surrounding Barnstaple:

The Barnstaple Fair meet held each year at Yarde Down by the Devon and Somerset Staghounds probably doesn't have much significance to many people, but over a hundred years ago, the Barnstaple Fair Staghunt was one of the main attractions of fair week, and it was the custom if possible to bring the stag into or near the town. Venison had long played a part in the ceremonies surrounding the fair. As far back as 1582 a note was made in the accounts of the collectors and receivers of Barnstaple for £1-14s-4d, which was paid to the Mayor for the cost of eating venison by the town council. At different times the Cheriton Otterhounds were also kennelled in Barnstaple, at Pilton House, Brynsworthy and the Barnstaple repository.

In the 1870s the Barnstaple Harriers were mentioned in the papers but there was no indication as to where they were kennelled. Later, in 1893, the Barnstaple and North Devon Harriers were formed, being kennelled at Brynsworthy and later at Sowden. In 1879 Sir William Williams got together a pack of beagles, in the same year promoting them to harriers, and hunting the country around his home of Upcott (Barnstaple) until 1883. He then bought the hon Mark Rolle's pack and hunted the Stevenstone country four days a week until 1892, during which time the hounds were known as Sir William William's hounds. Mr Rolle then wanted to hunt his own country again, and Sir William resigned the greater part of the Stevenstone to him, although he retained by courtesy a portion of the country. Meanwhile Sir William hunted one day a week on his own side of Barnstaple (the North), his kennels, which he erected at his own expense, then being at Springfield near Ashford. At the end of two years, Sir William gave up his slice of hunting country and took over the Mastership of the Exmoor Foxhounds until his death in 1903.

From more than one authority Springfield was also thought to be the kennels for the Barnstaple Staghounds at one time, this would have been quite feasible after Sir William Williams' death, as the premises would have been an ideal location to locate these hounds.

Barnstaple also had a Badger club known as the Barnstaple and North Devon Badger Club, formed in 1914. The last hunt to operate around the Barnstaple district was the North West Devon Drag Hunt, which was formed in 1934 and disbanded at the start of the war. Local meets included one in the town at North Walk. Other sporting activities in the town included early point to point races known as the Barnstaple and North Devon Races, and the Barnstaple Horse and Hound show.

The Quantock Staghounds.
Without transport years ago, the pack was kenneled at the nearest farmhouse.

CHAPTER 1

BARNSTAPLE AND ITS EARLY CONNECTIONS WITH HUNTING,
AND THE FAIR STAGHUNTS

S
ince the formation of a pack of staghounds on Exmoor,
the residents of Barnstaple who were keen sportsmen
joined in; the town being within easy distance of the
moor. The earliest record of staghunting on Exmoor was found
by Charles Palk Collyns, (the author of an 1892 publication on
the chase of the wild red deer). He discovered that in the year
1598, Hugh Pollard Esq, ranger of Queen Elizabeth, kept a pack
of staghounds at Simonsbath. Examples of Barumites following
the hounds on the moor are given below.

In 1872 at the opening meet of the Devon and Somerset
Staghounds, several carriages were seen to be making their way
over the moors including one from the Royal and Fortescue
Hotel in Barnstaple. The report goes on to say "we noticed
excelled turn outs from Bonds Wellington Hotel, from Davies
Red Lion, Dulverton, from Fitze's Royal and Fortescue,
Barnstaple, and a brake and four, with postilions, from South
Molton. On arriving at the meadow, in accordance with the
time-honoured custom, every corner was regaled with bread,
cheese and beer from the cellar of the Baronet of Killerton."

In 1879 the Prince of Wales attended a meet of the Devon and
Somerset Staghounds at Hawkcombe Head where 8 thousand
attended. At the end of the day the Prince dispatched the stag.
The newspaper report says that "it naturally excited great

15

interest in Barnstaple and the vicinity; a large number of people leaving for the scene of the hunt on Friday." Indeed, Barnstaple rather distinguished itself on the occasion, for not only were the two horses which the prince rode supplied by Mr W Gibbings, but Mr Williams of Joy Street was in at the end. Mr Gabriel Litson of Bedford Street, Barnstaple, a very familiar figure in hunting circles, was also there at the end and held the antlers while the Prince administered the coup de grace and was privileged to be present at tea with his royal highness and his party afterwards.

In 1881 the Devon and Somerset Staghounds met at Eggesford Station, the paper goes on to say that at least 500 people put in an appearance while some of the older huntsmen computed the number at 600 and the spectators at 1000. It was reported that 27 horses went off from Barnstaple.

The *Journal* from 1908 says "A very large number of vehicles, motor cars etc, left Barnstaple for the historic meet of the Devon and Somerset Staghounds at Cloutsham early yesterday morning. Messrs F Robbins of Pilton and Richard Crang of Bear Street, the veteran cyclists, who have attended for a number of years were again present. The journey is an arduous and rough one of over 30 miles, and Messrs Crang and Robbins are to be congratulated for their pluck." In 1912 it was reported that Messrs Crang and Robbins were prevented from visiting the opening meet at Cloutsham owing to the inclement weather. In 1913 they were able to attend the opening meet. The paper goes on to say, "Motor cars and conveyances of various kinds continued to arrive during the morning, until at midday some 130 motors were gathered on the open moors. Among the visitors were Barum's veteran cyclists Richard Crang and Mr F Robbins who, in spite of their seventy odd years, again undertook the journey. Leaving Barnstaple at 5 o'clock yesterday morning, they arrived in good time for the meet, reaching home last night at 10 pm."

While the Barumites were not staghunting, they were busy out with the local hunts which included a day out they had at Tawstock in 1872 with the Hon Mark Rolle's Foxhounds. A correspondent for the *Journal* wrote:

A day with the Hon Mark Rolle's Hounds

"Splendid! – magnificent! my dear sir!" – such was the exclamation of a friend of mine as together we trotted up Sticklepath Hill on Monday to the meet of the above hounds, all eager for the chase like an hungry man for his dinner. According to notice duly given the beautiful "lady" pack of the Hon Mark Rolle was to meet at eleven at Western Lodge, Tawstock, and half of Barnstaple turned out to see them, it being, as was epigrammatically intimated by the expression of my friend, "a most magnificent opportunity." The sky was clear, the air crisp, and the ground firm. No wonder, then, that so many of our Barum gentlemen – and ladies too – wended their way with us to the spot where all the sportsmen in the neighbourhood not otherwise engaged were expected to assemble. And not only did the Barumites come out in great force, but from all the country round came the people, both on horse and on foot, until a field had congregated such as really is seldom seen. It was verily a glorious sight. The spot selected for the meeting was one in which the different aspects of such a scene were well displayed. The red-coats and the other equestrians on their prancing steeds, the ever-moving and uneasy hounds, impatient for the run, the throng of people on foot "of all sorts and conditions of men" – the whole of these being grouped in one grand picture – formed a sight never to be forgotten. The meet was by far the most brilliant held in North Devon this season, save and except that time which will long be remembered, not only by sportsmen, but by all who know the worthy master of the pack

Sir William Williams' Foxhounds
November 1st 1889

As a preliminary to the opening meet of the above pack of hounds, a non-advertised meet took place on Monday at Horridge, near Barnstaple. The occasion was arranged mostly for the benefit of Sir William's tenantry, who came to Horridge in full force, and well mounted. In addition there were a few sporting friends from Barnstaple and the neighbourhood. The hounds came into Barnstaple from the kennels at Torrington about nine o'clock, stopping at Bradiford (Sir William's residence), and proceeding to Horridge, for a short time where the field assembled at 11 o'clock. Among the ladies were Lady Williams, Miss Hibbert, Miss Brown, Miss Willink and Miss Swaine. There were also Messrs E Hext, J Harper, R Vickery, Mullar, G Davey, JFR Morris, C Skinner, T Horn, W A Roberts,

W V Richards, T H Pitts-Tucker, R Pethebridge, King, J Elliott, G Ashton, Darke, and Mr and Mrs De Guerin. A most sumptuous lunch was provided for the tenantry, who were wamly welcomed by Sir William and Lady Williams by hearty shakes of the hand. The hounds were first taken off to Ash Wood, and on to the Old Warren, where we found our fox. Master Reynard showed good sport to those who were on foot, from the fact of his being seen so many times running up and down. He would not be roused very often, evidently imagining that never having been disturbed before he had more right to the Warren than anybody else. The result was that he was chopped there and then without giving a run, much to the disappointment of those who were well mounted. After this the Master, with his usual desire to show good sport, trotted the hounds in through Barnstaple to the other side of the bridge into Tawstock parish. There the hounds were taken to Yarnscombe where a fox was found in Court Wood. He gave a good spin of quite two hours, when darkness coming on the run finished, and all set out for home.

The Barnstaple sportsmen were also hunting the hare as we see from a meet at Roundswell in 1889 – a place we know so well today, but I imagaine it wasn't quite as busy then.

Hunt dinner and meet of the Ilfracombe Harriers
December 26th 1889

This pack met at Roundswell near Barnstaple on Thursday last, with about 40 horsemen and a like number on foot. The harriers drew for a radius of about five miles but the day proved blank. In the evening a dinner was held at the King's Arms Hotel.

The Fair Stag Hunts

The tradition of holding a staghunt during Barnstaple fair quickly became one of the chief attractions during the week's celebrations. In ancient times it was the custom, if possible, to bring the stag into or near the town. Newspaper reports referred to it as the "Fair Staghunt", and the custom of the fair stag hunt is still kept up today; the Devon and Somerset Staghounds always meet at the Poltimore Arms at Yarde Down near Brayford during fair week as they have for many years. The *North Devon Herald* of 27th September 1888 reports that James Richards and Francis Huxtable were summoned for being drunk and disorderly on the 20th August at the Poltimore

Arms, Yarde Down the day the staghounds met there. Venison had long played a part in the ceremonies surrounding the Fair. As far back as 1582 a note was made in the accounts of the collectors and receivers of Barnstaple for £1 14s 4d which was paid to the Mayor for the cost of eating venison by the whole town council. The Barnstaple records show a report from 1796: "September 22nd, Staghunting day nearly 400 horses out but did not kill."

There follows part of a poem which refers to the staghunt at Barnstaple fair, from the *Cave* periodical, 1824.

The French, alas! go à la Chasse in ron po shay and pair
But what's all that to Button Hill, to Barnstaple Fair.

For we will all a-hunting go, on horse, or mule, or mare, sir!
For everything is in the field to Barnstaple fair, sir!

To Button Hill, whose name to all the sporting world sure known is,
Go bits of blood, and hunters, hacks, and little Exmoor ponies,
When Lords and ladies, doctors, parsons, farmers, squires, prepare,
To hunt the stag, with hound and horn, to Barnstaple fair.

Then up and ride for Chillam Bridge, or on to Bratton Town, sir,
To view the rouse, or watch the Yeo, to see the stag come down, sir.

There follow newspaper cuttings from staghunts held during the fair week.

September 10th 1824
Fair Staghunt

We have great pleasure to inform our readers that every considerable interest is excited to preserve this truly noble diversion now only to be met with in the North of Devon, and which, combined with the majestic scenery of the country, presents to the admirers of field sports, a gratification not to be equalled perhaps in Europe. And we are authorised to say, that through the interference of several of the leading gentlemen of the hunt, a very respectable and numerous attendance is expected at the ensuing annual dinner at Barnstaple, on the first day of the fair, when a buck will be given on the occasion by a gentleman who has the prosperity of the staghunt much at heart.

September 24th 1824

The staghunt dinner at the rooms was very respectably attended
by the admirers of the chase. J Knight in the Chair supported
by the treasurer J Law esq. Our annual Fair Ball on Wednesday
was attended by nearly 200 of the most respectable families in
the town and neighbourhood. The Ball was opened by Miss
Burry and Car Clay esq, and the dancing was kept up to a late
hour. On Tuesday last the staghounds met at Bratton, and
turned a galloper from North Woolley, which was lost under
Yeotown, by three hinds starting up before the dogs, this together with the heavy rains rendered further pursuit impracticable,
and disappointed the expectations of a large field of sportsmen,
we are informed, to the number of 300.

September 1827
Fair Staghunt

Sir Arthur Chichester's Hounds met on Saturday last, according
to appointment at Bratton Town, about eleven o'clock onwards
of about 200 horses were in the field, and a great number of
pedestrians, the tufters were put into Smythapark Wood, and a
remarkable fine five year old deer was turned out, which made
off through Bratton Town to Haxton Down and Leworthy Bridge,
from thence to Buscombe, Shoulsberry Castle, Moles Chamber,
and over the forestry to Exford Town, and was killed about two
miles below Exford in the parish of Winsford. A finer chase could
scarcely be rode, the greater part of the time. Though so large a
concourse of huntsmen were present at the rousing of the deer,
not more than half a dozen were in at the death.

The Fair Staghunt 1830

The Stag Hunt, on Tuesday, afforded high gratification. At the appointed hour a field of several hundred sportsmen assembled on Bratton Down, and to prevent disappointment a Wild Stag had been previously secured and was turned out by Sir Arthur Chichester's huntsman. It was a noble animal, seven years old; and bounded off in full view in fine style; he took the direction to Highbray, and at the bottom of Braywood turned off and made for the Forest, over Wallover and Fullover Downs and Challacombe Common; when near Lynton, he turned and came back nearly in the same direction, and was killed after a very splendid and interesting chase, at the bottom of Little Bray Wood, about one hundred sportsmen being in at the death. To the public spirited conduct of Sir Arthur Chichester, the admirers of staghunting are especially indebted for reviving and perpetuating this sport, so peculiar to the North of Devon who at great personal expence harbours the game, and furnishes the hunt.

The Ball on Tuesday evening was attended by upwards of one hundred and sixty ladies and gentlemen; several of the country families of distinction were present; and so agreeable was the assembly, that they did not separate till four o'clock in the morning.

September 1839 – The Fair Stag Hunt

The stag was let off on Bratton Down, in the presence of a large field and shortly afterwards the Devon and Somerset hounds were laid on. The stag took the course across Leworthy Farm, down the bottom under Ovice, through Wort Wood and Little Bray to the river a little below Brayford Bridge where he was killed, about 15 horsemen were in at the taking. The run occupied about three quarters of an hour.

September 1840
(The Fair Staghunt)

The fair staghunt which was anciently one of the most attractive accompaniments of Barnstaple fair, was revived this year. It was intended to come off on Tuesday, but the very heavy rains indiced its postponement until Wednesday. The Devon and Somerset Staghounds met at Shallowford, near Castle Hill, at half past ten, the field comprised upwards of 200. Having tried the cover of Bremridge Wood without success the hounds were led up the valley to Withygate in North Molton and the tufters tried Bera Wood and roused a fine hind, which made across Yarde Down, where she was met by the whole pack scarcely ten yards off. She then went over the fence into the forest at the Western end and made directly across it above Simonsbath over Withypool Common to Hawkridge Cover and at the adjoining Coombe, about four miles from Hawkridge, the hounds lost the scent and were called off at half part three. The morning was very unpromising and there were heavy showers through the day and in consequence of the rains of the last two or three days the turf on the forest was in very bad state. Out of the field of 200 only eight followed the hounds across the forest, the rest going over by road to Simonsbath and Hawkridge. It is remarkable that out of the 8 horses which maintained the chase throughout, one was a grey pony only 11 1/2 hands high, ridden by Mr Geo Thorne junr of West Buckland, whose extraordinary speed excited general admiration. A large party of gentlemen from the return of the hunt dined together at Marsh's "Golden Lion hotel."

September 1850

The staghunt, one of the oldest – and formerly among the most admired and popular – amusements of the Fair week, took place on Saturday last. It was but a shadow of its former self; for instead of the red deer aroused in his native covers by the noble staghounds, whose deep-toned voice was wont "to make the welk in ring," a four-year-old stag, who had spent the last 18 months in captivity at winkleigh, was brought to Bratton Down enclosure and hunted by a merrie park of harriers. The field preserved some relics of its ancient glory, for it boasted the pleasure of every regular sportsman in the neighbourhood, and of every tyro who could get a mount for the occasion. The fixture was at half past ten, but owing to the heavy rains of the preceding night, the Master of the hounds (Mr Luxton, of Winkleigh), was unable to cross the River Taw – the rains having so much swollen the ordinary stream – until after a delay of two hours or more, causing an exercise of patience of the field for about the same length of time, which was taxed the more by frequent and drenching showers. At half past one the stag arrived and was uncarted on Sir Arthur Chichester's allotment. On leaving his conveyance, he quietly surveyed the assembled field, as if hesitating in which direction to escape; and after a moment's pause, made off at a good pace, clearing the shore fence on each side of the Combe Martin turnpike. After giving him twenty minutes' law, the pack was laid on. The scent was bad over the open, but improved towards the Arlington and Loxhore covers, which was the direction the stag had taken. It was hoped, by some who remembered the pleasure of the chase in the former days, when the stag was driven into and through the town of Barnstaple, that he would take the same course on this occasion, and that the townspeople might have the novelty of joining in the hunt. In this, however, they were mistaken, for it soon became apparent that the stag was too fat to run; and instead of bodily taking any decided line, he preferred dodging about the Didicombe covers, until finding them too hot to hold him, he went away to Bratton Down where he was very nearly captured, but succeeded in reaching Stoke Wood, and there dead beat, he yielded himself to his pursuers and was taken uninjured after a rambling and unsatisfactory chase of about two hours. It was now half past three o'clock, and the master of the North Devon Harriers, with that desire to afford sport which is always characteristic of him, announced his intention of trying for a fox in Shortland brake. The hounds were at Leworthy, and lost no time in unkennelling Mr Reynard, who went away in right gallant style across the moor, and after a short burst of twenty five minutes without a check, he was glad to seek shelter in Tinnery Earths.

Courtesy of Tom Bartlett's Postcard Collection
A Barnstaple Fair postcard from 1907

23

September 1851
The Fair Staghunt

The staghunt on Tuesday was a failure. In ancient times when this sport was in its glory, it formed one of the chief attractions of Barnstaple fair and it was always an object, if possible, to bring the stag into or near the town. Of late years however, the practice has not been kept up, although generally there have been fixtures made in the fair week for the gratification of those of the visitors who might incline to the amusments of the field. This year the Bath Staghounds, now hunting the Exmoor Country, had their meet at Yarde Down. To accommodate the fashionables, whose late hour at the ball the night before might make an eariler meet inconvenient, the hounds did not throw off until 12 o'clock, at which hour the tufters were thrown into Span Wood to draw for a stag which was reported to be there, but after a delay of two or three hours, no stag being found, the hounds were taken away much to the disappointment of a large field of ladies and gentlemen who were assembled to witness the find. The hounds then drew Cornham Brake, near Simonsbath, but the party were again doomed to disappointment and the largest party of the field turned their horses heads homewards and we understand the day terminated without any sport. To make it worse a party of 150 met at Leworthy Cross near Bratton for which, by error, it would appear the fixture was published.

September 7th 1853
Hunting
To the Editor of the *North Devon Journal*

Sir – Whilst you are gratifying one section of your readers by giving them the evidence extracted by the Commissioners, who are now sitting and unmasking the frailty of human nature, may I hope to entertain another portion by recording our splendid run of Friday, which may be mentioned amongst the most brilliant in the annals of the chase. The propinquity of the stars on the preceding evening foreboded unfavourable weather, and a more forbidding morning is seldom ushered in than was that of Friday. The rain for hours poured down in torrents, when not a patch of blue was visible in the sky to indicate a brighter prospect. However a ray of hope was lit up about 10 o'clock, by the wind shifting and blowing from the north, and soon after the horizon in that quarter had a brighter aspect; at length old Sol lent his aid and speedily the clouds disappeared.

Brendon was the appointed spot, and the much-esteemed master of the excellent pack, with his usual punctuality, was at his post with the welcome news that a stag had been harboured in and was lying in Parsonage Wood. He was speedily roused with the pack on his haunches, when with one bound the copse he cleared, and seemed to say "Little I value you all." By each stride the distance was increased between himself and his pursuers. He continued in view of the horsemen for a mile and half, and by his appearance and running showed that he was a galloping deer. He first made for Scobhill; then pointing towards Badgworthy, he reached to Trouthill on the moor. Here we nearly lost our valued huntsman in a bog. On we went to Larksborough, crossing Porlock Common, thence to Dunkerry Beacon, and Horner Hill, by the side of Pinchcombe; from thence to Porlock, through as beautiful a country as can be seen amongst nature's choicest prospects. Here he sought refuge in a mill stream, swollen by innumerable feeders from the adjoining hills, and rushing on with irresistible rapidly. It was bounded on either side by an embankment 20 feet high, with a cascade above and a tunnel below, through which the stream passed on towards a mill. Our object were to stop it and to interpose a ladder between the deer and the tunnel, which was effected and the stag was secured for our Barnstaple Fair Hunt.

Honoured names of departed ancestors! How this manly sport harmonised with their feelings! Cementing friendship and creating joy wherever their presence was obtained. The names of Acland, Bassett, Fortescue, Chichester and Fellowes were connected by the Patriarchs in the evening with Brendon, Badgworthy, Dulverton, and Horner, with as much glee as our old veterans of the Peninsula still revert to Talavera, Salamanca and Vittoria in connection with the great general of the time. – Exmoor is still wild and uncultivated; therefore the deer have not to fly like the aborigines of America at the approach of civilization: they are protected by formidable hills wood and water; and long may they exist and our noble sport continue to be the pride of our country!

I am, Sir, your obedient servant,
A LOVER OF HUNTING.

An advert from 1886 for Hon John Fortescue's book

HUNTING APPOINTMENTS
1853

The Devon and Somerset Stag Hounds will meet on Wednesday, the 21st of September, at Slowly Wood, at 11 o'clock; and on Saturday the 24th (being the Barnstaple fair hunt), at Challacombe village, at 12 o'clock.

THE DEVON AND SOMERSET STAGHOUNDS
Octber 17th 1889

A most successful meet of the Devon and Somerset Staghounds took place at Leworthy Post. It had been known for a long time that, by the kindness of Mr Comer Clarke, deer were being encouraged at Smythy Park, and in the Barnstaple fair week a good run was enjoyed as the result of a meet at this place. On Wednesday the Master (Mr C H Basset) again arranged a meet mostly to oblige sportsmen in and around Barnstaple. Although the weather was stormy a goodly muster made their appearance, including J Harper, S N Adams, H K Thorne, R Vickery, E Mugford, T Horn, W V Richards, E S Hext, the Rev Hole, the Rev J Chichester, Pugsley, Comer Clarke, besides Miss Kingslake, Mr J Huxtable, Rock (3), Lord Ebrington MP, Miss Beadon, and Mrs Lock, Roe. The hounds were kennelled at Mr W C Bowden's at Knightscott. Arthur put in the tufters, and the stag broke very quickly, going off through Teddicombe and Twitchen Wood, Westland, across the road, then after a few enclosres past Tinnerly then on to Chapman Burrows, then on to Lingstone, Pinkerry, Farley Water, across the road from Simonsbath to Brendon Two Gates to Badgworthy, across the stream, up over the Deer Park; afterwards to Chalk Water, Luccott, under Cloutsham, and to Horner, where the stag doubled back to Luccombe village. After this he was at bay in the road, making it very dangerous to horses and riders, but he crossed a field, jumped a fence, the hounds still following him, when he turned back and charged them. He then jumped another fence into the Parsonage Lawn, where he was killed. Most of the Barnstaple men were in at the kill. The distance from find to kill was, as the crow flies, about 22 miles, and the whole distance traversed was nearly 30 miles – done in about two hours and twenty minutes, which was admitted by all old hands to have beaten the record. The stag was a fine fellow, about eight years old. The next day he was sent back to Mr Comer Clarke.

Sportsmen will be sorry to learn that at the close of staghunting, and before hind hunting commences, the veteran huntsman to the Devon and Somerset Staghounds will retire. He feels that he is unable at his age to continue in the position. Mr Heal, or "Arthur" as he is familiarly called, has been connected with this famous pack the greater part of half a century, and his judgment and practical experience of every detail of the sport rendered his help almost indispensable.

Chase
Devon and Somerset Staghounds
29th September 1896

The meeting of the Devon and Somerset Staghounds on Saturday was at Yard Down. Anticipations ran pretty high, for on the corresponding day for two years past this meet has afforded excellent runs, the Master reserving Yard Down as the fixture for the day after Barnstaple Fair. Two years ago the stag took us from Highbray to Umberleigh Weir, and last year there was a very fast moorland run to the Doone Valley from the same spot. The meet was a large one, almost everyone in the district owning a horse and pretending to ever so little riding was present, and there could not have been many less than 300 horsemen at Yard Down. It is almost useless to give names, because one can scarcely mention a staghunting sportsman who did not put in an appearance. Among many others I noticed the Master and Mrs Sanders, the Secretary (Mr Evered), Lord and Lady Ebrington, Baroness Taintegnies, Mrs Muirhead, Captain and Mrs Curson, Miss Hurst and the Hon Copplestone and Mrs Bamfylde. Unfortunately, Goss, the harbourer, was unable to report anything but a young deer, the heavy stag which had been lying in the Bray covers for some time having left the neighbourhood. But in Fernham Wood he had harboured a three-year-old stag. So the hounds were at once taken to Gratton and kennelled, while Anthony with four couples of tufters, soon had the stag on foot. After two or three turns up and down the valley he finally broke cover from Wort Wood, and came up over Gratton in view of the whole field making for Whitefield Common. Hopes ran high, and they were not disappointed, that we should have a good moorland run. The Master galloped back for the pack, which was speedily laid, and the hounds carried the line up the stream, running underneath Beara Wood, the "field" having capital galloping ground over Whitefield Common. The stag, turning to the right underneath the Poltimore Arms, pointed for a short distance as though for Long Wood and North Molton, but, happily, when near Flydon he again pointed for Exmoor, taking us over Fivebarrows, where the horsemen encountered several patches of soft ground, which was the cause of more than one saddle being relieved of its weight. Nothing more serious occurred. The hounds now ran down to the Kenford water, carrying the line on to Sheardown and past Lanacre Bridge to Withypool. Just beyond there the stag was refound, and he retraced his steps to Lanacre Bridge, going up the Barle as far as Honeymead. The stag was killed half-way between Honeymead and Simonsbath, after a good and exciting run of 3¹/₂ hours. Taking the various points into consideration, without reckoning the contour of the hills, the distance covered was about fifteen miles, and is, so far, the best run of the season.

SPORTSMAN

The Devon and Somerset Staghounds, who still keep up the tradition of meeting during the Barnstaple Fair Week, at Yarde Down near Brayford, seen here is Dennis Boyles (Huntsman), alongside Bob Nancekivell (one-time Master) celebrating his 90th birthday at home in 1990. © *North Devon Journal*

The Barnstaple Fair Staghunt of September 2003.
The Devon and Somerset Staghounds meet at the Poltimore Arms, Yarde Down

Mr and Mrs Richard Austin gave a large crowd a most hospitable welcome at the traditional Barnstaple Fair meet at the Poltimore Arms, Yarde Down, on Saturday the 20th. Tufters were taken to Fyldon Wood, and were quickly away over Fyldon Hill to Lyddicombe and Yarde Wood. However, when this stag climbed out as if to cross the top road, it was decided to go back to

Poster from Barnstaple Fair 2003

the harbourer's second string in Sportsman's. Only a younger stag was on the move, but news now came of a suitable stag lying at the top of Durcombe, and so Donald took the pack there. Rousing him immediately, they came away to Sportsman's, and down past Barham to Mines and the bottom of Long Wood. Crossing the road to Radworthy Down, they hunted in to South Wood, dropped down to the Isle of Dogs, and hunted steadily all up Waterworks Combe almost to Tabor Hill Drive. Swinging back high over Barcombe Down now, they crossed the road under Brinsworthy and hunted down through Broomball Plantation to the Mole. The stag had made a complete circuit around under Court Place, and hounds worked up to him out of the water, to come out short of Cross Lane Cross into Oakford Copse. Hunting on to Venn Wood, they crossed the valley to Flitton Wood, and sailed away to Northland Cross, where they were held up and gathered together. Let go again, they took it on to Lowdy Cleave, and steadily down the valley, to cross the main road at the Lion's Rump and in to the Bray. Cast downstream to Brayley Bridge, the stag could be splashed for several hundred yards below, before hounds hit the line out over Park

Wood and out across the fields above Park, almost to Proutworthy Brake, before coming to another check. A forward cast failed and, with the hour getting late, home was blown after a most interesting hunt.

PRICKET

The Poltimore Arms at Yarde Down near Brayford where the Barnstaple Fair Stag Hunt has taken place for many years. The tradition is still kept alive today by the Devon and Somerset Staghounds.
© Richard Lethbridge

It was also traditional for the Cheriton Otterhounds to meet on the Saturday after the fair as seen from a meet in 1891

Cheriton Otterhounds Fair Meet

On Saturday the Cheriton pack (Mr W Littleworth, master) met as usual on the Saturday after the Fair, at Pilton Bridge. Hounds were put to water at Raleigh, and drew up as far at Pitt Farm, but failed to get on a trail. The Master tried every holt carefully, but failed to find the quarry at home. Snapper was reached without a find, and the Master then drew on as far as Bratton Cross, where he called off without hounds having had a "sniff" all day. No doubt this was due to the water being so low. A tasty luncheon was partaken of before the journey back to Barnstaple.

31

CHAPTER 2

THE RUNS OF SIR JOHN AMORY'S STAGHOUNDS, THE BARNSTAPLE & NORTH DEVON HARRIERS, AND PETER ORMROD'S STAGHOUNDS IN THE BARNSTAPLE DISTRICT

F our years before the formation of the Barnstaple Staghounds in 1901, regular staghunting was taking place in the Barnstaple district between the Barnstaple and North Devon Harriers, Sir John Amory's Staghounds (now known as the Tiverton Staghounds) and Peter Ormrod's Staghounds. At this time, deer were spreading beyond the boundaries of Exmoor which was hunted by the Devon and Somerset Staghounds. This led to the formation of Sir John Amory's Staghounds in 1896 and the Barnstaple Staghounds and the Quantock Staghounds both in 1901. There follows some reports of runs of the above mentioned hounds in the Barnstaple district during the period 1897-1901.

Sir John Amory's Staghounds,
The Barnstaple and North Devon Harriers and
Peter Ormrod's Staghounds in the Barnstaple district,
12 October 1897

Of late years deer have been increasing in number in the valley between Barnstaple and Arlington, and in consequence they have been doing a considerable amount of damage to the farmers' crops adjoining the large covers on Sir Arthur

Chichester's property. In seasons past the Devon and Somerset Staghounds have put in an occasional day, and some fine runs have been experienced from this neighbourhood, but the deer are now so numerous that it was thought desirable that more hunting should take place along the valley. Mr Basset made a representation to the effect to the Master of the Devon and Somerset Staghounds. The latter kindly permitted Mr Basset to invite Ian Amory, Master of Sir John Amory's Staghounds, to come down with the Tiverton pack, which he did on Monday last. Ample accommodation was provided for horses, hounds and servants at Pilton stables, while the Master and whips (Messrs De las Casas) were entertained at Westaway by Mr Basset.

Sir John Amory's Staghounds, 14 October 1897
– Stag hunt near Barnstaple
A Kill in the Taw

Sir John Amory's Staghounds concluded their complimentary visit to the west side of the Devon and Somerset district on Friday, when they had a very successful run from Loxhore Cot, where the pack was to have met on Thursday, the meet, owing to the severity of the run on the previous day being postponed to give horses and hounds extra rest. It being Barnstaple market day, and the meet only three miles away, there were not so many present as there would otherwise have been, although the attendance included quite 60 on horseback, while many came by carriage or bicycle. The introduction of cycles at a stag hunt was too much for one of the thoroughbreds. At the sight of them the animal became restive, and, eventually bolted, knocking over several cyclists, besides causing the upset of a trap party, although happily no serious injuries resulted.

A cartoon depicting an incident at a meet of Sir John Amory's Staghounds at Loxhore Cot.
© Terry Gable

Among the company present were the Master (Mr Ian Amory), Mrs Amory, Messrs De Las Casas (whips), Miss Hibbert, Miss Hurst, Sir Arthur Chichester, Mr C.H. Basset, Mrs Hugh Toller, Miss Smith and Miss Crang (Eastdown), Mr A.F. Seldon, Mr W. Penhale, Mr R. Lake, and Mr Speke. Among those on wheels were Mrs Chichester and party and Mrs Seldon and party. Two stags had been harboured, one by Sir Arthur Chichester's keeper in Youlston, and the other by Mr Litson. The latter, which was lying in Woolywood, was selected as being close at hand, and it did not take the tufters long before they had aroused a fine four year old stag, which at once pointed its head towards Barnstaple. The scent was so good and the tufters had gone such a pace that it was impossible to stop the whole of them. The pack was therefore taken by Mr Basset and Mr De Las Casas to Cross-tree, three miles from Barnstaple where they quickly took up the line by Blakewell Mills to Tutshill, where they turned into the wood to Westaway, where the stag was in full view, crossing Mr Basset's grass land to Raleigh, Frankmarsh and Stoneyard. Here it was thought the stag must have returned to the large covers by the River Yeo, where deer are known to be very plentiful, but refusing this shelter, he turned to the right, the hounds carrying the line across the Lynton and Barnstaple road, sinking into the valley by Maidenford and crossing the Devon and Somerset Railway to Bishopstawton, where, after crossing Whitemere it got down to the tidal waters of the Taw, exactly underneath Tawstock Court. The stag was killed here, it proving to be that of a powerful specimen with brow and bay, two on top one side, and one on the other. Thus concluded about as successful a week as any the Tiverton pack has had. Mr Pile, of Eastdown, had a nasty fall during the run, fracturing his ankle.

October 16th 1897

Having a bye day, Sir John Amory's Staghounds tried the Loxhore Valley near Barnstaple on Saturday, to endeavour to capture a very old and heavy deer. So wily is the old deer, that he has baffled the Devon and Somerset Staghounds when they have hunted the neighbourhood. After the severe work of horses and hounds during the past week, it was decided that nothing but the old stag would be run. Hounds were kennelled at Chelfham Mills, the tufters drawn and taken to the woods. Immediately opposite the Mill, and the woodlands drawn from this point to Loxhore Cott. A number of young stags, of about the age and size of those hunted during the week, were found, but the heavy stag was nowhere to be seen, though he had been distinctly slotted in several parts of the covers as recently as a fortnight since, probably he had moved higher up the valley, and will have to be reckoned with on a future occasion. The Master (Mr Ian Amory) decided to call off at one o'clock and hounds returned to Westaway (Mr C H Basset's), their head quarters during the visit, afterwards leaving for Tiverton. Barnstaple people hope the day is not too distant when they may be favoured with a reputation of the good sport they have enjoyed with this pack.

2 December 1897
Sir John Amory's Staghounds in the Barnstaple District

Amongst the followers of the sport of staghunting in the Exmoor Country including the district of Barnstaple, the presence of many staghounds in the Loxhore Valley and woods belonging to Sir Arthur Chichester, Bart, is viewed with great satisfaction. Sir Arthur, a few days ago caught sight in his park one of the finest stags he has ever seen, and Fred Goss, the keen harbourer to the Devon and Somerset Staghounds has given his opinion that it is the biggest in the Exmoor Country. Sir John Amory's Staghounds have been invited down from Tiverton and they are now being kennelled at the farm of Mr C. H. Basset, Westaway, near Barnstaple, who was a former Master of the Devon and Somerset Staghounds. A meet took place on Saturday at Chelfham near Barnstaple. The tufters were taken to Woolley Wood, opposite Loxhore Cott. On the way the tufters broke off after a big stag and a young male deer. Eventually they found their hind and raced down a stream of water to the bridge at the bottom of Bratton Hill, where she crossed the road and made for Smithapark Wood, the pack was there laid on, and as the deer was taking the line generally taken by deer for the forest, the field were hopeful of a moorland run, but this was not to be. Scent was good, and at a fast pace the hounds carried the line over Smithapark and Riddle to Loxhore village. The deer bore away to the right and again down to the River Yeo, near the point where she first left it, and she held a course to Chelfham Mills, down the water to Coxleigh Wood, hounds carrying the line to Kingdon Gardens. They broke out over the top on to Coxleigh Farm, and through Brightley Cott down over the hill, crossing the Shirwell road into the valley leading down to the Playford Paper Mills. Hounds were now racing very hard, the course now to Roborough overlooking the town of Barnstaple. Here she rested amongst some shrubs at the back of Raleigh House, now turning left handed and came down underneath Mr Basset's farm, Westaway. Here the field had some capital galloping over Mr Basset's meadows, racing the hind in view as far as Bradiford

from where she followed the stream to the Braunton road close to Barnstaple. She held the road for some distance down, and just before reaching Strand House she broke over the fence and crossed the Barnstaple–Ilfracombe railway. She was slotted to the water edge of the River Taw, where further there was none. The dangerous river for fording here is well known, but a bold adventurer, Mr Speke, led the way at a point just below Sir William's Salmon Weir. The bulk of the field followed, but on the other side there was no trace of the deer. She must have been gifted with the same forethought as Robert the Bruce, and successfully waded or swam some distance down the river. At any rate the line could not be recovered. Rain came on just now and the Master was reluctantly compelled to abandon the pursuit.
Red Coat

2 December 1897

The deer which eluded Sir John Amory's Staghounds on Saturday by swimming away in the Taw near Strand Houses was captured in Appledore Pool on Sunday. Some men walking on the sand hills at Instow disturbed the deer, which bounded into the water and swam towards the pool. The capture was effected by fishermen, who placed their prize in a shed at the Beaver Inn.
Mr Vigors
Mr C. H. Basset, of Westaway, telegraphed on Monday, and on Tuesday the deer was forwarded to Barnstaple, afterwards being transferred to Tiverton. At Appledore the animal was photographed by Miss Pike of Richmond House.

Above: Hazel Down displays antlers which where left at Fordlands, Tiverton, where she once lived. At one time Jack Yandle lived here and as his father Tom used to harbour the deer for Sir John Amory's Staghounds while they were hunting the Barnstaple district, the antlers might have been left by his family. It would be nice to think this was a Sir John Amory head.

Right: The inscription on the antlers. If this was a hunted stag, this date coincides with the time Sir John Amory's Staghounds would have been hunting the Barnstaple district.

Both photos © Richard Lethbridge

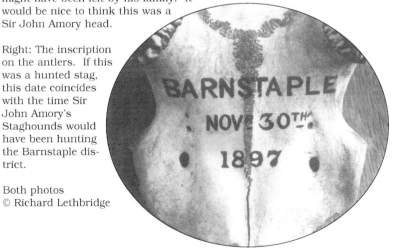

February 10th 1898
The Chase
Sir John Amory's Staghounds
Fine run in the Barnstaple District

Deer are still very plentiful in the Barnstaple district, and, at the invitation of Mr C H Basset, Sir John Amory's Staghounds have again paid a visit to this country. For the second time in the week, they met on Saturday at Chelfham Mills.

The meet was again a very large one, not less than seventy or eighty mounted being present. The weather for the time of the year was brilliant, and this, combined with the good sport afterwards, fully compensated for the trials and sorrows of Wednesday. Among those present were the Master (Mr Ian Amory), Mr De Las Casas (one of the whips) unfortunately the other whip, Mr M De Las Casas was unable to be present, as he is indisposed by a severe attack of influenza. Mr C H Basset, Mr and Miss Hext, Mr and Mrs G H Gould, Miss Crang, Mrs Penhale, Mr W Speke, Mr B Fanshawe, Mr W Smith-Ford, Mr Litson, Messrs Robins (2), the Rev F L and Miss Sprye, Mr Burden, Mr W Penhale, and a great many more. Sir Arthur Chichester's keeper again reported that deer were lying in Woolley Wood. The pack was consequently kennelled at Chelfham, and three couple of tufters taken on in the direction of Loxhore Cot. Cot Wood was first drawn, and then the tufters were taken to Woolley Wood. A three-year-old hind was soon on foot, and came out over Cot Down, turning back over the top of the ridge, and then into North Woolley Wood. The tufters here broke away after other deer. Three large stags came into view, two enormous fellows, with very fine heads, coming out in front of some horsemen on North Woolley; and although they had evidently had a severe bustling by the tufters, they took it pretty leisurely over the open, affording a fine sight to those who were on the spot. An enterprising butcher present, with an open eye, at once gauged them to be thirteen score each. The tufters were promptly stopped, and taken down to the stream, where the hind had previously been seen to take to water. She went down the valley for a distance, but

SIR J.H.H. AMORY'S
STAGHOUNDS.
FOUND. HIGH BRAY–FILLEIGH.
KILLED. UMBERLEIGH.
SEPT. 7TH 1907

subsequently again turned back into the Arlington Woods. The tufters, however, gave her no rest. She pointed eastward, and came out on the open at Mr Vicary's, of Coomb's Head. Crossing the Lynton-road, she ran on for the Tidycombe covers, whence she came down to the water and was observed by some men who were working near to lie down in the stream. The tufters in the meantime had gone off after a stag in the Tidycombe Wood. They were ultimately cleverly stopped by Mr F W Taplin as far as Wistlandpound. He was later on rewarded for his success by Mr Amory with a slot of the hind. The tufters, brought back speedily, re-found the hind. The latter ran a circle round Twitchen and Tidycombe, which afforded a capital gallop, though a severe one for the horses, as some of the coombes were very steep. One horse dropped from loss of wind. The hind then made for Smithapark, pointing down the Bratton Valley. The scent seemed very bad along by the water, and the hounds were unable for a time to own the line. Mr Amory now waited for a short time for Mr Las Casas, who had gone for the pack. On the hounds being brought up, the hind was reported to be a long way down the valley, nearly to the Lynton road. She was there re-found, in view of the whole field, and they raced her some time up and down the watered meadows, and in and out of the Youlston Woods, a fine view being thus provided for spectators on the opposite side of the valley. She made a final effort by running up towards Shirwell Rectory, but, finding the climb too steep, she turned with fast-failing strength down to the water by Shirwell Mills, where she was speedily taken and killed. It may be gathered, therefore, that the party were given a very good run. The covers passed through evidently contained a very large number of fine stags, augering well for sport in the future.

An advert from 1901

39

August 25th 1898
Red Deer Near Barnstaple

As Mr James Gooding, of North Woolley Farm, Shirwell, was cutting a field of oats on Monday last, there was found lying in the best part of the corn a fine young hind. It remained in its bed until the machine came very close to it – not more than two or three cutting breadths – when it jumped up in view of the harvesters, causing great excitement. There were also seen by a reliable informant nine huntable stags in one herd in the adjoining Arlington Coverts, which augers well for the present hunting season. All the sporting community are anxiously looking forward to the first meet of the Staghounds in the neighbourhood, and sincerely hope that the day is not far distant. The deer are getting very plentiful in the surrounding coverts, and doing considerable damage to the tenant farmers, who are anxious that the sport of Kings should be followed here as well as in other parts of the Red Deer Land. – NIMROD

An advert from 1892 promoting a book on fox hunting which was obtainable at Marks Brothers Bookshop, Barnstaple

13th October 1898
Staghunting near Barnstaple

Sportsmen in the Barnstaple district will be delighted to hear that Mr Ian Amory, knowing how plentiful red deer are, and how keen a hunting spirit prevails, in the neighbourhood, has determined not to abandon the country. Two meets have at present been arranged – one for Wednesday next, the 19th October, and the other for Saturday the 22nd October. The meets will be in the Yeo valley at 11 o'clock. It will be remembered that Miss Chichester declined to have the Arlington covers hunted, and it should be unnecessary to ask the field to respect this decision. Good sport may be safely anticipated, as reports as to fine deer being seen in the vicinity are frequently received. The hounds (Sir John Amory's) will be brought from Tiverton to Barnstaple on Monday. Mr Tom Yandle, the harbourer from Tiverton, will be in attendance, and will be assisted by Mr Gabriel Litson as local guide – both will-known yeoman and life-long staghunters. Mr Amory (Master) and Mr De Las Casas will be the guests of Mr C H Basset at Westaway during their visit.

SYMONS & CO.,
COACHBUILDERS,
Summerland Street, Barnstaple.

A NUMBER OF

NEW & SECOND-HAND CARRIAGES IN STOCK.

ESTIMATES SENT FREE.

Tom Yandle from Riphay nr Dulverton, who came down with Sir John Amory's Staghounds and was harbourer for them while they were in the Barnstaple district.

October 20th 1898
Staghunting near Barnstaple

Yesterday's meet of Sir John Amory's Staghounds near Barnstaple was a great success. in spite of drenching rain there was a field of some seventy or eighty horsemen with a score of carriages. Mr Tom Yandle, the harbourer, came from Tiverton on Tuesday, and was driven over the scene of operations along the Loxhore Valley by Mr C H Basset, a former Master of the Devon and Somerset Staghounds. From numerous indications which his practised eye observed, Mr Yandle was convinced that there were several warrantable stags in the neighbourhood. At daybreak yesterday, Mr Yandle was again on the alert, and he succeeded in harbouring a fine

41

stag in Sepscott Wood, just above Collar Bridge, the property of Sir Edward Chichester, Bart. The hounds, which had been taken care of at Westaway, arrived punctually at eleven at Chelfham Mills. The field included Mr Ian Amory (Master), Messrs De Las Casas (3) the Whips, Mr C H Basset, Mrs Curzon, Mrs Eyton, Mrs Hugh Toller, Mrs Gould, Miss Smith (Ford), Mrs Penhale, Miss Crang, Rev C and Mrs Chichester, Rev J Dene, Captain Laurie, Dr Raby, Messrs W Penhale, A F Seldon, M Squire, W L Ashton, J Berry, D Smoldon, G H Gould (Barnstaple), W H Speke, S Heard (Bideford), H Turner (Instow), Comer Clarke (Loxhore), Parminter and Robins (Highbray), Smyth (Wistland Pound), J H List (Sherwill), &c. The pack was kennelled at Chelfham Mills, and the tufters were taken to Sespscott Wood through the Youlston covers. The stag was at once found, and he pointed straight towards Barnstaple, running through Coxleigh Wood to Kingdon Gardens (close to the borough boundary). There he turned to the right and went back again through the head of the cover until opposite Bratton Cross, where he came down through the wood, crossed the river Yeo, and made over the Lynton road for Smithapark. Here the stag was joined by two hinds. The tufters pushed him on at a good pace into Mr Comer Clarke's covers. Mr Amory now waited for the pack, which meanwhile was being brought up by the whips. After posting the whips around the wood so that the hunted deer might be viewed away, Mr Amory laid the pack on in the cover, which was literally alive with deer. Fortunately the hounds at once settled down to the hunted stag, but were almost immediately again drawn off by a hind and yearling. After being stopped they were again laid on to the stag, which was pointing up the water for Hunnacott. The pack raced him through the wood nearly to the Lynton and Barnstaple Railway. Here he turned sharply back, and was finally taken in the stream just before reaching Smithapark. He proved to be a magnificent deer, with brow, bay and tray, with three on top one side and two on the other, and with very massive beam.

When the field left Smithapark Wood another fine stag looking quite beaten, was viewed from the top of the hill. Mr Amory decided to lay the pack on to this deer. The hounds carried the line slowly for a mile or so, but unfortunately the stag turned into the forbidden Arlington Woods. Mr Amory thereupon calling off the hounds. But for this, another stag would doubtless have been added to the day's sport.

Mr Tom Yandle and Mr Gabriel Litson are of opinion that there are plenty of heavy stags in the Loxhore Valley – enough, at any rate, to ensure another good day's sport next Saturday, when the hounds meet at Chelfham at eleven.

BARUMITE.

Notices.

LYNTON & BARNSTAPLE RAILWAY
Opening Ceremony.

THE RAILWAY WILL BE OPENED

Wednesday, 11th May, 1898,

BY

Sir George Newnes, Bart.

(Chairman of the Company.)

PROGRAMME.

The Mayor and Corporation will assemble at the Guildhall at 10.15, on the morning of the 11th May, and proceed to the New Station in the North Walk, where they will meet the Chairman and Directors of the Railway Company.

An Address of Congratulation will be presented, and Opening Ceremony will then take place.

The Mayor and Corporation, with the Directors and their friends, will leave by the first train for Lynton, starting at 11.15 a.m.

The Children from the Elementary Schools of the Borough will be massed in the North Walk, and as the train leaves the platform will sing the National Anthem.

The Borough Chamberlain will then be fired.

The return train will arrive at the Barnstaple New Station at 7.30 p.m., when a Procession will be formed consisting of the Band of the 4th Vol. Batt. Devonshire Regiment (by kind permission of the Commanding Officer, Col. Walcot, &c.), the A and B Companies of the Regiment, the Barnstaple Fire Brigade, and Inhabitants of the Borough and Neighbourhood, which will proceed to the Market.

THERE WILL BE A

FREE CONCERT IN THE MUSIC HALL

FROM 8 TO 9 IN THE EVENING, AND

Free Admission to the Market,

WHERE THERE WILL BE

MUSIC, DANCING & GAMES FROM 8 TO 10.

(Mr. J. Bater has kindly consented to act as M.C.)

The Mayor hopes that the Inhabitants of the Borough will co-operate in making the Opening Ceremony a Success, and invites them to join in the Procession both to and from the Station, and to decorate their establishments.

C. E. ROBERTS CHANTER, MAYOR.

The Guildhall, Barnstaple, April 28th, 1898.

GOD SAVE THE QUEEN.

The opening of the Lynton and Barnstaple Railway in 1898 was to play an important role in the history of the Barnstaple Staghounds, with the hounds crossing the line many times. Unfortunately it closed in 1935. The trains were used to transport riders on their way to the meets and on occasions the hounds and horses and even a stag carcass was transported. The staghounds also met at some of the stations en-route, including Blackmore Gate, Bratton Fleming and Woody Bay. At the time of writing a section of track has been relayed from Wooda Bay Station, giving rides for the first time since 1935.

27th October 1898
Staghunting near Barnstaple

There was an enormous field to meet Sir John Amory's Staghounds at Chelfham Bridge, near Barnstaple, on Saturday, notwithstanding the downpour of rain. It was probably the largest assembly in the annals of staghunting in the Barnstaple neighbourhood, there being about 122 horsemen besides a goodly number in carriages and on foot, many of the latter coming by the Lynton and Barnstaple Railway to Chelfham. The sport was not quite as good as that of Wednesday, although there was a good deal of pleasure and excitement during the day, and the horses had enough to do. Under the existing circumstances the very best possible use of the day was made. Owing to the heavy rains we have had during the past week harbouring was found to be difficult. Mr Basset took Mr T Yandle over the locality on Friday, and the latter was again at his work at daybreak on Saturday, yet no warrantable stag was exactly located. There was, however, plenty of evidence of a heavy deer being in the neighbourhood. Rumours were brought to the meet that a large

Horsemen ready to board the Barnstaple-Lynton Railway
on the way to the Chelfham meet.
©Terry Gable

Sir John Amory's Staghound trophies, courtesy of Mark Amory.
© Richard Lethbridge

stag had been seen near Smithapark Wood and another at Youlston Wood, but owing to the difficulty encountered in securely harbouring them, long and tedious tufting had to be carried out. The pack was again kennelled at Chelfham Mills, and Mr Amory started with five couples of tufters for Smithapark. After going through the covert, and thoroughly making sure of every portion of it, which occupied a good deal of time and patience, a move was made for the deer lying at the upper end of Youlston Wood underneath the Old Park, where Mr Orlando Chichester's keeper had a few hours before, seen the slot of a good stag. The field learned afterwards that the big stag which was supposed to be at Smithapark was all the time lying in Button Wood, just across the valley, and close to the Bratton Railway Station. Rumour says it was a large and heavy stag equal to or better than the one killed on Wednesday. Before going into the Youlston Wood, Mr Amory took a fresh lot of tufters, the hounds he had been using having by this time became somewhat tired. On taking them into the wood they were not long in rousing a stag, which proved to be a galloper, with two on top on one side, and one on the other. Like the stag on Wednesday, he at first pointed towards Barnstaple and came very nearly the same course towards Kingdon Gardens, being joined during the run by several other deer. He turned back through the covert, and came down to the water at Bratton Cross, where he evidently intended to make for Mr Comer Clarke's coverts, but owing to the great crowd of carriages, horsemen and pedestrians in the road, again turned up the valley. The pack was now brought on and raced him through the woods on to Cot Down when he turned to the right and crossed the valley and then over the top of Loxhore Cot Hill. Mr Amory had lost a great deal of time in getting to his hounds through not being allowed to ride through the Arlington grounds. Before he could again reach the pack they had carried the line on to Smithapark, and down to the Bratton Water, where they drew up; but no one being exactly present. It was difficult to know what had become of the deer, as hounds could make nothing of it. Mr Amory tried up and down the water for some time, and being unsuccessful, and it getting late, made for home. As Miss Chichester appears to be so averse to deer being hunted on her property, one could hear that it would be a gratifying thing if she would fence those parts of her woods where the deer are inclined to pass. Lord Lovelace in the Porlock district, has had put up a cheap kind of wire fencing on a large scale around many of his farms where the deer did a considerable amount of damage, and which has proved effectual in preventing the deer from crossing on to the land. Among those at Saturday's meet where

Mr Amory, Messrs De Las Casas, Mr C H Basset, Mrs Curzon, Miss Hurst, Mrs Eyton, Mrs Penhale, Miss Smith, Miss Crang, Mrs Gould, Miss Turner, Mr Speke, Mr Penhale, Captain Laurie, Messrs Comer Clarke, R Parminter, M Squire, W L Ashton, A F Seldon, Ash, Gillard, Chamings, Robins, Hunt, J Baker, W Burden, J Cole, Stanley Heard, H Turner, G H Gould, Keall, German (2), D Smoldon, Peard, Stanbury, and a number of others, including many from Tiverton and Wivelliscombe.

17th November 1898
Staghunting near Barnstaple

Sir John Amory's Staghounds met, by permission, at Chelfham, near Barnstaple, on Saturday, the field being large. The pack was, as usual, kennelled at Chelfham Mill, and seven couple of tufters were taken to Youlston Wood, where a three-year-old was soon found, and as very much larger deer were known to be lying in the adjacent valleys, the tufters were promptly stopped at Youlston Old Park by Mr M De Las Casas. Woolley Wood and Cot Wood were then drawn but without result, and a move was made for Mr Comer Clarke's covers at Smithapark. Tufters were no sooner put into the upper part of the wood than a hind and yearling were on foot and came across some turnips in view of the field. The hind left the yearling in the wood below, and ran down the valley for some distance, when she again turned back and ran up Bratton Water as far as Nightacott and up to the Lynton and Barnstaple line. With a falling glass and rain coming on, scent was naturally very bad and finally died away altogether, so that nothing could be made of this deer. Mr Amory again went back to Smithapark Wood, where a large stag, with three on top was at once found. He also ran down the valley as though tending for the River Yeo, but again turned back and ran up the Bratton Water. Scent by this time had improved considerably, and the hounds pushed him along at a good pace, when he turned left-handed and came up the valley to the Lynton and Barnstaple coach-road, and then ran at a great pace to Loxhore Cot. The tufters were here joined by the pack, which had been previously sent for. This was a critical moment for the hunt, for if the stag turned up the valley he would be in Miss Chichester's grounds, where they were not allowed to hunt; but if he ran down, a good run with almost a certain kill. Without other views, Mr Amory's only course was to make good on the right and left of the valley down the water, which he did with great patience and perseverance, but after a time a message came down that the stag had been viewed near Miss Chichester's ornamental water. The sport had accordingly to be abandoned, much to the regret of all. During most of the day the rain fell in torrents, and everyone returned home drenched to the skin, for the morning being bright no one was provided with a waterproof. Besides Mr Ian Amory, there were also present Messrs De Las Casas (whips), Mr C H Basset, Captain Laurie, Messrs Speke, W Penhale, J Comer Clarke, A F Seldon, R Lake, T Coop, M Squire, W L Ashton, Garman, Crang, H Gould, W Burden, Taplin, Crang, Dalling, Robins, Gillard, Catford, Bale, the Rev H Braund, Dr Raby, Messrs M Ridd, Smith (Wistlandpound), Litson, Smith (Ford), and others, as well as many who were present in carriages including Mr F A Baker and party, Mr J G Hamling, Mrs Buckingham and party, and an unusually large number of cyclists. There were also several ladies mounted, amongst them being Mrs Eyton, Mrs Gould, Mrs H Toller, Miss Smith (Ford), Miss Smith (Wellclose), and Mrs Giles (Eastdown).

23rd February 1899
Staghunting near Barnstaple

Thanks, principally, to Mr C H Basset, Sir John Amory's Staghounds are again hunting this week on the Barnstaple side, the hounds being, as usual, kennelled at Westaway, the Barnstaple residence of Mr Basset. A very good beginning was made on Tuesday, when, in splendid weather, the meet took place at Chelfham, about four miles from Barnstaple. There was a large field. Deer were reported lying on the wooded spur of the hill, exactly opposite the meeting place, and in sight of the viaduct. Mr Amory took three couples of tufters and three deer were almost immediately on foot. Pointing for a short distance down the valley towards Barnstaple, they turned sharply to the right, going up to Youlston Old Park and back through Long Timber Wood to Cot Hill, and through Cot Wood, crossing the stream to Deerscombe at a good pace. The deer then pointed for Smithapark Woods, crossing the Lynton Road on Loxhore Cot Hill, through Mr Comer Clarke's covers, and back again to Loxhore Cot Wood. Here the hind had left the two stags behind her. She was closely followed by the tufters, almost in sight, and ran through the woods down the valley nearly to Barnstaple, turning shortly back by Kingdon Gardens, and coming down to the River Yeo and through the marshes, when she again went up to the cover, through Coxleigh Wood, and over the open field at Sepscott, where she was viewed by the whole field. The pack was now brought up by Mr Amory and laid on. The hind by this time showed signs of giving in, but unfortunately the hounds, in again going through the covers towards Loxhore Cot, changed on again to two stags and a hind. In coming through Cot Wood the deer separated, the pack keeping to the line of a fine stag. For a time he ran the same line as the hind in the morning to Smithapark, where he came down the Bratton Stream, being killed a few yards above the bridge at Bratton Cross. It was now four o'clock, the hounds having thus been running hard almost without a check for five hours. Both hound and horse had apparently had enough. The stag had all his rights of brow, bay, tray, and two on top, on each side his antlers showing signs of having engaged in many a combat. The field included Mr Ian Amory (Master), Messrs De Las Casas (whips), Mr C H Basset, Mr E J Soares (who was "blooded" after the run, this being the time-honoured method of initiation to staghunting). Dr and Miss Raby, Mrs Eyton, Captain and Mrs Tomlin, Rev F W and Mrs Toms, Miss Giles, Mrs Hugh Toller, Mrs C Guppy, Mr W and Mrs Penhale, Captain Laurie, Messrs A F Seldon, R Lake, W H Speke, Comer Clarke, Everett, S Adams, D Smoldon, Pugsley, J H List, Kent, Litson, R Parminster, F Elliott, Robins, Taplin, Crang &c.

A dull early morning was, somewhat unexpectedly the precursor of brilliantly fine weather yesterday, when the meet was again at Chelfham. At ten o'clock, or half-an-hour after the field had assembled, there was a big find in Woolley Wood – no less than three stags being turned out. Attention was centered on the one which proceeded down the valley, and the pack was at once laid on. The stag had not gone far when it entered the stream, standing still in view of many persons, but this was premature, and it was promptly re-started. As though refreshed, it went off at a rattling pace towards Chelfham, and then made its way in turn towards Collar Bridge and Kingdon Gardens. Here it continued its course further to the right by ascending to Roborough, and then it swept to the left through Westaway. Anchor Mills, and behind Bradiford House. Here the major portion of the field was led to believe that the stag had gone on towards Prixford (in which direction they proceed) but as a matter of fact the animal ran under Upcott, and then descended until it reached Braunton road. Here it crossed and made for the river, but, probably balked by the Ilfracombe railway, it soon retraced its steps, and was seen to cross the road and to clear a very high fence with the greatest of ease. With the field diverted in its course, the stag was thus given a little rest. This it took in a kind of dyke, and it then moved away towards Heanton Punchardon. A seven-year-old, with three on top, the animal showed to great advantage as, moving leisurely up over steep fields, with the sun striking upon it, it made for the highest point at Heanton Punchardon. A few minutes later the whole field came down the Braunton road, and re-found. The stag was turned out of Eastacombe Orchard, and it then went on to Wrafton, being killed just after twelve o'clock in the middle of the stream at Wrafton Farm (Mr J D Reed's). A good proportion of the large field were in at the death. The pack returned to Tiverton in the afternoon. There will be further meetings in the Barnstaple district on Friday and Saturday.

2nd March 1899
Staghunting near Barnstaple
A Grand Run

One of the finest runs which followers of the staghounds could wish for was the good fortune of those who accompanied Sir John Amory's Staghounds on Friday last. The meet was at Chelfham Bridge, about four miles from Barnstaple. Mr Basset, Mr Amory (the Master) and the whips (Messrs De Las Casas) were met by a large assemblage, it being a glorious morning. Mr Amory proceeded to Loxhore Cot with five couples of tufters and drew down the valley as far as the viaduct. On the way, the tufters picked a line, and just at the point where we found on the previous Tuesday they roused a three-year-old stag. He at once turned back, and ran up to Cot Wood, where the tufters changed on to a hind. She came down on the line the stag had gone up. On passing Chelfham Mills, the pack were taken out by Mr De Las Casas, and laid on. They ran nearly to Collard Bridge, when the hind suddenly turned, and again ran up the Yeo as far as Bratton Cross, where she was viewed by a crowd of spectators crossing the river and it is marvellous how she managed to cross the Lynton road without being seen. This occasioned a slight delay, as it was presumed she must have gone back into the wood. But in a few minutes Mr Amory, feeling sure she had gone up the Bratton Valley, took the pack over the road, and into Little hill Wood, where the hounds caught up the line and came out at the top of the cover, and raced towards Smithapark. The "field" saw hounds were in earnest, and began to ride their best. We found, however, we were only just able to keep with the pack, which, from Little Hill Wood right on to the Doone Valley, at least seventeen miles off, were never checked for a moment, but were running their very hardest the whole distance. As if by magic, Mr Amory managed to extricate himself from the deep woods and intricate combs lying between Smithapark and the Friendship, and obtain a lead which he held for many a mile, notwithstanding that many of those familiar with the district were doing their utmost to get on the high open moorland beyond as quickly as possible. We were fortunate enough to catch a view of the hind going over Westland after she had crossed the Lynton line, and we knew then that we were, in all probability, in for a first-class run. The pack raced on to Tinnerlycombe, over Woodbarrow and Butterhill. As the pace was so great we were hoping the hind would turn down to Woolhanger. But she held on straight for the open forest, by Hoar Oak, Farley Combe, Cheriton Ridge and Brendon Two Gates. Alas, there were no second horses at this point. If there had been they would have realised good prices for the moment. The pace had now become so fast that no horse could live with the leading hounds, and it was only by now and again catching sight of the tail of the pack that we were able to hold on. By and bye the Deer Park came into view, and we sank down into the Badgeworthy Water in the Doone Valley, where about half-way between Shepherd's Cot and Malmesmead, and just below the celebrated Water Slide, where she was speedily taken, and killed, at about a quarter to four o'clock in the afternoon. Only thirteen of the original number of about eighty riders besides the Master and whips, came in to the finish. They were Miss Blake, Mrs Eyton, Miss Beadon, Mr Taplin, Mr Stanley Heard, Mr Southcombe, Mr W Smyth (Ford), Mr W Speke, Mr W Penhale, Mr Renton, Captain Laurie, Mr Comer Clarke, and Mr W Crang. Mr E J Soares just missed the end, his hunter being "done" a mile and a half from Badgeworthy. It was fortunate, in going over the moor, that we did not change on to other deer, for we passed at least three large herds, numbering a total of over fifty. One little calf, more inquisitive than the rest, came up to within fifty yards of the riders, and curiously gazed at them. We now had to turn our faces for home, most of those present having to get to Barnstaple, a distance of twenty-three or twenty-four miles. The pack finally reached Westaway, Barnstaple, about nine o'clock.

Staghunting near Barnstaple
September 28th 1899

Sir John Amory's Staghounds met by invitation at Chelfham Near Barnstaple on Saturday and a very large field testifying to the popularity of the fixture. Among the mounted company, in addition to the Masters (Mr Ian Amory and the whips Messrs De Las Casas) were Mr C H Basset, Captain Curzon, Miss Curzon, Mr E J Soares, Mrs Eston, Mr W H Speke, Mr Nicholas Snow (Oare) Captain Laurie, Mr F H Toller, Miss Blake and Mr Blake (Tiverton), Messrs J Comer Clarke, S N Heard (Bideford), D C J Bush (South Molton), W E Pitts-Tucker, A F Seldon, H Incledon-Webber, J Incledon-Webber, J Cole (Bideford) R Clogg, F Clogg,

R Longstaffe and C Longstaffe (Mortehoe), G Litson, C H Sperry (Isle of Wight), Smyth Bros (Wistlandpound), J Fry, R Penhale, Raby (Son & Junr), W L Ashton.

A three year old was soon found, but it was not until a few minutes past one that the tufters started the grand stag, which gave the field a fine run. The stag which was found at Warren, Wooley, Shirwell went away through the Arlington Covers crossing the Ilfracombe road near West Down and traversing Hallrainger Down. A heavy shower here caused a slight check by deading the scent. The line was picked up and it carried the field across the railway, the stag having made for Wrafton Marshes. The stag passed close by Wrafton Post Office and was killed in a duck pond near Mr Perryman's house on the Manor belonging to Sir William Williams. It was a magnificent stag with twelve points. There was a second meet on Monday when there was an enormous field, large number of people going to Chelfham by rail and road in order to witness the start. The hounds were kennelled at Chelfham. The covers adjoining Bakers Folly, the Warren and Kents Woolley, tried in succession, all proved blank but a very fine stag was eventually found in Woolley Wood. The animal at once took the field up the zigzag and down Goslings Woolley. Doubling, it retraced its steps

Wrafton Post Office where the stag passed close by.
Courtesy of Steve Knight, from the R L Knight collection

somewhat, and after working up and down the valley for some time it crossed on the other side of Arlington Covers, and thence proceeding to Commbeshead Park and Smythapark Wood. Hence the animal roused no less than four hinds. After a brief halt in the wood, the stag turned towards Arlington Covers and ran right through the churchyard. Revisiting Smythapark Wood, the quarry then made right down Lower Loxhore, and took to the stream near the drinking trough at Loxhore. He again ran to Smythapark, and from this transverted the covers at Chelfham and Kingdon Gardens and then dashed right down the stream through Pitt and Frankmarsh Farms. Retracing the ground slightly the stag went through Frankmarsh and into Derby road by Zephyr's Cottage and jumped the high wall of the meadows adjoining the cemetery. It then ran down to Derby proper and it is thought that but for some children who had gathered, its course would have been right through Vicarage Street and the town. Instead it leaped a garden wall and made across a couple of fields. It was soon captured after trying to negotiate the new cemetary wall in Mr Bryant's poultry run adjoining Bicton Street. The field galloped through Derby, reaching Bear Street by way of Gaydon Street, the unusual occurrence causing a great sensation. Many hundreds of persons quickly assembled in the vicinity of Bicton Street, the sight of a staghunt ending in the town being a novel one. The Master, who was accompanied by Mr Soares was the first horseman on the scene. The dashing run occupied over three hours, the last forty minutes being most exciting. It was a five year old with brow, bay and tray and two or three on top. A number of stags were seen during the day, and there seemed to be a difference of opinion as to whether the animal killed was the one first started. Some contend that it was recognising the animal by the peculiar formation of one of its horns, whilst others affirm that it was a fresh stag which was turned out of Smythapark. The hounds will return to Barnstaple three weeks hence.

SIR J.H.H.AMORY'S STAGHOUNDS.
BEMBRIDGE WOOD.
SEP. 15TH 1906

Loxhore Cott, a regular run of the Barnstaple Staghounds. Photo courtesy of Tom Bartlett's postcard collection.

2nd November 1899
Staghunting near Barnstaple
A Kill at Loxhore

The second meet in connection with the latest visit of Sir John Amory's Staghounds to the Barnstaple district was at Chelfham on Friday. The weather was very unfavourable, with the result that the field which met Mr Ian Amory and the Whips (Messrs De Las Casas) was not so large as that of Wednesday. The neighbouring covers were drawn without success, but there was a find at Smythapark. Getting away promptly, the stag travelled round Arlington and then made off in the direction of Barnstaple. When just the other side of Roborough it turned, and doubling back headed for Loxhore, where it was eventually killed. It was a very fine specimen. For the concluding meet on Saturday the hounds were kennelled at Loxhore Cot. It was a fine morning, and the field on this occasion was a large one. the tufters were taken to a warren belonging to Sir Edward Chichester at Shirwell, where a hind was soon roused. She made up under Bratton on to Smythapark, where a stag broke away and pointed towards the moors. Laid on under Wistlandpound, the pack crossed the Bratton road and afterwards proceeded in turn to Longstone and Woodbarrow. Here the stag (which had apparently taken a rest) was "caught up" and it dashed off just in front of the hounds. Travelling at a great pace, the course lay through Oare Oak, Brendon, straight to Mr Nicholas Snow's deer park. Here the field had the satisfaction of witnessing a large herd of deer, but sport for the day was at an end, the stag having become merged with the herd and showing no inclination to restart. The run, however, had been a capital one, having lasted without a break for a couple of hours. Mr Amory returned to Tiverton with the hounds a little later in the day.

A kill at Bratton Cross in the Barnstaple District from a meet at the Gidley Arms near Meshaw
13th February 1900
Sir John Amory's Staghounds
(The hounds were kenneled at Mouseberry, now the home of the Tiverton Staghounds)

On Wednesday these hounds met at Gidley Arms, the weather had been so severe that no one imagined that the hounds would be able to hunt. However at 12 o'clock Mr Amory determined to make the attempt, and hounds were taken to Mr Murch's at Mouseberry and there kennelled. The field was not a large one, consisting as it did – in addition to the two whips – there was

only Mr Renton, Mr Dunsford and Mr John Selley of Hilltown – a very different sized field from that which generally turns out to meet these hounds when they hunt in that part of the country. Miller had harboured three young stags in Week Cover, where tufters quickly found them, and, after one turn around by Odam Moor and the Gidley Arms, they drove one of them through West Week and in the Weekson Wood where they were stopped, and at 1.30 the pack was laid on. Hounds soon settled onto the line and in Bycott Wood fresh found their deer. They went away over Horridge Moor, and leaving Chulmleigh on the left made for South Molton Road Station and on through King's Nympton Park, across the River Mole to the village of Chittlehamholt. There they swung right handed and made their way straight to Lord Fortescue's coverts at Castle Hill. In the River Bray which runs through the park they fresh found their stag and raced him through the deer park with its herd of fallow deer to Filleigh Station and down beside the Devon and Somerset railway to Swimbridge near which they crossed the line, and going by Fenscott and Stoke Rivers found themselves in the country usually hunted by these hounds during their visit to Barnstaple. It was now rapidly becoming dark and it seemed probable want of light would again – as it did just a week ago – put an end to the run before the stag could be killed, but in this instance so unsatisfactory a finish was not destined to take place. Hounds were heard (at the time it was hardly possible to see them) to be baying their stag in the River Yeo, and at 6.30 he was killed at Bratton Cross in exactly the same spot as the last stag that was accounted for in the Autumn when the hounds were at Barnstaple. He proved to be a young stag with brow, bay and uprights. Hounds were now 30 miles from their kennel, so it was decided to stay the night at Barnstaple. The run was a wonderful one, lasting as it did from 1.30 till 6.30 and covering such an extent of country. How many miles were traversed by hounds in the course of the run it is impossible of course to estimate, but the distance measured straight across the map from the point where the stag was found to the place where he was killed was 15 miles, and anyone who is accustomed to riding up and down Devonshire coombes, whether along the roads, on a bike, or across the fields on a horse will know how much be allowed on this score, in addition to which, naturally, the stag made many points in the course of the run, which were considerably out of the straight line, from Week to Bratton Cross.
Roadster

15th March 1900
Staghunting near Barnstaple

Sir John Amory's Staghounds are visiting the Barnstaple district for four days' hunting during the present week, Mr Ian Amory (the Master) and Messrs De Las Casas (whips) being the guests of Mr C H Basset at Westaway. Weather in connection with the first meet at Chelfham on Tuesday was very fine, and there was an exceptionally large field (mounted) whilst hundreds were in carriages and on bicycles. The pack was kennelled at Chelfham Mills, and Mr Amory, prompt to time, drew four couples of tufters, and proceeded to Youlston Wood, in which Sir Edward Chichester's keeper had reported a large number of deer to be lying. The moment the tufters entered the Wood five hinds and a stag were roused. Four of the hinds made over Youlston Park towards Coxleigh, the remaining hind and stag going up the valley towards Cot Hill. These were pursued by the tufters through Shirwell Mills and Long Timber Wood, and considering the capital pace it was hoped that scent would be good, but in this respect disappointment was in store. Running through Cot and Woolley Woods on to the top of Loxhore Cot, both deer then turned to the left to Wistland Pound, with the tufters in close attendance. At Wistland Pound the hind crossed the Lynton Railway embankment and headed for Exmoor. Provided the pack could now have been laid on there would undoubtedly have been a long run and a good day's sport, but having regard to the fact that the Devon and Somerset Staghounds were meeting at Exmoor on the following day, Mr Amory decided to now turn his attention to the stag. This animal turned left-handed down into the Kentisbury Valley, crossing the small stream into the rectory Wood, Eastdown; and here the tufters were stopped. Mr Amory had meanwhile ordered Mr De Las Casas to bring the pack to Loxhore Cot, and soon the welcome notes of his horn were heard at Cot Hill. At a good pace the pack was taken to Rectory Wood and laid on, but it soon became apparent that scent was very indifferent, the pack only just managing to hold on to the line. No doubt, too, scent was interfered with by reason of the fact that one or two tufters had managed to steal ahead. The field proceeded through Ford and Shortacombe, crossing the valley on to Brockham, where news was received that the stag had turned into Woolley Wood. Mr Amory accordingly took the pack into the Wood. Unfortunately, however, the Wood was found to be full of deer, and the pack divided in several directions. Some hounds, however, stuck to the hunted stag, and he was finally brought to bay and killed. Most of the

57

field had left for home. The stag was a fine specimen, with three on top on one side and two on the other.

The meet yesterday at Loxhore was largely attended. A stag was soon roused in the Wood between Loxhore and Chelfham Bridge, and went down the stream. Hounds were laid on at twelve o'clock. The stag turned off at Chelfham towards Stoke Rivers Wood. He ran to Bratton and on to Smythapark, turning back into the Loxhore Valley, where he was killed after a run of 2 1/2 hours. The stag was about six years old, with two on top on each side and all his rights.

We now turn our attention to Peter Ormrod's Staghounds. In 1900 steps were taken to establish a permanent pack of staghounds for the Barnstaple district. Peter Ormrod from Lancashire with his pack of staghounds volunteered to hunt the district which he did off and on for nearly a season. There follows some of his runs.

September 20th 1900
Mr Ormrod's Staghounds
Extraordinary Incident and a Narrow Escape

The second meet of Peter Ormrod's Staghounds at Chelfham on Saturday was attended by very good sport, following a remarkable occurrence at the outset. The weather was brilliant and there was a large attendance, the Master (Mr Peter Ormrod) and Miss Ormrod, being supported, among others, by Mr C H Basset, Miss Curzon, Captain Laurie, Major Raby and Mr W L Ashton (joint Hon Secretaries), Miss Hurst, Miss Gillard, Miss Smoldon, Miss Squire, Miss Furnival, Mr and Mrs Smoldon (on wheels), Captain Tomlin and party (on wheels), Messrs E J Soares, T W Smith (Eastdown), M Squire, E German, B Raby, E A Arthur, J Comer Clarke, G Litson, J Stanbury, A J Gillard, A W Gaydon, A E Arnold, F Taplin (Challacombe), Tarr (Arlington), Saunder (Ashford), Sanders (Pilton), Tamlyn (Orswell), Tamlyn (Rosehill), Pugsley, Marquis, Lewis, Ridd, Fry, Berry, and Master Chichester (Youlston). There was also a number of cyclists and pedestrians present from Barnstaple. With an addition of three or four couples of fresh hounds, the Master arrived in good time, the hounds having been kennelled at Woolley Barton. Four-and-a-half couples first drew Cot Wood and the Warren, but nothing reliable could be seen. The harbourer (Mr Litson) felt sure some warrantable deer were to be found at Mill Wood, and accordingly the tufters were trotted thither, two "warrantables" being as the result soon on foot. The largest of the two made down the valley under Youlston Old Park on the Sepscott Wood, but the other was responsible for an extraordinary occurrence. Endeavouring to leap the fence, it broke its shoulder, and, moreover, knocked down young Mr Chichester, who, fortunately escaped uninjured. The injured stag (which proved to be a four-year-old) having been despatched, attention was paid to the other animal which had started off. The tufters were in hot pursuit of this stag, and the Master sent back to Woolley for the pack. The stag, a fine animal, raced under Sepscott, through Coxleigh Wood and down to Kingdon Gardens. Here the tufters were stopped until the arrival of the pack, the deer making off through Pitt Farm, Barnstaple, the Brewery Marsh, over Pilton Lawn, and on to Westaway. The stag attracted a large number of Barumites who had a fine view of the animal as it proceeded over Pilton Lawn; the stag leaped from the roadway into the Lawn. The pack was now laid on, but owing to the time that had elapsed, and the distance, hunting became very slow. Considering the drought, too, it was a decided marvel how the hounds went on at all, but they proceeded though Westaway meadows, to Tutshill Wood, through the farm to Blakewell, then crossing the road near Springfield Lodge. They eventually worked the stag to Whitehall Mill and Pippacott, but as it was then 5 o'clock, the field gradually dispersed, and hounds were drawn off.

For the first time, Mr Ormrod's hounds met at Bratton Fleming Railway Station on Monday. There was a large field present which included the Master (Mr Peter Ormrod), Mrs and Miss Ormrod, Lord and Lady Ebrington, Mr Comer Clarke, Mr Ernest Arthur, Major Raby, Messrs Ridd and Baker, Bratton Fleming, and W Smith, Ford. – In calling for three cheers for Mr Ormrod, Mr Ridd mentioned that he had hunted in the locality for the past sixty years with the Devon and Somerset Staghounds, while he had also hunted with the late Rev John Russell, and he could only hope that Mr Ormrod would have as good sport as he (the speaker) had hitherto enjoyed. Three hearty cheers were then given for Mr Ormrod. – Mr Comer Clarke came with the news that he had harboured two deer in Smythapark Wood, one being a fairly heavy deer, and the other a galloper. The pack was kennelled at Button Farm, and the tufters were taken across the valley to Smythapark Wood. Hitherto, Mr Ormrod had succeeded in forcing the stag from cover with the tufters in a particularly short time, and Monday proved no exception to the rule. A stag was soon on foot from the lower part of the wood, as well as a number of hinds and several calves. The hinds scattered in all directions, one coming out at the top and parting for Arlington, being followed by a calf and a couple of tufters. Returning to the

Wood, the tufters followed the line of the stag, which proceeded up the valley, holding on at a good pace along the Lynton and Barnstaple Railway, which he crossed at a point between Hunacott and Thorne, and pointing for Kinnerley Coombes, where two hinds were also seen going up the valley for Exmoor by way of Wistlandpound, Mr Ormrod sent back for the pack from Thorne, but held on with the tufters to Friendship Inn and over the large grass enclosures at Wistland Pound, on to the head of Kinnerley Coombe, and thence to Chapman Barrows and Longstone. Owing to the excessive heat and the drought, the scent up to this time had been very bad, but on the forest it improved considerably and the hounds began to run at a capital pace. The course now lay over the combe at the end of the Long Stone, across a small stream, and up the steep sides opposite and on to Shallowford, (where the stag passed high up over the head of the combe), and on to Ilkerton Ridge. Matters were becoming exciting, when the animal turned downwards as though pointing somewhat for Lynton, going down to the water at Hoare Oak. By this time the stag had got a long way ahead, and inasmuch as the scent was again indifferent and there appeared little hope of killing. Mr Ormrod decided to stop the hounds, and return to Barnstaple. Despite the fact that the party were 20 miles from home, a goodly proportion of the field were present at the dispersal, most on arrival home having been in the saddle nearly eleven hours.

Bratton Fleming station, where Peter Ormrod's Staghounds
met for the first time.

September 27th 1900
Peter Ormrod's Staghounds

The meet on Thursday was at Chelfham. Fine weather prevailed, and those present included the Master, (Mr Peter Ormrod), Capt Laurie, Major Raby, Messrs A Chichester (Youlston), H Turner (Instow), F Taplin (Challacombe), H Waldron, W L Ashton, G C Western and Family, Rock (Suffolk), Goss (Langtree), Rev O Ramsay (Loxhore), A Hill (Bratton), Tamlyn (Orswell), Dyer and Webber (Bishopsnympton), E German (Pilton), G Densham (London), Robins (Barnstaple), B Raby, Furnival, W Smith (Wistlandpound), C Everett and G Litson, Mrs Rock (Suffolk), Mrs Tamlyn (Orswell), Mrs A F Seldon and party (Barnstaple), and Mrs G C Dennis.

Mr Litson reported two or three big stags in Cot Wood, but harbouring was difficult by reason of the dry weather. The pack was kennelled at Woolley. Cot Wood was drawn, and it was evident that during the morning deer had crossed into Mr Orlando Chichester's property near the Arlington covers. The tufters accordingly put in and a stag was soon viewed away below Woolley. It ran into Cot Wood, but some of the horsemen got in front of both hounds and deer, with the unfortunate result that instead of pointing for Shirwell covers, the stag was headed back into Cot Wood. Here several hinds and other deer were, as a matter of fact, roused, but they were all unwarrantable. The first named proceeded to the bottom of the Wood by Loxhore Cot, with the hounds 'Friendship', 'Foreman', 'Artist' close upon him. This was only noticed by a few people, the major portion of the pack and field being in Cot Wood. Some delay was consequently caused in following up, when the whips got as far as Shirwell Old Park, the leading hounds were stopped. The stag proceeded up under Bratton stream, and the pack was soon after brought and laid on. There was a grand chase from Bratton stream to Mr Comer Clarke's wood. A fine view of the animal was here afforded, and it proved to be a grand old stag, possessing a beautiful head. Closely pressed, the animal crossed close to the farmyard pointing for Wistlandpound with the hounds in close attendance. After some little hesitation, the stag turned to the left, its course lying along the Lynton old road for Arlington covers, and thence by Arlington Cot to Cot Wood – the starting place. It then ran across Woolley and round the Old Warren. His time appeared to be short but he succeeded in rising to the higher part of Woolley Farm, while he then dropped into Arlington covers. This is forbidden ground, and the Master, determined to respect the wishes of Miss Chichester, decided to call off the hounds. – Many warrantable stags were seen during the day, and there can be no doubt that with the hounds daily improving, good sport is in store for the pack.

October 2nd 1900
Staghunting near Barnstaple

A large field assembled in beautiful weather on Saturday to meet
Mr Peter Ormrod's Staghounds at Chelfham Mills. Mr Litson
had slotted a fine stag in Cot Wood the night before, but could
find no evidence of him in the morning. Mr Ormrod, however,
thought he would tuft the wood on the chance of finding him.
Accordingly the pack were taken to Loxhore Cot and kennelled.
Mr Ormrod tufted Cot Wood thoroughly, but found no trace of
the deer. Stags are very restless at this time of the year, and will
often shift after being harboured, and doubtless this one had
moved away. Mr Comer Clark had come to the meet with the
news that he had a good five-year-old stag lying in Smithapark
Wood   So the pack were now taken on to Smithapark and
kennelled. Mr Ormrod commenced to tuft the lower part of the
Wood, and he very soon had the stag on foot. He ran up the valley nearly to the end of the wood, and then lay down until the
tufters were nearly on him – all in full view of a crowd of people
who were watching the hunting operations from Bratton Station.
The deer jumped up and turned shortly down the valley going at
great pace through Riddell and over Upper Loxhore Ground into
Leywood. The tufters had been stopped by Mr Gabriel Litson at
Riddell, and the pack were brought by Mr Ormrod and laid on.
Scent was evidently very good, and hounds ran at a tremendous
rate across the Loxhore and Lynton road just at the five-mile-
post. After crossing the river Yeo, the stag turned down the valley through Youlston Wood.   He came out on the top on to
Youlston old Park, still pointing towards Barnstaple, and ran
nearly to Collar Bridge, where he entered Coxleigh Wood. Both
hounds and stag were still running without a check right on to
the end of the wood above Kingdon Gardens, where a fresh stag
jumped up and turned back towards Loxhore with about two-
thirds of the pack after him. The remainder of the pack held on
to the hunted deer, which came out at Brightleigh, over Coxleigh,
down to the Shirwell road. The few hounds which were running
him were here stopped. Some of the larger hounds of the harrier pack had been kennelled at Chelfham Mills in case of an
emergency, and these were now brought up to augment the
smaller number of staghounds remaining, and the combined
packs were again laid on to the line of the deer, which crossed
the valley, over the Shirwell road, on over Hardpiece and Sloley,
rising the hill, and again sinking into the valley near Plaistow
Mills. He crossed the Ilfracombe road and stream, and dived into
Kinnacott Wood, coming out on the top, and running on to Kings
Heanton and then to Prixford, where he again turned short back

A stag slot from the time
Peter Ormrod was hunting in
the Barnstaple district. The
inscription reads:

G R Litson
Peter Ormrod's Staghounds
Oct 25th 1900
Chelfham Mill
Run 3$1/2$ hrs

(Mr Gabriel Litson was the
harbourer at the time)

Photographs © Simon Eggleton

and dodged about, finally coming to Blakewell nurseries (pointing for Mr Basset's of Westaway), where he was blanched by a shooting party, and again turned up the valley. Darkness coming on the chase had, reluctantly, to be abandoned. The run had been a very good one, and for two-thirds of the way fast. The stag was beaten, and if there had been a little more daylight there can be no doubt that he would have been taken.

February 28th 1901
Staghunting near Barnstaple

Peter Ormrod's Staghounds met at Chelfham Mills on Tuesday, Mr C H Basset acting as Field Master in Mr Ormrod's absence in Lancashire. A hind found in Woolley Wood afforded a fine run, but eventually got into Arlington Coverts, a kill thus prevented. The new pack of hounds ran splendidly.

February 28th 1901
Staghunting near Barnstaple

Followers of Peter Ormrod's Staghounds had a pleasant day yesterday, when the meet was at Chelfham. Capt Peter Ormrod (the Master) being in Lancashire, Mr C H Basset acted as Field Master. A stag reported by Mr Comer Clarke at Smythapark Wood was tufted out, and it raced towards Loxhore Cot. Hard pressed it turned right-handed back over the top of Smythapark Covers, and ran on to Wistlandpound where it crossed the railroad, on to Woodbury. Here, however, the pack divided, a portion hunting the stag on to Brendon Two Gates, where Mr Basset decided to call them off. The new pack of hounds are proving that they can hunt deer remarkably well, while they are very fast; and some very fine sport may, therefore, be anticipated.

March 4th 1901
Staghunting near Barnstaple

The largest field of the season assembled to meet Peter Ormrod's Staghounds, in brilliant weather, at Chelfham Mills on Saturday. Mr Ormrod being away in Lancashire, Mr C H Basset acted as Field Master. The hounds were looking exceptionally well after their severe run on Exmoor on Tuesday, when they drove their deer to sea at Porlock, where it was taken by a boat. We were pleased to see Mr Gabriel Litson at the meet after his indisposition, and he brought the welcome news that there were three hinds in Cot Wood and a large stag in the Warren. As Mr

Sanders (Master of the Devon and Somerset) wishes only hinds to be hunted at this season of the year, the tufters were taken to Cot Wood. The hinds were soon on foot, one breaking away over Cot Down and into Arlington. The tufters were promptly stopped and again taken into the Wood, when two hinds took off in the direction of Shirwell. The tufters pushed the hind on to Youlston Old Park. The pack was not taken out, the tufters still driving the deer on over New Barn and Sepscott. Here we viewed the deer crossing some fields near the farmhouse coming down to Sepscott Lane, where the pack was laid on. The hounds dashed through Coxleigh Wood, and on Brightleycott Down, to the right of Smokey-lane on to Pitt Wood. Hounds came down over Pitt Farm to the River yeo, where there was a slight check in the water. The line, however, was soon recovered towards Ivy Lodge. Crossing the Lynton road, hounds ran on towards Westacott, at the back of Landkey. They turned to the left through Birch valley, skirting West Buckland to Stone Cross, and then down the Hakeford Valley, and again to the River Yeo. Unfortunately, the deer now proceeded up the valley and into Arlington covers, where the hunt had to be stopped in obedience to Miss Chichester's wishes. It was a long run extending over several hours, and the first portion of it was fast. Scent over ploughed land was, however, somewhat indifferent.

March 21st 1901
Staghunting near Barnstaple
A Long Run

Peter Ormrod's Staghounds met at Collard Bridge on Tuesday, Mr C H Basset acting as Field Master. Mr Litson had harboured deer in the Warren, and the tufters were taken on there from Chelfham. A deer was soon on foot and ran very fast over to Youlston and crossed to Bratton Wood. Running by the side of the line, which it crossed at Chumhill, the deer made towards Bratton village over Peacepark and out into the road again, turning left handed into Button Wood and going down to the water at Button Bridge. Several hinds were here on foot, so the pack was taken on to Wistlandpound (in order to avoid interfering with Miss Chichester's coverts) and laid on. From here they ran, almost without a check, straight out over the forest of Exmoor to the Badgeworthy Water in the Doone Valley – a run of over 25 miles. It was a very fast and exciting chase, but at Badgeworthy there were so many deer on foot that the pack had to be called off and taken back to kennels.

March 28th 1901
Staghunting near Barnstaple

Peter Ormrod's Staghounds met at Bratton Cross on Tuesday. There was a field of over 40, Mr C H Basset acting as Master. The tufters raised a fine stag from Woolley Wood, it breaking away close by the Warren, and going across to Youlston and into Coxleigh Wood. From here it turned towards Barnstaple, by way of Kingdon Gardens and Frankmarsh, going right into the Derby road and across the Brewery Marsh. From the Marsh it was observed by many people to get out into the Raleigh road and jump up into the Pilton Lawn – a high leap – and make off over Roborough, coming down by Brightlycott and into Coxleigh Wood again. It now made off in the direction of Snapper quarry and on to Chelfham, going up the valley to Woolley Wood, the starting place, where it was killed in the stream. It was a fine day's sport, the run being fast and exciting. This concluded the season's hunting, the meet arranged for Saturday next having been cancelled.

There is general satisfaction among lovers hunting in the Barnstaple district at the withdrawal by Miss Chichester of Arlington Court, of the threatened legal proceedings against Mr Ormrod for alleged trespass in the Arlington coverts in the course of hunting.

ESTABLISHED 1836.

GIBBINGS AND CO.,
COACH BUILDERS,
BARNSTAPLE.
[1400]

The Barnstaple and North Devon Harriers were also hunting the Red deer at intervals but their main quarry was, of course, the hare. They also had a go at hunting a fallow deer from a meet at High Bickington in 1897:

The North Devon Journal, September 23rd 1897
The Barnstaple and North Devon Harriers at High Bickington
Hunting a Fallow Deer: A Brilliant Day's Sport

Tuesday may well be termed a red-letter day for this pack, which
met for the first time this season at High Bickington to hunt a
fallow deer, which, like others in former years, had made its
home on Burriott Farm, where it had been well preserved by Mr
Bedford, who is a well-wisher to all sport – whether it be fox-
hounds or harriers. At 10.30 Mr Eyton (the Master) and Mr
Speke arrived with 12 couple of hounds, as fit as one could
expect at the start of a season, and amongst the very large num-
ber on horseback who turned up to meet them were Mrs Eyton,
Captain F A Barton, Captain Laurie, Mr J H M Furse and son
(Dolton), Messrs German, Stanley Petter, Lake (2), Richards,
Roads, Irons, Ashton (2), Squire (2), Mugford, Davis, Gillard
(Barnstaple), Ridd (Bratton), B Thompson, G Penny, G Gardiner,
E and B Cole, Chugg, Harris (3), Pickard, Tucker, Brothers
Hellyer and son, Cousins, Slee, Murley, Pedlar and sons, J
Miller, Featherstone (High Bickington), Davis (Winkleigh), G
Arnold, T Chaming, Westacott (Beaford), G Boundy, J Harris, W
Callard (ashreigney), S Potter, Manning (Burrington), F Veysey, J
Thompson, Howard and Son (Chittlehampton), J D Squire, T
Folland (Roborough), Hooper (2 Huntshaw), Hookway (2 St
Giles), Oatway (2), Dockings, Down (Atherington), and about
twenty others whom I did not know. At 10.45 a move was made
to the covert's side, where the Master soon had his hounds busy
at work, and not ten minutes had elapsed when a view "Hallo"
was given, and sure enough he was at home (strange to say, not
many yards from where the stag was found last year, and which
gave us such sport in the run to Huntshaw Cross), but the deer
dodges back into the gorse, and although Mr Eyton quickly had
the pack on the line he could not be persuaded to leave his snug
quarters. But hark! there is a hound giving it a little higher up,
but it is only a puppy, which seems to be trying its hand at rab-
biting. Now Mr Eyton casts down the valley, but all to no purpose. No, he cannot have left his quarters, so try back is the
game, and sure enough old "Leader" rouses him at last, opposite
Pulley Mill. Now you should hear the scores of feet, people test-
ing their lung power as he breaks cover away over the fields,
under Burriott, in full view of the "field" down the valley, turning
left, skirting Lee Wood, crossing Yelland meadows, by Lower
Yelland. Now my Nimrods, ride if you please; but hold hard, here
he takes to the road, turning right-handed away to Lee and
South Heal, through Heal Brake as if heading for Langride Ford.

But no, he had been turned, and comes up straight for the leading horsemen to the Sherwood Green road, to which he sticks on by Way Barton; here he turns left-handed, jumping the fence to Hill Farm. Now for empty saddles – especially did I notice one venturesome sportsman on a grey, whose heart seemed nearly, but not quite, as big as the fence – but its all right, up again, and on we go, down the valley to Dadscott Wood, crossing at the top of the mill-pond, where he sailed to Bridge Copse, on to Winscott Barton, then down into the valley again, with hounds in hot pursuit, to Honeyford Mill; here he clears the gate in style, on the road towards St Giles, with hounds and horsemen in full view; now the deer is being pressed so close as to cause him to turn sharp in the road, passing 3 or 4 of the foremost horsemen pretty near to be comfortable, another jump over the fence down the meadows back to Stoneyford Mill once more, where he again scales the gate side by side with hounds, but this time comes to grief, and the Master, as quick as thought, had his whp around his antlers, and Captain Barton gave him the *coup-de-grâce*. Time from start to finish, without a check, 45 minutes, and as fast as the most ardent could wish. All those who were at the finish were delighted with the sport which had been shown. Being yet early in the day the Master decided to draw for a hare so back we trotted to Vauterhill Farm, and in a few minutes Puss was set on foot, running around Shutley and back in the direction of the find, but scent is not good, and slowly they hunt her – I beg his pardon, I think it was Jack – to Natty Cross where he takes to the road for a mile to Deptford and up the valley to Week Down, where he saved his scent. Hark! there is another "Hallo" on Sugworthy Moors, just opposite, and hounds are soon on the line, and after running her smartly for 15 minutes they kill her. Now my Nimrods this is enough for one day, so the popular Master decides for home, as hounds and horses have had quite enough. May Mr Eyton long continue to show such sport with this smart little pack is the wish of "For'a'd Away"

Hind Hunt Near Barnstaple
26 May 1898

Some of the Red deer having been doing considerable damage in the neighbourhood of Braunton, Mr Speke took the Barnstaple and North Devon Harriers down a couple of weeks ago, but nothing was found. On Saturday he returned, and after half an hour found a hind in Buttercombe Wood. She went off towards Putsborough, and rounded Baggy Point. Here scent failed, but the line was quickly hit, and the hind was driven past Croyde

Village and round Down End to Braunton Burrows, where there was another brief check. She was soon hit across Saunton Links and Braunton Field, when she turned and made for the Marshes. Doubling back somewhat, she again took to the Burrows, reached the Crow, and swam the Taw at low water to Instow. Hounds were taken over in a boat with some of the field, but the hind had a good start, and horses had to be procured. The hind was scented past Mr Turner's Farm, past the rear of Tapeley Park, and beyond Newton Tracey, where she is apparantly lost, though hounds still went on. It was a very long and a very rough run, the burrows and marshes being in a wretched condition. A portion of the field had to walk home to Barnstaple.

Barnstaple and North Devon Harriers
29th March 1900

This popular pack, now under the temporary mastership of Mr E Arthur, met on Wednesday, at Iron Letters, near Ilfracombe, when a large field of ladies and gentlemen turned out to welcome them, including Mr C H Basset, of Watermouth Castle, who was able to say that he thought there was a stag in the Watermouth covers. So hounds were taken to Ettiford Plantation, and, as the tenant cheered us with the statement that he had seen three deer returning from their morning feed, we became convinced we were in for a sure find. In a few moments hounds were busy in taking up a stale line on to Woolscott Cleave, through the big woods, when a burst of music from Favourite and Lacer announced that the quarry was about. Now there was a holloa near Woolscott House, and a good four-year-old was seen to break away, with hounds on good terms, through Woolscott Farm to Hill Farm and Berrynarbour. Turning westward he left Watermouth, and went on to Haggerton, to Hele, up the valley under Warnscombe, and on to Two Pots. Here there was a slight check, but they were soon past the old Ilfracombe kennels to Great Shelfin, crossing the road to Cheglinch, away right hand-ed to Mullacott, by the Ilfracombe Railway, as if straight for the sea. But he came across the railway fence, and went on by Campacott and Bamage Farms to Mortehoe Station. He contin-ued his course away by the line, over Trimstone Barton, Westdown, away to Dene. Then he crossed the line to Buttercombe, on to Woolacott Hill, to Tucker's Down, thence to Spreacombe House. He went down the drive, and the hounds hunted him to a big wire fence, which must have turned him to below Pickwell Plantation. Hounds were now only slowly able to own the line down the stream, and as we had had a long and smart run the Master thought it best to call off.

The following announcement from the newspaper indicates the time the Harriers were hunting the deer.

The Barnstaple and North Devon Harriers will meet on Saturday April 21st 1900 at Blackmoor Gate (for deer) at 10.30 am

April 26th 1900
Hunting
Barnstaple and North Devon Harriers

By the kind permission of Mr Sanders, Master of the Devon and Somerset Staghounds, these hounds met at Blackmoor Gate on Saturday, in response to the invitation of farmers on whose land deer had been doing a considerable amount of damage of late. There was not a large muster, but especially pleased were those present to see Mr Basset come over and superintend the busi-ness of the day. Amongst those present were Mrs F Toller, Miss

70

Hurst and Miss Curzon, Mr Comer Clarke, Major Raby, and Mr Raby junr, Messsrs G H Gould, Ashton, Smith (Eastdown), Smyth (2, Wistlandpound), Tamlyn, Taplyn, and others. A long jog brought us to where the deer were supposed to be lying, viz, close to the Hunter's Inn near Wooda Bay. The pack having been kennelled, tufting commenced in Invention Wood, and after a wait of about three-quarters of an hour we were rewarded by seeing three fine hinds come out over the brow of the hill, making in the direction of Colley Wood. Mr Basset decided to lay the pack on, and away we went to the above-mentioned wood, where the hounds divided. After some delay hounds were got together and laid on by the Combe Martin road to a single hind going away towards Wistlandpound. Hounds ran steadily past Kentisbury as if for Smithapark, but turning to the right, skirting Arlington, we find ourselves at Loxhore Cot. Our hind was viewed here hard beat, going down towards Chelfham, but hounds unluckily put up an old stag in the Cleave, and before being able to stop them ran through the Warren, across the Shirwell Road, away to Sloley Plantation. Here hounds fresh found him and crossed the Ilfracombe Road nearly on to Prixford, but then turned right handed and ran through the Muddiford Coverts on to Whitefield, where hounds were whipped off after a hard day.

HORSESHOE

November 8th 1900
Barnstaple and North Devon Harriers

The Barnstaple and North Devon Harriers have been having some capital sport during the past week. On Wednesday the meet was at Aylescott Cross, Burrington. As Mr Harris, of Hole, brought word that an outlying stag had been paying a visit to his roots during the previous night, it was thought best to give him a pipe-opener. Accordingly, hounds were taken to Hole Wood, and in less time than it takes to tell he was set on foot. Right merrily did the hounds charm him away to Church Water, to the right by Riddlecombe, back through the wood, over Heal, where the quarry came in full view of the field. A good four-year-old he appeared to be as he leaped the fence into the road. Down he went to the stream under Crabdown and Woodrow. Crossing the road by Teddywater, down the valley to Callard, Ashwoodland, Bidefin Common, hounds worked out the line at rattling speed. Over Hook Farm, crossing the road to Bourne and Bridge Farm, taking to the river at Bridge Reeve, hounds followed close on his haunches. Now the huntsmen had some little difficulty, the game stag swimming down the river Taw for three miles. Landing again under Bourne Down he led the hounds through Hansford Farm to Hansford Mills, down the river under Churchanger, where the stag was once more viewed opposite South Molton Road Station. He crossed the road to Bridge Farm, on to Catham Wood. Here we evidently changed the quarry for a younger deer, with uprights only – very likely the three-year-old stag that Mr Ormrod's Staghounds ran from Smithapark Wood to the river Taw on the 23rd ilt. We re-crossed Bridge Farm, over the marshes opposite South Molton Road Station, down the turnpike by Poole Farm. We next climbed the hill to Bouchland Farm (where the Burrington ploughing match had been held the previous day), followed the hounds on under Hill Farm to Ley, farther down the valley under Mrs Cooper's garden to Kingford Farm. We had a slight check in Northcote Wood, but Fancy hit the line to the stream above Hannaford, which he stuck to up under Gratley Wood and Ash Farm, now turning to the right over Gratley Farm and the valley to Snape wood and Farm to Witherhill. Down we ran under Nethergrove House to the stream, through Middlewood Farm, to Weir Marsh, where hounds were called off, as both horses and horsemen had had quite enough for the day. Our friend, Mr Harris, gave us all a good refresher, and we returned home well pleased after a thoroughly enjoyable day.

Gone to sea

CHAPTER 3

THE EARLY DAYS

The first meeting for the purpose of considering the advisability of establishing a pack of staghounds for the Barnstaple district, 19th July 1900

A public meeting was held on Friday afternoon with Mr C H Basset (JP and former Master of the Devon and Somerset Staghounds), presiding over an attendance of about sixty sportsmen who were present from all parts of North Devon.

The chairman explained that the meeting had been called for the purpose of considering whether it was advisable to continue staghunting in the Barnstaple district which for three or four years had been so successfully carried on by Sir John Amory's Staghounds. Deer were plentiful in their woods and he was sure many sportsmen would be willing to support the proposed pack if it could be established. there could be no doubt that it would be a good thing for Barnstaple and the district generally. Mr W Penhale read a letter from Mr R A Sanders, the present Master of the Devon and Somerset Staghounds, who promised that the only stipulation he should make was that the Barnstaple pack should not run the forest side of the country on the days he hunted, generally Wednesdays and Saturdays. He could let them have two or three old hounds which might help to teach the others and he would also let them have one or two more at the end of the season.

Mr E J Soares thought that they were all extremely anxious that a pack of hounds should be established in the Barnstaple district (applause). The principal matter they had to consider was ways and means and he should be prepared to open the subscription list with £25 a year (applause). On the motion of

Mr R A Sanders,
Master of the Devon and
Somerset Staghounds
(1895-1907)

Photograph from
Devon and Somerset Staghounds
by E T Macdermot, 1936

the chairman it was unanimously resolved that a pack of staghounds be established for the Barnstaple district. Mr Basset promised a subscription of £10, and thought he could provide the kennels. Also providing a subscription were Mr B Jones (£10-10s), Mr E Arthur (£10) and Dr Raby (£5). Mr B Fanshawe asked whether Farmers were to be compensated for trespassing on the land, the chairman replied that for three years they had compensated farmers whose land was ridden over, last year £32 was granted, in 1899 £30, and in the year previous, about £25. Mr Soares said he would propose a resolution which he knew would meet with the hearty approval of everyone, it was that Mr Basset be asked to take the Mastership in the first year (applause). Mr Basset in reply said it would afford him much pleasure to be field Master for the first year, he could not undertake to hunt the hounds as they would have to keep a good huntsman. On the motion of Mr G W F Brown, seconded by Mr C N Skinner, it was decided that a committee of management be formed consisting of the chairman, Messrs E J Soares, Comer Clarke, W Penhale, B Jones, W Arthur, E S Hext, W Smith (East Down), and G W F Brown. Mr Morris presumed that Sir John Amory's Staghounds would not again visit the Barnstaple district, the chairman was very sorry he did not believe they would, he moved that Mr Penhale be asked to act as secretary which he

74

accepted. Mr F Chanter asked if they had any idea what the staghounds would annually cost. "What do you think now?" said the chairman amidst laughter. Mr Basset added that they would do it as cheaply as they could. He proposed to find a steady huntsman, some hounds and after that, to find some deer ("hear! hear!" and laughter). The subscription list was handed around the room and promises were given amounting to about £115. Meets of the staghounds at Barnstaple are very interesting, the sweetly pretty valley of the Yeo being usually hunted. It is no uncommon thing for the deer to pass through the northern end of Barnstaple making for the Taw.

<hr>

9th August 1900
BARNSTAPLE STAGHOUNDS

THE BARNSTAPLE STAGHOUNDS COMMITTEE desires to Thank all those who have promised to Subscribe for the establishment of a Pack of Staghounds, and the Farmers who have preserved the Deer, but the Committee regret to announce that with the means at its disposal it has been unable to devise a satisfactory plan for carrying out the scheme at present.

WILLIAM PENHALE, Hon. Sec.

<hr>

A STAGHOUNDS PACK FOR BARNSTAPLE
HOPE TELLS A FLATTERING TALE

Alluring Prospects of a Hunt Being Established
in the District. – Two Rumours. Which is True?

Special to "The Herald"

It would seem that the establishment of a pack of Staghounds for the Barnstaple district, so ardently hoped for, is not to be abandoned altogether without one more brave effort being made. As announced in our last issue, the primary efforts to secure sufficient financial support in the immediate district have ended in temporary failure, some of those from whom the most ready and generous assistance had been expected backing out at the last moment. While perfectly ready to participate in the enjoyment of the hunt if it could be organised, they seemed rather inclined to stay their co-operation right there, apparently being contect to leave the paying powers to others. Since then, however, two alternative suggestions have been made, one being that Mr Ian Amory should be induced to come back to this district, and hunt it as before, and the other that the offer of a wealthy Lancashire gentleman should be accepted, which practically meant that he should come here and run the pack at his own expense, the surrounding neighbourhood extending to him their most coridal welcome in return for the provision of the very necessary expenditure upon his part.

In regard to the first suggestion, we may remind our readers that Mr C H Basset very emphatically stated at the Guildhall meeting, in response to an enquiry put to him, that there was little or no hope of Mr Amory coming back to this district. It is now stated, however, but precisely upon what authority we are unable to say, that Mr Amory may yet return; but that before he finally consents to do so he very properly will ask a guarantee that no more opposition or threats of legal injunctions shall be encountered from Arlington. As there is little reason to beleive that Miss Chichester is any more favourably disposed to stag-hunting to-day than she always has been, this guarantee is little likely to be given; so Mr Amory's return – welcome as it would undoubtedly be – can be dismissed as altogether improbable. We are, therefore, thrown back upon the second resource, in connection with which it is rumoured that an opulent and enthusiastic sportsman from the north has generously offered to act as a "deus ex machins". It is reported that he arrives in Barnstaple on Monday next; and that, provided everything be found or can be arranged in accordance with what he requires (what that just is we are unable to state, for the best of all reasons that we do not know!), he will consent to bring down thirty couples, kennel them, and pay all exes incidental to the maintenance of the hunt in a becoming manner, and that he will, in a word, run the whole show as it has never been run before.

All this sounds most promising, and we sincerely hope that it is not too good to be true. The very obvious question which one will put is – "why should this generous and enterprising gentleman consent to bear all the expense?" Upon the principle that it is an ungracious thing to look a gift-horse in the mouth, one may possibly be condemned for putting the question which is one that is certain to be asked, sooner or later. One thing, however, is sure, and that is if the report prove true, and Barnstaple is to be favoured in the manner stated, it will be difficult for the neighbourhood to show its appreciation too pronouncedly. We feel convinced that sportsmen will know how to respond in the proper spirit, and that our prospective benefactor will have no reason whatever to regret his magnificent enterprise. We hope shortly to be able to mention that one or the other of the suggested undertakings has become "un fait accompli."

30th August 1900

Barnstaple is, after all, to be made a staghunting centre forthwith. The local attempt to establish a pack of staghounds having failed. Some of those from whom the most ready and generous assistance had been expected backing out at the last moment. While perfectly ready to participate in the enjoyment of the hunt if it could be organised, they seemed rather inclined to stay their co-operation right there, apparantly being content to leave the paying powers to others. We can now say that a wealthy gentleman devoted to sport has stepped into the breach. The gentleman to whom the sportsmen of the district are thus indebted is Mr Peter Ormrod, of Preston, Lancashire, who has made arrangements to bring down his pack of staghounds and to hunt the district at once. Mr C H Basset has kindly undertaken to find kennels. Mr Ormrod will bring down 30 couples next week, and the first meet (of which due notice will be given) will take place in the following week. We understand that if Mr Ormrod likes the hunting this season – and as red deer are very plentiful and the district has a high reputation for the excellence of its hunting we suppose this may be taken as a foregone conclusion – he will be prepared to make permanent arrangements for hunting the district regularly. Nor is this all. He will also hunt the Barnstaple and North Devon Harriers for the Committee during the absence of Mr W H Speke (the Master) at the front. There will be great rejoicing in local sporting circles.

Red deer are very plentiful just now in the Bratton Fleming district. Any morning or evening half a dozen or so can be seen, and early on Sunday morning last, Mr C H Godden, who lives at Bratton, on looking from his bedroom window described no fewer than twenty-one in a meadow belonging to Mr Comer Clarke, JP.

September 6th 1900
Staghounds for Barnstaple

The announcement made in last week's *Journal* that Mr Peter Ormrod, of Preston had offered to bring down his pack of Staghounds and to hunt the Barnstaple district afforded the liveliest satisfaction in local sporting circles. it is scarcely necessary to add that the generous offer was most cordially accepted; and a well attended meeting to discuss details in connection with the management, and to obtain support towards a damage fund, was held at Barnstaple on Friday. In regard to the damage fund, there should not be the slightest difficulty, inasmuch as when an effort was recently made to establish a pack of staghounds locally subscriptions were promised amounting to over £200. At Friday's meeting a large general committee was appointed, whilst eight gentlemen were selected as a sub-management committee. Major Raby and Mr W L Ashton consented to act as joint hon sec.

Mr Ormrod arrived at Barnstaple on Tuesday, bringing with him thirty couples of hounds. Mr C H Basset (for seven years Master of the Devon and Somerset Staghounds) with his usual kindness has placed his kennels and stables at Pilton at the disposal of Mr Ormrod. The pack is a splendid one, Mr Ormrod having spared neither time nor expense in order to bring it to its present state of perfection. On numerous occasions he has travelled hundreds of miles in order to procure animals which he thought would be suitable for his pack. The hounds are chiefly of the old southern strain, and have shown fine sport in the north country, not only with carted deer, but with outlyers. Standing from 24 to 25 inches in height, the animals are not rounded, and they are particularly remarkable for their beautiful heads, which show a distinct trace of the bloodhound strain. There is not a mute hound in the pack, whilst there is probably no pack in England whose music can be heard so far; frequently they have been heard at a distance of five miles. With deer plentiful, good sport should thus be in store in the Barnstaple district. Mr Ormrod has been in the habit of hunting carted deer in and around Wyresdale, and he is coming to North Devon in fulfilment of a long-cherished desire to hunt the red-deer in its natural state. Mr P Ormrod is a large landed proprietor, and manages his entire estate with the aid of a secretary. He is a thorough sportsman. At Preston he has the largest fish-breeding establishment in the world. It is an interesting fact that Mr Ormrod's schooldays at Harrow were spent with Mr Sanders, the present Master of the Devon and Somerset Staghounds. Mr Ormrod has recently been spending a little time with his old friend at Minehead, where staghunting is now in full swing. During his stay in North Devon, Mr Ormrod intends to reside at Ilfracombe.

Mr Ormrod has made considerable sacrifices in order to come to North Devon, and he expresses the hope that the result of his visit will be beneficial not only to sport, but to the people of the district. It was the wish of Mr Ormrod in coming to hunt the district to put himself entirely into the hands of Mr Basset (to whom he is most grateful for services rendered up to the present), and

Mr Basset will accordingly make the arrangements for the whole of the hunt meetings.

Mr Ormrod's pack will meet two days a week for staghunting, and as often as required for hindhunting. The opening meet will be at Chelfham Mills early next week. There is every promise of a large field, and Mr Ormrod can rely on having a most cordial reception.

Mr and Mrs Ormrod, with Miss Ormrod, are staying at the Imperial Hotel, Barnstaple.

The Imperial Hotel where Mr, Mrs and Miss Ormrod stayed on their visit to Barnstaple.

§

The name of Rowe has been associated with the world of taxidermy in Barnstaple since 1810 as seen in the advert below. James Rowe died in 1914 at the age of 72, and was succeeded in the business by his son Mr W W Rowe.

JAMES ROWE,

GUN MAKER, FISHING TACKLE MANUFACTURER
and TAXIDERMIST,

69, HIGH STREET BARNSTAPLE.

GUNS on any principle made to order, Stocked. Browned, or Converted in the shortest possible time. Breech-Loading (Double Guns) from Five Guineas and upwards, Loaded Cases, and every requisite for the Sportsman of the best manufacturers.

J R. has many opportunities of selling Dogs, should gentlemen have any to dispose of.—Established 1810.

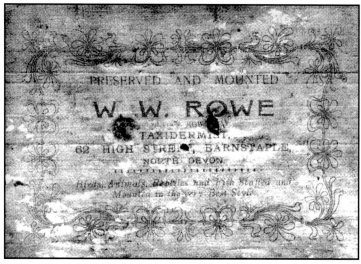

An advert for Mr WW Rowe, Taxidermist of Barnstaple. No longer trading, but I expect many a Barnstaple Staghound trophy would have passed through this business.

It reads: "Preserved and Mounted, W W Rowe, Taxidermist,
62 High Street Barnstaple, North Devon. Birds, Animals, Reptiles
and Fish Stuffed and Mounted in the Very Best Style.

I have seen a trophy from 1954 which has a W W Rowe advert on the reverse, so he was still trading at that time.

Below is an advert from 1914 for R C Orchard, taxidermist from Porlock.

Stags heads, skins, slots and other trophies of the chase, dressed and mounted to suit every requirement at the shortest possible notice. Good sheepskins in stock, suitable for motor rugs, hearth rugs.

R C Orchard, Porlock

The tradition of taxidermy in Barnstaple today is carried on through the work of Mary-Ann Knill.
Photo ©Richard Lethbridge

§

CHAPTER 4

PETER ORMROD'S STAGOUNDS

As stated in the last chapter, Capt Peter Ormrod brought down his hounds from Lancashire in 1900 to hunt the Barnstaple district when plans were being discussed in forming a permanent pack of staghounds. He did this until 1901 when the Barnstaple Staghounds were established with their own pack of hounds. This chapter contains some of the sport which Peter Ormrod provided. Below is a description of his staghounds at the time from the Baily's Hunting Directory.

MR PETER ORMROD'S STAGHOUNDS

Master – Peter Ormrod, Esq., Wyresdale Park, Scorton, Lancashire.
Honorary Secretary – Edward C Cadman, Esq., Scorton, Garstang, Lancashire.
Huntsman – The Master.
Whipper-in – E C Cadman, Esq., and Fred Reeves (2nd and K.H.)
Deer-keeper – W Ling
Thirty couples of hounds. Over 100 red deer and a herd of fallow.
Kennels – Near Scorton.
Deer Paddocks – Wyresdale Park.
Telegraph Office and *Railway Station* – Scorton, half a mile distant.
Days of Meeting – Two a week.
Mr Ormrod's country, which lies in North Lancashire, consists almost entirely of pasture and moorland with small coverts. there is wire, for

removal or marking of which arrangements are being made. No fox-hounds hunt the country.

A private pack, owned by the Master, who accepts subscriptions.

Mr Ormrod's Staghounds were established in 1899 with the best of Mr Allen-Jeffrey's pack and with hounds purchased from various kennels, notably the Penistone Harriers. Mr Ormrod's pack consists chiefly of the Old Southern Hounds, which stand from 25 to 26 inches.

In September and October, 1900, Mr Ormrod took his pack into Devonshire to hunt the Barnstaple district of the Devon and Somerset territory.

Mr Peter Ormrod entertains
at the Golden Lion Hotel, Barnstaple
September 13th 1900

Mr Peter Ormrod of Preston, whose generous offer to hunt the Barnstaple district with his pack of staghounds has been cordially accepted and he entertained 50 farmers and others at dinner at the Golden Lion Hotel, Barnstaple on Friday. In the quaint dining-hall, with its beautiful plaster ceiling, the coversation was all of the hunt, the advantages which it brought to a district, the ready market it provided for agricultural produce, and the difference it made to the Minehead and Porlock district, where, although the land was comparatively poor, yet good rents could be paid, in consequence of the money spent by the supporters of the Devon and Somerset pack. Some capital hunting stories of the old days were related, and one sturdy old farmer stated that one season he had been in at the death of three stags, two hinds, three otters, five foxes, and two hares – a good all round record, which it was generally conceeded it would be hard to beat.

Mr G W Lindsley took the head of the table, and was supported by Mr Peter Ormrod, Mr G W F Brown and Mr E T Soares, while among those present were Messrs Stanley Heard (Bideford), M Squire, G H Gould, A J Hutton, W E Squire, R Matta, E Berry, and T H Stevens (Barnstaple), T Copp (Ilfracombe), J Baker, W Yeo (Bratton), T Yeo (Loxhore), W Western, Friend, Beard, Ackland (Sherwill), W Beard, G Pike, W Heal, A Hill, J Tucker, W Tucker, J Pike, W Beard, Tucker, Gammon and W B Hunt (Bratton), G Smallridge, J Smallridge, W Yeo, N Smallridge, Champion (Tawstock), Brooks (2), Tarr (Arlington), T Dallyn (Parracombe), H Ridd (Challacombe), J Alford (Goodleigh), J Fry (Plaistow Mills), W R Berry-Torr (Westleigh), W Smith (East Down), J Robbins (High Bray), J S Chamings (Coxleigh), G Litson (Woolley), and S Gile (Loxhore).

Mr Peter Ormrod's Staghounds at Wyresdale Park, Lancashire

The 'Tufters' stopped. Master and Huntsman changing horses
before laying on the pack
from The Red Deer of Exmoor by Archibald Hamilton pub. Horace Cox 1907

The Barnstaple and Lynton Railway

INTRODUCING MR ORMROD

An excellent menu was provided by host Lindsley, and then when the overflow from the coffee-room had come back to the larger room, he said that Mr Ormrod had done him the honour to ask him to undertake the very pleasing office of introducing that gentleman to those who had gathered there. No doubt they would get a straightforward English speech from Mr Ormrod as to what his intentions were, and as it was impossible to intro-duce them individually, he would do so collectively, and trust to their having many pleasant meetings on the hunting field in the future. (Hear, hear.) Mr Ormrod came to them a stranger from the same part of the country as Mr Soares, and he hoped he would be equally good company. (Hear, hear.) Mr Ormrod's intention was to hunt the Barnstaple country, which would fill a much-felt want, and he (the speaker) was perfectly certain from what he had seen of Mr Ormrod, that he would do his utmost to show sport, and if they did not properly support him, well, they did not deserve to have a pack. (Applause.)

A CORDIAL WELCOME

A round of cheers, punctuated with "field halloas" greeted Mr Ormrod, who thanked them very heartily for his cordial recep-tion. He came to Devonshire six or seven years ago, and but for his pleasant experience of Devonshire farmers in the Lynton dis-trict he should not have had the cheek to come and introduce himself in a strange country. He had not anticipated being looked upon as a sort of public benefactor – (laughter) – as he was not used to encouragement in his own country, where he started a pack of staghounds. In fact he met with a good deal of opposition, and so he came down to Devonshire mostly to please himself, as his hounds were doing nothing at home and he want-ed to kill a few wild deer. (Hear, hear.) It was while reading his "Field" that he saw they were trying to start a pack of staghounds for the district, and he thought there was only one man to do it, and that was Mr C H Basset. (Applause.) He took the opportu-nity of saying how indebted he was to Mr Basset, who offered him his stables and found a place for his hounds. Mr Basset would carry a horn and do all he could to help him he knew. (Loud applause.) It was his intention to come round and make the acquaintance of each individual farmer over whose land he was going to ride, thinking that was the best he could do, but after paying three or four visits he had to give it up – their hos-pitality was so great it was more than he could stand. (Loud laighter.) He was pleased to meet so many of them, and hoped to know them all better in the future, and could only thank them for the way they had received him. (Loud applause.)

TOASTING A SPORTSMAN

Mr E J Soares chaffingly protested against the chairman's refernce to him as a stranger. (Hear, hear.) Some of them were anxious to listen to him, whom he found it difficult to whip up on other occasions – (laughter) – but on such occasions as that politics were not in it. (Loud applause.) They had nothing whatever to do with politics that afternoon, but were a company of sportsmen ready to welcome a brother-sportsman who had come into their neighbourhood, and was going to do his best for them. (Hear, hear.) Mr Ormrod had begun very well, and was evidently determined to get on the right side of the farmers, and he would find them real sportsmen – (Hear, hear.) – and although he might set them a hot pace they would all keep as close to the tail of his horse as they could. (Applause.) If Mr Ormrod's hunting was as good as his hospitality it must be very good indeed, and he was sure they would all join him in cordially thanking Mr Ormrod for his hospitality and speech and drinking to his health. (Applause.)

Mr Ormrod received another very hearty demonstration of good will and expressed the hope that he would kill his first wild deer on the morrow. He knew he had much to learn, only having hunted carted deer, and looked to them to assist him as much as they could.

This concluded a very harmonious and cordial gathering, and it was evident Mr Ormrod had made a very good impression on those present.

On the left is the Golden Lion Hotel where Peter Ormrod entertained farmers of the district and where many a meeting followed regarding the Barnstaple Staghounds. Today the building is a restaurant known as The Bank. Around the corner is the Golden Lion Tap, thought to be where the servants lodged.
©Tom Bartlett Postcard Collection

Sale of the Golden Lion in 1885.

FOR SALE TO-MORROW
"GOLDEN LION HOTEL."

TO BE SOLD by AUCTION, by Messrs. SANDERS and SON, on the Premises, The Golden Lion Hotel, Barnstaple, on Friday, the 4th September, 1885, at 3 for 4 o'clock in the afternoon, the following Valuable FREEHOLD PROPERTIES:—

All that old-established high-class Family and Commercial Hotel and Posting House, known as the "GOLDEN LION HOTEL," together with the Coach-Houses, Stabling, Yard and Premises in the Rear, situate in Barnstaple, in the occupation of Mrs. Ann Marsh.

Also, all that Fully Licensed Tap, known as the "GOLDEN LION TAP," adjoining the Hotel Yard, in the occupation of Mrs. Charity Blight.

The whole of the above is let on a lease to Mrs. Ann Marsh, for a term which expires at Michaelmas, 1886, when the Purchaser can, if he desires it, obtain possession. The Land Tax is redeemed.

N.B.—The GARDEN in Silver Street, Barnstaple, in occupation of Messrs. Lewis, WILL NOT BE OFFERED FOR SALE at the Auction, as previously advertised.

To View Lot 1, and for further particulars, apply to the Auctioneers, to Messrs. Gould and Webb, Architects, Barnstaple; to

Messrs. POTTS & POTTS,
Solicitors, Broseley, Shropshire;

or to

Messrs. FFINCH & CHANTER,
Solicitors, Barnstaple.

Dated Barnstaple, 25th July, 1885.

Opening Meet of Peter Ormrod's Staghounds
at Old Youlston Park, Shirwell.
September 14th 1900

Any doubts Mr Peter Ormrod may have had as to the kind of reception he was likely to meet with in North Devon must have been completely dispelled by the splendid send off at the opening meet of his fine pack on Tuesday. It was originally intended to hold the meet at Chelfham, but this was altered to Youlston Old Park on the estate of Sir Edward Chichester, Bart, and the change proved to be a wise one. There is a magnificent panorama to be obtained from the summit, all the well known haunts and coverts of the deer and the valleys branching from the Yeo being unfolded and affording a grand idea of the scope of the country over which Mr Ormrod will hunt. From an early hour there was a constant stream of arrivals, and the park was soon the centre of a most animated scene, there being 60 or 70 carriages and brakes, about 100 horsemen, and a host of cyclists and pedestrians. Punctually at eleven o'clock Mr Ormrod, looking smart and businesslike in his hunting outfit, put in an appearance, with his two whips and about thirty couple of hounds. Mr R A Sanders, the Master of the Devon and Somerset Staghounds, Mr C H Basset, an ex-Master of the same pack, and other capable critics were present, and during the parading of the pack, the hounds came in for close scrutiny. On the whole they created a very favourable impression, more particularly Gulliver and Friendship. Meanwhile on the park, yet more people assembled until there must have been quite 600 or 700 present, many of whom took advantage of this wait to partake of luncheon with the east wind and brilliant sunshine the conditions were none too favourable, but Mr Gabriel Litson of Tiverton who is doing the duty as harbourer, despite the difficulty of the drought making it almost impossible to slot the deer, and so ascertain the size and whereabouts of the stags, came to the meet with the information that he had two stags lying in Cot Wood and several others in the Warren, the property of Mr Orlando Chichester. Accordingly, the pack was taken to Mr Kent's farm, Woolley Barton, and kennelled.

Mr Ormrod decided to first try Cot Wood, and it was not very long before the tufters got on the scent and forced the deer into the Warren. Just afterwards a fine stag broke away over the large field to East Plaistow, pointing towards Bittadon, and Mr Basset, having stopped the tufters, blew his horn as a signal to Mr Ormrod, who speedily brought up the pack. There was little delay, and the dreary time of waiting, which is usually encountered by tedious tufting was in this instance avoided. Laid on in a large grass enclosure adjoining the upper Lynton road at Shirwell, the hounds at once took the line, travelling away across East Plaistow to Upcott Farm at a good pace.

The stag soiled in the mill pond at Upcott, coming out on the opposite side, and after negotiating a deep coombe, ran on to Viveham and Bowden. The lemon and white hounds (particularly Artist) ran remarkably well but some of the heavier black and tans found difficulty in getting over the large Devonshire banks, to which they have not been accustomed. No doubt, with a little practise they will be able to take them as well as the other hounds. The line of the stag was now straight on to Whitefield Woods, then pointing north to Hartnoll Woods, near the half-way house on the Ilfracombe road, where he came down to a small stream which is a tributary of the Chaddiford river at Barnstaple. The deer came down the water and then took a westerly direction. Very pretty hunting ensued, the stag holding on his course over Marwood, Halsinger, and a little east of Braunton, on to Wrafton, pointing for the river Taw, where he took the water in the estuary of the river, and was captured by some boatmen in Appledore Pool.

On reaching Upcott on the ride home, Mr E J Soares invited the field in for refreshments, and on their leaving hearty cheers were given to Mr Soares for his kind hospitality.

Mr Ormrod is proving himself to be a thorough sportsman and it is interesting to note that he says that if the southern hounds – the old hunting hounds of England, and the same breed as comprised the original pack of staghounds on Exmoor 80 years ago – are unable to kill the wild red deer, he will procure hounds which will bring the deer to bay, that being his object in coming into North Devon.

Our Appledore correspondent thus describes the capture of the stag in the estuary: Two fishermen named Jenkins, on Tuesday afternoon, whilst fishing in the Appledore Pool, saw a fine stag come running across the sands on the Instow side, and then take to the water. They quickly pulled their boat to it, and with great difficulty managed to secure it. They got it into their boat at last, and brought it across to Appledore, where it attracted great attention. It was secured in an outhouse of the Globe Hotel, and on being examined, was found to be a fine animal, apparently about five years old. It had a fine pair of antlers. News of the capture was sent to Barnstaple, and in the evening four gentlemen came down to take charge of the animal, and reward the fishermen. As they were unable to take it away alive without a lot of trouble, the animal was killed, and the carcass taken across to Instow, and thence to Barnstaple. This is the third stag that has been captured here in like manner at different times.

The dead stag was taken to Westaway on Tuesday night, and was dressed off for the purpose of distribution among the farmers in the neighbourhood of Youlston. He had a fine body but a stunted head. The bay and tray antlers were absent, but he had three on top on each side. Mr Basset considered he was a six or seven year old deer.

There was a by-meet at Chelfham Mills on Saturday, when, despite the fact that the meet was as early as 7am, a large number were present, including Messrs C H Basset, E J Soares, German, M Squire, F Gillard, J Alford, Tamlyn (2), D Smoldon (junr), W L Ashton (joint secretary), Mrs Exton, Miss Chichester (Tree), Miss Tamlyn (Stoke), and a great many others. The pack was kennelled at Chelfham and after half an hour's tufting, two deer were found just under Youlston Old Park. They ran through the woods down to the water, then to the right, and up over the Specott. Crossing the fine old park, they then made off towards the Warren, when the tufters were stopped. Mr Ormrod soon brought up the pack from Chelfham. It was decided to kennel at Mr Kent's at Woolley, taking a few couples of fresh hounds to lay on in the Warren. Many more deer were soon on foot, when the pack, which gave charming music, was laid on. The pack ran on to Loxhore Cot, back to Youlston and down to Kingdon Gardens, where the hounds were called off.

FIRST ANNUAL SALE OF PETER ORMROD'S HUNT HORSES

SANDERS AND SON have been honoured with instructions from Peter Ormrod, Esq, to Sell by Auction in the Cattle Market, Barnstaple, tomorrow (Friday), October 26th, 1900, at 11.30am, his STUD of HUNTERS, comprising: 11 First class Mares and Geldings, aged from 5 to 7 years, and from 14.2 to 15.2 hh.

The above Horses have been regularly hunted with Mr P Ormrod's Staghounds and have carried the Master who hunts his own Hounds and rides 15 stone. All the Horses have been ridden by a Lady, are broken to double and single harness, in rare condition, free from vice, and open to Veterinary inspection prior to Sale.

18th October 1900
HUNTING
Staghunting near Barnstaple

Mr Peter Ormrod's staghounds met at Chelfham Bridge on Saturday, when a good field assembled. Expectations were running high for a good day's sport, as Mr Comer Clarke had given out that he had what he considered to be the biggest stag in red deer land lying in Smithapark Wood, where he had successfully harboured him that morning. Mr Ormrod accordingly took the pack and kennelled at Smithapark. Bringing the tufters on to the wood, he was successful, within a few minutes, in rousing this enormous stag with a very fine head. He immediately began the usual tactics of old deer by endeavouring to procure a substitute, rousing eight or nine hinds in the hope that they would draw the tufters from his line. But the hounds were not to be eluded in this manner. They stuck to him remarkably well, and forced him to the open on the top of Smithapark Wood. In the meantime Mr W Smyth and Mr Gabriel Litson had kennelled the pack and brought them on to the top of the cover, so that they were laid on to the line of the deer immediately. They ran him very hard over the enclosed country, but the stag, unfortunately, headed for Arlington, and Mr Ormrod had to call off his hounds. Mr Clarke had another stag of lesser size, but a good deer, harboured in the plantation at the lower end of Smithapark Wood. The pack were again kennelled at Smithapark, and Mr Ormrod tufted out the second deer, which was surrounded by a number of hinds. He came down the valley, over Smithapark and Riddell to the river Yeo, where he was viewed by Mr E J Soares (the newly-elected MP for the Barnstaple Division), who sent back word to the Master to say the deer was down the valley. He kept down the valley through Longtimber and Youlston Wood and on to Kingdon Gardens, where he again turned short back and came up the water as far as Snapper, then pointing for Goodleigh and on to Yard in Stoke Rivers parish. But darkness unluckily coming on, the chase had to be abandoned.

Peter Ormrod's Staghounds
October 25th 1900
Staghunting at Chelfham

A large field welcomed the Master, four or five deer were soon on foot, and hounds went after the one that went towards Cott Wood. He went on through Loxhore and Smithapark, where it was seen that he was a magnificent specimen. The stag crossed Loxhore road to Long Timber, then turning to the right towards

Shirwell. He then made for Kingdon Gardens, entering the borough of Barnstaple. Going on to Pitt, a young hind put up the finer deer and took to the river Yeo. The quarry breasted the hill behind Frankmarsh, and crossed Bear Street Road near Well Close. He passed Sowden and crossed the Devon and Somerset railway and struck the Landkey Road just below Broadmead. The deer had been within the borough boundary ever since he passed Kingdon Gardens, and he went on to Rumsam passing close to Rosehill, making his way to Bishops Tawton. He mounted Codden Hill, whereupon the Master called the hounds off, being of the opinion that deer should be encouraged to spread more over the Barnstaple district. Mr Ormrod returns to Lancashire next week, if agreeable to the local hunting people and this, of course, is a foregone conclusion he will return to Barnstaple in April when he will hunt for a month, then suspending operations until September.

THE FUTURE OF STAGHUNTING AT BARNSTAPLE
Mr Peter Ormrod to again visit the district
November 1st 1900

For the purpose of considering a proposal by Mr Peter Ormrod, Master and Proprietor of the Staghounds which for the past two months have been hunting the Barnstaple district, a public meeting was held in Barnstaple Guildhall on Thursday afternoon.

On the motion of the Mayor (Mr J G Hamling), seconded by Mr W Penhale, Mr E J Soares MP was voted to the chair and among those present were Miss Raby, Mr Peter Ormrod and his brother, Major Raby and Mr W L Ashton (Hon Secs), Dr J Harper, Messrs M Impey, R I Bencraft, T R Seldon, Raby junr., J H List, Castelo Wrey, J Alford, J D Young, D Smoldon, J N Brewer, F Elliott, R W Mairs, Ackland, T W Smith, M Watts, R Ashton, T Garland and J Lock.

Mr C H Basset wrote regretting that he was unable to attend the meeting. He understood Mr Ormrod would ask for a certain sum of money if he continued to hunt the district. If this was decided upon he would be quite willing to pay his share, but Mr Ormrod must agree to hunt the district with a proper staff and an efficient pack of hounds. So far, he had given them some very pleasant days and many good gallops, but farmers would not preserve deer unless they were hunted and killed.

Mr Ormrod agreed with everyone that his hounds were not suitable for the district, in his own country he had endeavoured to get hounds as slow as possible with heaps of music and great

93

hunting power, but in this country they must stick to the stag and force him at a good pace if they wanted to kill him.

The Barnstaple country was not large enough to hunt the whole of the season. What he proposed to do was to obtain an efficient pack, and to hunt in the months of September, October and April. That meant a larger staff of servants and next year stables would have to be provided. It would cost him over £1000, and he must therefore, ask them for a little help; he suggested that they might manage to furnish him with £200 in addition to the damage fund of £30 or £40. He would guarantee to bring down a pack of hounds they would be proud of and a credit to the district.

Mr Ormrod then left the room, and in his absence the position of affairs was discussed. It was suggested that Mr Ormrod should be offered £100 instead of £200.

Mr Raby proceeded to interview Mr Ormrod, and shortly afterwards he came back with the reply that Mr Ormrod was prepared to accept the lower sum mentioned.

Mr Penhale thought they could raise the £100 and possibly more.

Mr Ormrod was called into the room and a resolution was passed to the effect that he should be paid the sum of £100 – He agreed to the proposal, amid applause, and spoke of the kindness he had received from sportsmen, especially Mr Basset.

The Chairman remarked that Mr Ormrod had acted most generously (applause). To hunt the district would cost him a good deal of money. Staghunting would be a splendid thing for the town, and they owed their grateful thanks to Mr Ormrod for coming forward in the manner he had done. It was a pleasant duty to present Mr Ormrod with a horn, as an emblem of a silver horn which would be given to him later. He felt sure that a token of the kind had never been given to a keener sportsman or a better man. (Applause.)

Mr Ormrod expressed his thanks for the emblem, of which he said he felt utterly undeserving. (Voices: "No, no.") It afforded him great pleasure to think that he should return to the district in a few months. He again thanked Mr Basset, one of the finest sportsmen in the country, for the assistance he had given him, and said that Mr Smith, Major Raby, Mr Ashton, and, in fact, everybody, had rendered every assistance. (Applause.)

☞ TO-DAY. ☜
——o——

MR. PETER ORMROD'S
STAGHOUNDS.
——o——

ALL INTERESTED IN STAGHUNTING ARE
REQUESTED TO

ATTEND A MEETING
— AT THE —

GUILDHALL, BARNSTAPLE,
TO-DAY, (THURSDAY).

Chair to be taken at Three o'clock by C. H. BASSET,
Esq.

Staghunting the Barnstaple country will be discussed. It is also intended to present Mr. Ormrod
with a slight souvenir as a token of the appreciation
of his having hunted the country for the past two
months.

J. A. RABY AND W. L. ASHTON,
HON. SECRETARIES.
[762]

A Stag Hunt near Barnstaple
17th January 1901

A large party of local sportsmen turned up on Saturday at
Chelfham Mills for a day's staghunting. The meet was not advertised, but the increasing number of stags causing some complaint among the farmers it was found expedient to have a by-
meet. Mr C H Basset, as acting Master, was punctual, and the
field were glad to welcome him. Mr W L Ashton was present as
huntsman. Four couples of tufters were sent away into Sepscott
Wood. It was not long before as many as eight very fine stags
were afoot. They crossed the Old Park in full view of the field.
One deer went ahead in front of the tufters to Woolly Barton, and
then into the Arlington covers, which is forbidden ground to the
hunt. The hounds were consequently soon stopped, and it was
seen that the remaining seven stags had made off in other directions. The field returned some distance, via Loxhore Cot, when
news was given by that keen young sportsman, Sir Edward
Chichester's son, that a good stag had been seen in Mill Wood.
Mr Basset gave orders to bring up the pack. They were soon laid

on, and ran in good form to Long Timber. In a short time they were down to Pitt, in the borough of Barnstaple. Only one sportsman was even with them, and that was Henry Hitchcock. The stag, completely pumped, had got into the millstream. Five or six miles had been run at terrific speed, but the field was up in no time. The stag lost no time in slipping down into the river Yeo, and then, being somewhat refreshed, he crossed up to a little planting by Ivy Lodge. The hounds were foiled by the water. There was a halloa to Ivy Lodge planting, and hounds reached there in a moment, the wily animal had succeeded in shoving out a hind to draw off the hounds, while he secured safety by remaining in the planting. The hind went straight across to Ackland Hill, then to Landkey covers, to Bradninch and Gunn. Crossing to Hutchington, the stag ran down to Stoke Cross, and then to Yarde, in the parish of Stoke Rivers. Going through Stoke, he made his way back to Chelfham Mills. Darkness now setting in, hounds were called off, and the hope was expressed that an early opportunity would be given in a similar manner of meeting again.

February 14th 1901

In consequence of deer doing much damage and causing farmers considerable trouble in the Barnstaple district, Captain Peter Ormrod, has returned to North Devon from Lancashire for hunting purposes a month earlier than was originally arranged. The pack of hounds he has just brought to Barnstaple is an entirely new one, Captain Ormrod having at great trouble and expense collected 25 couple of hounds which, it is considered, will be suitable for hunting in North Devon. The hounds have all been drafted for size from various packs of foxhounds, and they include some of the best blood in England, coming chiefly from the famous Oakley, Brocklesby and Warwickshire strains. Captain Ormrod has also brought ten new horses – they are all thoroughbreds, and are larger than those which he used last season. Mr C H Basset has again kindly placed his kennels at Captain Ormrod's disposal, and the horses will be stabled at the Horse Repository (Mr Ash's) in Braunton-road. Captain Ormrod is still hunting his own hounds in Lancashire (where, it is interesting to note, he is adopting Devonshire methods in connection with outlying deer, and tufting with two or three couple of hounds) and in his absence next Wednesday (when the meet will be at Chelfham Mills) his huntsmen will take charge of the hounds. After next week, Captain Ormrod will hunt the district regularly two days a week until the end of March. Deer are exceptionally plentiful in the district, and some fine sport is anticipated.

STAGHUNTING NEAR BARNSTAPLE

A FINE RUN AND A KILL

14th March 1901

There was a very noteworthy run in connection with Peter Ormrod's Staghounds on Saturday. The meet was at Chelfham, and Mr Comer Clarke reported to a large field that deer were lying in Smithapark Wood. Mr Ormrod kennelled a portion of his pack at Chelfham Mills in case the deer came inwards, and the remaining portion were taken on to westland, near the Friendship Inn, should the deer go to the forest, which has occurred frequently of late. The tufters, however, were taken into Smithapark Wood, and were soon on the line of the deer. Mr Basset viewed a hind away over the top of the wood, pointing for Exmoor. She was followed by another hind and calf, and a male deer. These at once made off for Arlington. The tufters, however, stuck to the line of the first hind, and pushed her on as far as Hunnacott. Just beyond this some furse was on fire, and this undoubtedly turned her back again. She recrossed the top of the hill, passing in front of Mr Comer Clarke's house, and down the valley by the Bratton stream, crossing the road near Bratton Cross, into Youlston Wood. Tufters were running very hard, and were pushing their deer along at a great pace. When opposite Chelfham Mills the portion of the pack kennelled were liberated, taken to Youlston Old Park, and laid on. It was at once evident that scent was exceptionally good, for the hounds went away with tremendous dash, on through New Barn and Sepscott, coming down to Collar Bridge and into Coxleigh Wood. The hind, with the hounds in full pursuit, ran very fast along the top of the wood, and it was now simply a race for several miles, the field galloping along parallel to the aqueduct of the Barnstaple water-works, as far as Kingdon Gardens, where the hind came to the river Yeo, and ran for some distance down the water, coming out near Pitt Farm and ascending the hill towards the residence of Mr George Brown, Mayor of Barnstaple, turning however, again to the left, and passing near the filter beds over Raleigh Park. There was a slight check here in the numerous lanes in to the locality, but the hounds soon hit off the line in the Park, running over Mr Basset's meadows of Westaway, passing east of Pilton, across the River Yeo, and up the valley between Frankmarsh and Gorwell, to Stoneyard, where the hind crossed the main road, near Waytown, pointing for Landkey. There was some difficult ground to cross, the country being very close, and a number of banks had to be negotiated. But there was no time to be lost, as the hind had been viewed passing between Mount Sandford and Mr C E R Chanter's residence. The Great Western Railway line was crossed, the course then being on to Chestwood (where the hind was plainly viewed by a number of spectators in the Barnstaple football field) to the top of the hill which overlooks Bishopstawton, with Coddon Hill lying immediately to the left. The hind went down to the water here, where she soiled. Doubtless she would have gone to Coddon Hill, but there was a good deal of gorse burning, which turned her down the valley. Hounds puzzled out the line through the water in capital style, and forced her along on the back of Bishopstawton village, where she jumped into Mr G C Davie's lawn and was killed, after a chase of three hours. A large crowd assembled to see the finish. Mr Basset ordered the carcass to be taken to the Barnstaple Station to be returned by the Lynton Railway to Mr Comer Clarke, who will distribute it among the farmers in the valley.

On Monday the pack was taken to Lynton by Mr Peter Ormrod to hunt the following day on Exmoor, through the kind invitation of Mr R A Sanders, Master of the Devon and Somerset Staghounds.

The old Friendship Inn, now renamed Friendship Farm. The Barnstaple Staghounds frequently passed by this old Inn during their runs. Hunting Appointments from newspapers refer to the Barnstaple Staghounds, the Barnstaple and North Devon Harriers, the Devon and Somerset Staghounds and Sir Bruce Chichester's Foxhounds all meeting here at different times.
© Richard Lethbridge.
Thanks to George & Ann Douglas of Friendship Farm

Peter Ormrod's Staghounds

The recent meet of these hounds will long be remembered by those fortunate enough to be present as one of the best days seen for a very long time after deer in the Barnstaple district. Owing to complaints having been made of damage done by deer in the Bratton Valley, these hounds, with Mr Ashton as huntsman, met at 11 o'clock, and trotted off with a select field to draw Smithapark. The pack having been kennelled at Westland (in the hope of a moorland run, which was afterwards fully realised), tufters were put into Mr Comer Clarke's coverts, and soon roused four hinds, which made away through Titecombe, across the Lynton road, skirted Arlington, and came back through Smithapark and Titecombe, and on to Titchen, and up the valley, across the railway line past Wistlandpound, where the pack were laid on almost in view of the deer. Racing up over Longstone (one of the hinds was viewed lying down here, hounds went across Farley Water, and on to Hoar Oak, where the deer were successfully headed off from the deer park, and came back over Woodborough and Pinkery Pond, across the Chains to Farley Water. Here hounds fresh found the deer lying under a thorn bush, and, pressing the three over Lincombe, down to the Lyn Valley, on to the railway line almost into Lynton Railway Station, they divided. One hind, unable to jump the high wire fence, with the pack in close pursuit, ran up the valley almost to Woolhanger, where she turned and after a check of half an hour, was fresh found lying under a bush. Hounds raced her up as far as Farley Water, where this gallant hind was taken at 5 o'clock, after running since 12 o'clock. The distance run, judging by those who know the country well, was computed at not less than thirty-five miles. Those in at the finish of this grand run were the hunstsman, to whom great praise is due. Major Raby, Messrs Stanbury, F Taplin, B Raby, Impey, W Smith and T Dalling.

New Pack of Hounds

By August 1901, Peter Ormrod had finished hunting the Barnstaple district. Newspaper reports give his last season as being inglorious and there was "no desire to resume the connection upon either side". This lead to the formation of the Barnstaple Staghounds under the Mastership of Captain Ewing Paterson of Bickington Lodge and Mr Arundell Clarke of Fremington. In 1904 Peter Ormrod returned to North Devon and became Master of the Exmoor Foxhounds for a season. At the same time he brought down his staghounds to hunt on the moor by kind permission of the Master of the Devon and Somerset Staghounds Mr R A Sanders, erecting temporary kennels for them near Oare house, and with the aid of his north country kennel huntsman, Jack Greenway, an absolute embodiment of James Pigg, he succeeded in killing twenty deer in the 1904-05 season, two of them stags, the rest mainly hinds from the Cloutsham district. In 1905, while both hunting on Exmoor, Peter Ormrod and the Barnstaple Staghounds met up at Porlock Water.

In the hunting appointments of 1905 we see there are five packs of hounds advertised, including Peter Ormrod's and the Barnstaple Staghounds who were hunting at the same time. A newspaper report follows of Mr Ormrod quitting the Barnstaple district and a few misinformed rumours that were going around at the time.

The Present and Future Condition of he Hunt

Whoever supplies the local hunting notes and comments to our contemporary "The Field" should endeavour to be a little more accurate and less imaginative with his information. This authority declares that "Mr Peter Ormrod may become Master of a fourth pack of hounds in the Barnstaple district." May he? This will be news to most individuals, and to none more than Mr Peter Ormrod himself. The connection between that gentleman and the Barnstaple district, brief as it was, afforded little, if any, encouragement for its continuance or renewal. True, at the period of his last departure certain quidnuncs intimated that "next season Mr Ormrod intended to return with a fine lot of hounds," but as was pointed out in these columns at the time, Mr Ormrod's departure was probably destined to be final; and so we believe it will prove to be. The season proved inglorious, and we can ascertain no evidence of any desire to resume the connection upon either side. The new Masters, Captain Paterson, of Bickington Lodge, and Mr Arundell Clarke, of Femington, may be depended upon to give every satisfaction, and if the Hunt can flourish under any auspices it will certainly do so under theirs. How long it will be after the commencement before trouble again breaks out over the forbidden ground, cannot be foretold. Every effort will, however, be made so that the slightest pretext for complaint or interference many be avoided.

Hunting Appointments of 1905 when Peter Ormrod was
hunting with his staghounds on the moor.

HUNTING APPOINTMENTS.

DEVON AND SOMERSET STAGHOUNDS.

Thursday, February 9 .... Hawkridge.
Friday, February 10 .... Winsford Hill.
Monday, February 18 .... Dunkery Hill Gate.
Tuesday, February 14 .... Mountsey Hill Gate.
Thursday, February 16 .... Hawkridge.
Friday, February 17 .... Winsford Hill.

At 10 a.m.

PETER ORMROD'S STAGHOUNDS.

(BY INVITATION.)

Friday, February 10 .... Meet cancelled.
Tuesday, February 14 .... Cloutsham.
Friday, February 17 ... Shepherd's Cot, Badgworthy.

At 10 a.m.

QUANTOCK STAGHOUNDS.

Saturday, February 11 .... Quantock Farm.

At 10.30 a.m.

SIR JOHN AMORY'S STAGHOUNDS.

Saturday, February 11 .... Hele Bridge

At 10.30 a.m.

BARNSTAPLE STAGHOUNDS

Saturday, February 11 .... Chelfham.
Tuesday, February 14 .... Challacombe.

At 10.30 a.m.

Taking the
Tufters to
covert, by
Whitestones
*from The Red
Deer of Exmoor
by Archibald
Hamilton pub.
Horace Cox 1907*

CHAPTER 5

BARNSTAPLE STAGHOUNDS

I n the second part of the 1901 season – the year in which the Barnstaple Staghounds were established – we see a withdrawal of Peter Ormrod's Staghounds and newspaper reports inform us of this new pack constituted under the joint Mastership of Capt Ewing Paterson (Adjutant of the Royal North Devon Imperial Yeomanry) from Bickington Lodge, and Mr Arundell Clarke of Fremington. Below is a description of the pack from Bailys Hunting Directory.

BARNSTAPLE STAGHOUNDS

Masters – Captain Ewing Paterson, and Arundell Clarke, Esq.
Huntsmen – The Masters
Whipper-in – C Tucker
Harbourer –
Sixteen couples of hounds
Kennels – Sowden, Barnstaple
Telegraph Office and Railway Station – Barnstaple 1 mile distant.
Days of Meeting –
The Barnstaple Staghounds hunt the same country as the Barnstaple and North Devon Harriers.

The hounds are owned by the Committee. The Masters have no guarantee: the minimum subscription is one guinea: capping is not practiced.

The pack was established in 1901 to hunt the district in which deer from Exmoor had become increasingly numerous.

102

Collecting flesh for the Tiverton Staghounds from Douglas A
Gratton, family butcher, of Boutport Street, Barnstaple. 2003.
Left to right, Guy Loosemore (whipper-in 1998-2003), David
Gratton (butcher), John Norrish (huntsman).
100 years ago flesh would have been collected around
the town for the Barnstaple Staghounds.
© Richard Lethbridge

DEVON & SOMERSET
STAGHOUNDS.

RATES OF PAYMENT FOR FLESH AT KENNELS:

HORSES (ALIVE)	15/- to 21/-
(DEAD)	10/- to 15/-
BULLOCKS AND COWS	7/6 to 10/-

The above Prices are for when sent for by Kennels. Extra Payment when delivered by Owners at Kennels.—Apply :
            S. TUCKER, THE KENNELS, EXFORD.

An advert from 1907 showing prices
paid for flesh at the Devon and
Somerset Staghound kennels

August 22nd 1901
Staghunting near Barnstaple

Barnstaple Staghounds virtually opened what promises to be a highly successful season yesterday, when a bye meet of the newly-formed Barnstaple Staghounds took place at Heddon Mills near Braunton, for the purpose of entering young hounds. The pack has recently been constituted under the joint Mastership of Capt Paterson (Adjutant of the Royal North Devon Imperial Yeomanry) of Bickington Lodge and Mr Arundell Clarke of Fremington, both Masters attending yesterday's meet. Among those also present were Mr C H Basset, Mrs Curzon, Miss Hurst, Misses Arthur (Marwood), Mr E J Soares MP, Messrs W L Ashton, J H List, Armer, and German. Starting just after 8 am, a four-year-old stag was soon disturbed in Buttercombe Wood, and he gave the field a fine gallop. The quarry headed for Lee, near Ilfracombe, and he was hunted back to Mortehoe, where he entered the sea. He was lost sight of, but he soon returned, scent being picked up again at Lee. He raced to Morte and then made his way back to Spreacombe. As the pace had been pretty hot for four hours, Capt Paterson called off the hounds. The pack (which numbered fourteen couples) went remarkably well, and it promises to become very smart. it was reported that there were several deer in the woods round Spreacombe yesterday, and it is evident that this part of the district will show some good sport. Red deer are this season very plentiful in the Loxhore valley.

The opening meet has been fixed for Monday September 2nd, in Youlston Old Park.

The Barnstaple Staghounds hunt button.

We are very lucky that the ancestors of the late William Lawrence Ashton, who later became Huntsman, still retain some of the hunt buttons. The inscription on the small button on the right reads "prosperity to staghunting".On the reverse of the buttons the makers are recorded with the name of Firmin & Son of 108 St Martin's Lane, London

September 5th 1901
Barnstaple Staghounds
Opening Meet

On the breezy heights of Old Youlston Park (the property of Sir Edward Chichester), the first meet of the new Barnstaple Staghounds was held on Monday. Surrounded by timbered and pasture lands, Old Youlston Park is an ideal spot for the purposes of a hunt meet, and from different parts fine views of Exmoor on the one hand, and Dartmoor on the other, can be obtained. The morning was rather threatening and decidedly nippy, with a keen north easterly blowing. Not at all an ideal morning for late summer, good as it might be for scent. The new joint Masters of the hunt are Mr Arundell Clarke and Captain Ewing Paterson (Fremington). Carrying the horn, Captain Paterson brought a mixed pack of fifteen couples to the meet, and he had the pleasure of seeing about 300 persons present, about 150 of whom were mounted. They included representatives of all classes and many on cycles with a good show of pedestrians, and numbers in private and hired carriages. Great things are expected of the hounds, many of which have been procured at considerable expense from different parts of the United Kingdom. On Monday the animals looked very smart, and were generally admired. the new hunt dress – scarlet coat and canary waistcoat, with buttons bearing a slot and the initials "B.S.H." – was, too, an object of considerable interest.

Among the first to arrive was Mr C H Basset JP, ex-Master of the Devon and Somerset Staghounds, who had consented to act as field master for the day. Among those present were Lady Chichester (wife of Sir Edward Chichester of Youlston), the Misses Chichester, Miss Hurst, Miss Curson, Mrs Arundell Clarke and party, Misses Hext, Ashton, Berry, Bury Russell, Smoldon, Mrs Hutton, Mrs Tamlyn, Mrs Beckwith, the Misses de Guerin, Mrs Smith, Mrs Bencraft (in carriages), the Misses Lovell, Mrs F H Toller, Mrs W Penhale, Miss Crang, Miss Arthur, and Miss Tamlyn, &c. Sir Augustus Warren, Messrs Las Casas, M Squire, W L Ashton, W Penhale, J H List, J Baker, W M Burridge, Kelland, Studd, Rowe, R Vickery, A and T Thomas Randall (Swindon), A T Hutton, G Bale, H Waldon, J Fry, Sydney Reavell, W Boson, E R Berry-Torr, Berry, Smyth, the Revs J Dene, Albany Wrey, and E G Beckwith, Messrs C Marsh, W V Richards, L Cooke, Copp (Ilfracombe), J Q Tamlyn, J R Harper, W E Arthur, J Western, De Lautour, Hill E Chanter, Smith, Comer Clarke, H Dalling, Chamings, Crang, German (Barnstaple), German (South Molton), Chubb, M Ffoulkes, Mr P Evered (Secretary of the Devon and Somerset

Staghounds), Mr Greig, with Sydney Tucker, the whip.

Mr Shapland, Sir Edward Chichester's keeper, came with the news that a large stag was lying in New Barn Wood. Mr Basset decided, however, that as the Warren was in full view of the spectators at the meet, it should be tufted first. The pack was accordingly kennelled at Woolley, and Captain Paterson took three couples of tufters, and proceeded to draw the Warren, which was, unfortunately, found to be blank. The pack was then taken on to Chelfham Mills and kennelled, and a fresh relay of tufters was taken into Youlston Woods, where a large number of hinds were found. A good stag was also roused, and two tufters ran it over Youlston Old Park, and on to Cot Wood, thence into Woolley Wood, adjoining Miss Chichester's Arlington coverts, which the hunt are prohibited from entering. As the wire fence (which is being erected at the expense of the hunt) around these coverts is not yet finished, it was decided not to lay on the pack, which might go at once into the Arlington coverts. Mr Comer Clarke reported that he had a good stag lying in Smythapark Wood, but as the day was getting far advanced (it being nearly 4 o'clock) it was decided that the hounds should be taken home, the next meet being fixed for Saturday at Smythapark. Although there was no kill the day's sport afforded much satisfaction.

Captain Paterson, ably supported by Mr Arundell Clarke, negotiated banks, gates and rails as they came, and worked hard to rouse a runnable deer. A deer calf that recently died of injuries caused by wire fencing was come across in the course of the day's tufting. Deer are plentiful in the district, and a very successful season is anticipated.

Woody Bay Station, where the Barnstaple Staghounds used to meet

Old Youlston Park, where the Barnstaple Staghounds had their opening meet.
Photo courtesy of Tom Bartlett's postcard collection

September 12th 1901
Staghunting near Barnstaple
A kill in the borough

In the second meet on Saturday, the new pack of Barnstaple Staghounds established under the joint Mastership of Captain Paterson and Mr Arundell Clarke were rewarded with a kill. Saturday's meet was at Smythapark Wood, Loxhore (the property of Mr Comer Clarke), a well-known cover for deer. A good many spectators viewed the proceedings from different points, the wood overlooking the village of Bratton Fleming and the main road to Barnstaple. Among those present were Master Ted Chichester (Youlston), Messrs W L Ashton, Rafarel, German (Barnstaple), Berry jun, Comer Clarke, J H List, Liston, Huxtable, T W Smith, Taplin, W Richards, J Stanbury, Hobbs, R Vickery, S Petter, A E Arnold, German, Hallett, W Smyth, Mrs J Smyth, Mrs F H Toller, Mrs Arundell Clarke, Miss Clarke, Misses Paterson, Mrs German, Miss Crang &c. Mr C H Basset acted as field master, while Captain Paterson and Mr Arundell Clarke (joint Masters) were huntsmen, and Charlie Tucker (brother of the well-known "Devon and Somerset" whip Sidney) was whip.

The pack was kennelled at Chelfham. Five couples of tufters were put into the coverts, but during the first hour and a half they only succeeded in rousing a hind and calf, although there was plenty of evidence of the presence of a stag in the neighbourhood. Eventually the tufters were taken from the covers to New Barn, near Youlston Old Park, the property of Sir Edward Chichester, Bart, whose kindness in allowing sportsmen to cover his property is much appreciated by them. Here a good four year old stag was soon roused. Hounds being laid on, he was run down to Collar Bridge, and returned to the meadows below. He went over New Barn and Youlston Old Park, and made straight for Woolley and the Warren, thence through Cott Wood and Woolley Wood, pointing for Arlington Covers. here he attempted to jump the fencing. Coming back through Cott Wood he once more headed for the Warren, under Woolley, and Mill Wood, New Barn, Sepscott, and Coxleigh Wood to the back of Kingdon Gardens, where he was viewed crossing Coxleigh Cleave. He next turned his attention to Roborough Plantation, and crossed the Shirwell old road. Having made an entry into the lawn of the residence of his Worship the Mayor of Barnstaple (Mr G W F Brown), he led the hounds out at the back, and was seen pointing for the Shirwell new road. The stag made off over the hills, crossing under Westaway, the residence of Mr C H Basset, in the borough of Barnstaple, and was killed in the pool. It was a fine stag, with brow and bay and one on top. Among those in at the finish were Mr Basset (who was very well pleased at the kill taking place at Westaway), Mr Arundell Clarke, Miss Clarke, Miss Smoldon, Messrs Dalling jun, Ashton, Taplin, Hallett, Tucker (the whip), Smith, Litson, S N Petter, German, and others. The party was subsequently hospitably entertained at Westaway by Mr Basset, who remarked that he had heard there was a kill at the same spot about 100 years ago.

The hounds did their work well, and the run, lasting about four hours, was a very exciting and enjoyable one.

The Mayor of Barnstaple, Mr G W F Brown. During the 12th September 1901 hunt, the stag made an entry into his lawn

September 12th 1901

So far, the utmost satisfaction has been expressed at the manner in which the Barnstaple Staghounds is being managed; and the extraordinary difference noticed in the handling of the hounds, and the conduct of the hunt generally, today, compared with what they were last year, have drawn forth universal comendation. The open-handed liberality of Sir Edward Chichester in allowing the hunt to cover his property, is much appreciated, and is compared with the attitude of some other land owners in this district. Every encouragement is being shown, and we trust will be continued, to the successful maintenance of the Barnstaple Hunt, and at no time has it been upon a sounder basis than it is today. The usual howl from the sickly sentimental and professedly "humane" individuals, people who sometimes go away for weeks together and leave their unfortunate cats to starve, and who think everything of what they disapprove should be abolished, has not as yet made itself heard. But we expect it. Immediately the dull season commences the customary dismal wails from "Constant Reader," "Devonian," "Fiat Justitia," and other anonymous scribblers make themselves a nuisance, and there is no reason to suppose that we shall escape them this year. Where, also, are the thunderous denunciations of our old friends Reginald Ottley, "De renroi," "Spectemur Agendo," and others? Anyhow their opinions have but little weight and produce small effect with anybody, while the hunt continues merrily all the same. Under the auspices of the present Masters, the Barnstaple Staghounds seem destined to enjoy a thoroughly successful season.

Kingdon Gardens
Kingdon Gardens became a regular run for the Barnstaple Staghounds.
On a recent visit, I could sense the history of the place and what it might
have looked like in its heyday. Mr and Mrs Morgan, the owners, are slowly
restoring it to its former glory.

Kingdon Gardens
In 1910 the Minehead Staghounds killed a stag here.

Photos © Richard Lethbridge

110

September 14th 1901

Mr Arundell Clarke and Captain Ewing Paterson have accepted an invitation from Mr Sanders (the Master of the Devon and Somerset Staghounds) to meet at Brendon Two Gates on Monday the 23rd inst, when they and their hounds will be the guests of Lord Ebrington at Simonsbath House. Mr Ian Amory of Sir John Amory's Staghounds will meet in the same neighbourhood by invitation on two days in the same week, and the Devon and Somerset will put in the other three days, so that the forest deer, by end of this combined week, should have received a pretty complete scattering.

September 26th 1901
Barnstaple Staghounds

Blackmoor Gate, in the neighbourhood of which deer have been doing considerable damage of late, was the meeting place of Barnstaple Staghounds on Tuesday. The pack was kennelled at Kemacott, and following the finding of a hind and calf on the eastern side of the valley, three stags were roused on Heal Farm. One of these animals crossed the valley, a memorable run by way of Combe Martin Common, Woolhanger, Shallowford, Lynton, Hoareoak, Brendon Two Gates, and Langcombe, eventually taking the stag into Badgeworthy wood, and thence into the far-famed Doone valley. Many deer had been seen on the way, and owing to their multiplicity here, the field had the mis-fortune to get off the line of the hunted stag, Capt Paterson, who had been supported by a large field, decid-ing to "draw off". Mr Nicholas Snow of Oare, put in an appearance at Badgeworthy, and received hearty congrat-ulations on recovery from his recent accident.

October 24th 1901
Hunting
Barnstaple Staghounds

These Staghounds met at Larkborough by the invitation of Mr Sanders, Master of the Devon and Somerset Staghounds. The hounds were taken to Simonsbath the night previously, the joint Masters (Captain Paterson and Mr Arundell Clarke) being the guests of Lord Ebrington. The pack was kennelled at Tours Hill, Lord Ebrington acting as field master. There was a fine run, the stag being run to a point near Porlock Weir. As daylight was fail-ing, hounds were called off.

An article from the *North Devon Journal* 21st November 1901, which refers to staghunting in Barnstaple as mentioned in Philip Evered's book *Staghunting on Exmoor*

When Mr Philip Evered was writing his charming book on "Staghunting on Exmoor" the establishment of a pack of staghounds at Barnstaple had probably not been definitely decided on. But, as a matter of fact, with the commencement of the present season staghunting was resumed in the Barnstaple district under highly promising conditions. That Mr Evered fully appreciated, however, the nature of the difficulties that lay before the hunt is shown by the following paragraph:

"As time passes it may confidently be predicted that the Barnstaple district will not be satisfied without the establishment of a pack on similar lines to those already carried out with such success. Suitable coverts, and a noble herd of deer in close proximity to the height of Exmoor, afford such certainty of good sport as can never long be allowed to remain idle. The history of staghunting contains many instances of individual landlords exhibiting animosity to the chase which brings health to some and affluence to others of the neighbours, but public opinion and the welfare of the many have sufficient influence and weight in modern England to ensure the ultimate victory of the will of the many over the prejudices of the few. The time for exercise of even the most ordinary rights and privileges is passing fast into the limbo of other long-forgotten feudal habits, but old-world ways and customs linger still among the hills and fogs of Exmoor, along with the cheery courtesy and pleasant welcome which might better be preserved than some of the rough and ready old-world customs that have prevailed since times before all history."

Staghunting in the Barnstaple district has just been deferred pending the result of an action commenced by Miss Chichester, of Arlington Court, against the Masters of the Hunt.

A meet at Venniford Cross of the Devon and Somerset Staghounds. This would have been a typical scene of carriages etc at Barnstaple Staghound meets also.

A typical seen from a Tiverton Staghounds run, 2004 shows a number of quad bikes out hunting.
© Richard Lethbridge

February 27th 1902
Barnstaple Staghounds
Two Hinds Taken

From a meet at Chelfham Mills a hind was killed in Woolley Wood. It being still early in the day – about 2 o'clock – hounds were taken on to Smithapark, the pack being kennelled at Combe Farm. Captain Paterson commenced to tuft Smithapark Wood. There was soon a "halloa" up the valley, and the tufters ran a hind right up to Wistland Pound, where just beyond the Lynton and Barnstaple Railway they were stopped. In the meantime Charlie Tucker (the whip) had gone back for the pack, and brought the hounds on to the Friendship Inn. Scent was still good, and hounds ran remarkably well over Woolhanger, the field going by Longstone, and down over Butterhill and Lynton Common. Hounds continued to run at a good pace to Shallowford, and thence gave a splendid gallop to Hoar Oak, over Cheriton Ridge, and down to Farley Combe. In consequence of the growing darkness, it was now decided to call off the hounds. A good many of the riders and pack returned to Barnstaple by train from Blackmoor Gate, the field being well pleased with two kills and the first rate moor gallop.

The venison of one of the hinds was distributed among farmers of Shirwell, and that of the other among those of Loxhore and Bratton Fleming.

HUNTING
6th March 1902
Barnstaple Staghounds
A Run Through the Borough

The Barnstaple Staghounds again had good sport on Thursday. The pack was kennelled at Chelfham Mills, and the tufters were taken by Captain Paterson on to Mill Wood, near Loxhore Cot, where a hind was soon found. She raced down the valley on to New Barn Wood. The pack was taken out and laid on. The hind led the field through Coxleigh Wood, pointing for Barnstaple. Hounds and deer ran at a great pace over Frankmarsh and across the Bear-street (Barnstaple) road, just above the cemetery. Crossing the Devon and Somerset line under Sowden, they made for Chestwood. Above Bishopstawton there was a slight check. Mr Willie Smith, however, succeeded in slotting the hind down over some allotment ground near the Law Memorial Buildings. Hounds carried the line down to the banks of the river Taw, but were unable to hunt further. Capt. Paterson tried up and down the water for some time without avail. Thinking the deer had probably crossed over to the Tawstock covers, he crossed the river, but hounds were unable to recover the scent, and after searching about for some time they returned to kennels. A large company attended the meet. The pack was taken to Lynton on Saturday and kennelled at Messrs Jones's stables.

March 6th 1902
Barnstaple Staghounds

The red deer of Exmoor have become so increasingly numerous during late years that they are extending their bounds in all directions. For some time they have been seen in the Tiverton district, where their range has increased towards Chulmleigh and Eggesford. In the Barnstaple district the deer have become so numerous as to occasionally be within the bounds of the borough itself, whilst along the Martinhoe and Lynton side they have advanced into the rugged valley of Heddon's Mouth. The Barnstaple Staghounds met in this valley two or three times last autumn, whilst, numerous deer having been reported of late, there was a further meet at Hunter's Inn on Monday. A large field assembled to meet Mr Arundell G Clarke (who is at present hunting the hounds). Mr C H Basset acted as field master, and among those also present were Mrs Curzon, Miss Hurst, Messrs B Fanshawe, Litson, H Medway, T Jones, and many others, those driving including Mrs Arundell Clarke and children, and Mr W Riddell and party. The pack was kennelled at Kemacott on the Wooda Bay side of the valley, and Mr Arundell Clarke proceeded opposite with a strong draft of tufters, taking care to avoid two fine stags which were known to be lying further down. Before long a hind was roused, and after a considerable time she put up and down the valley. Subsequently crossing to the Martinhoe side she came out on the top and was viewed away towards Martinhoe Church by Mr Basset, who ordered the pack to be taken out. The hounds at once took up the running. Scent was not over good, but the hounds proceeded at a fair pace past Martinhoe village on to the Lynton golf links, then bearing away to the right, at first as though for Woolhanger, and then down the valley to Barbrook Mill. Again pointing to the left, the hind recrossed the Lynton Railway not far from Lynton Station, going over the hill and dropping into the far famed Valley of Rocks. She now pointed her head straight for the sea, scrambled down the almost inaccessible cliff at a spot between the Castle Rock and Lee Abbey and swam out to sea. Mr Basset sent Mr Litson to Lynmouth for a boat, which after a short delay, worked round to the Northern Cliff, the hind being taken and speedily dispatched. The run, lasting three hours, was over a rough and broken country, but nevertheless was a most enjoyable one. Mr Arundell G Clarke is to be congratulated on the manner in which he hunted the pack on this, the first day in which he actually took personal command, the opinion being expressed by those who are well able to judge that he handled the pack remarkably well. Monday's kill made the fifth hind taken within a month.

LYNTON & BARNSTAPLE RAILWAY.

---o---

EXCURSION TICKETS

--- TO ---

LYNTON, WOODY BAY, AND BLACKMOOR

EVERY WEEK-DAY,

FROM BARNSTAPLE TOWN, at 6 20 a.m. and 10 30 a.m. DAILY ; at 9.5 a.m MONDAYS, WEDNESDAYS, and FRIDAYS only ; at 12 38 p.m. TUESDAYS, THURSDAYS, and SATURDAYS only. Return from Lynton by any train on day of issue.

C. E. DREWETT, General Manager.

March 13th 1902
Barnstaple Staghounds
A kill in the borough

Barnstaple Staghounds met at Chelfham on Thursday. There was a good field. Tufters were taken to Smithapark, but the wood was drawn blank. Crossing the River Yeo, Long Timber Wood and Null Wood were drawn, two hinds being started from the latter.

In view of a portion of the field, they made for Woolley Wood, the larger of the hinds getting through the wire fencing around the Arlington Estates. The tufters were at once stopped.

The smaller hind was again aroused in the wood and broke away towards Shirwell closely followed by the tufters. She crossed Youlston Old Park and Collar Bridge. The hind kept close to the Yeo, and raced towards Raleigh and through Roborough and Pitt Plantations.

Turning right handed through Coxleigh Wood, the hind led at a hot pace over the moors under Pilton Lawn. Here she took to the water and swam along the stream as far as the pond outside Pilton Park, where she was taken.

© S A Hesman (Scenic Prints)

The Barnstaple Staghounds
10th April 1902
Concluding Meet
Preparing for a move to the new kennels at Brynsworthy, Fremington

At the invitation of Mr Sanders, Master of the Devon and Somerset Staghounds, the Barnstaple Staghounds met on Tuesday at Nadrid Cross, North Molton, for the last day of the season. Among those present at the meet, besides the two Masters (Mr Arundell Clarke and Capt Paterson), were Miss Paterson, Miss Bull, Miss Arthur, Mrs Turner, Mrs Penhale, Sir William Williams, Mr John Williams (Master of the Fourburrow), Col Henderson, Mr F Day (Mayor of South Molton), Messrs E Arthur, W Penhale, Kelland, Moor, Williams, W L Ashton, Stanbury, German, Pearce, W Smyth, Robins, H Turner, Slader, Burnell, and several others.

The pack was kennelled at West Park Farm. Mr Slader reported several deer to be lying about Hacche Wood and adjacent covers. Capt Paterson proceeded to tuft down the valley, and two fine stags were soon on foot, crossing the North Molton road, which runs to the station. One of the stags turned away to the right, the other pointing on for Burcombe. The pack was soon brought down and laid on this deer. Hounds at once settled down to their work, and ran at a great pace to Whitechapel, Whitecott, and then into the great Molland covers. Unfortunately, in Molland Wood several deer were on foot, and this old stag here found a substitute. He put up a three-year-old, which the hounds followed up on by Cuzzicombe Posts and Molland Common, and then down to Lyshwell. They ran on down the Danesbrook, underneath White Rocks, where five or six

Mr Charlie Slader who did the harbouring for the Barnstaple Staghounds while they were in the South Molton district. He is seen here while he was hunting the South Molton Staghounds during the First World War,

hinds got in front of them. But some of the hounds stuck to the hunted stag, and carried it over Hawkridge, down to the river Barle, and up water to Tarrs Steps, where, unfortunately, he was lost. There was never a check from the time the hounds were laid on at North Molton until the Barle was reached at Hawkridge.

Mr Arundell Clarke and Capt Paterson are already making arrangements for another season, carrying out considerable alterations in the kennels at Brynsworthy, where the pack will be shortly moved, and are obtaining strong drafts of hounds form the Limerick and Rescommon packs.

April 24th 1902
Barnstaple Staghounds
A Bye Meet

Barnstaple Staghounds met at South Molton Station on Saturday, by kind invitation of Mr Sanders the Master of the Devon and Somerset Hounds. Mr A Clarke and Captain Ewing Paterson, the joint Masters, were at the trysting place at 10 o'clock sharp, the latter carrying the horn, with 17 couples of hounds, among which appeared for the first time a fresh draft from Ireland.

Mr Charles Slader, of Hacche Barton, who so kindly harbours in this district, reported five deer in West Park Wood, into which four couples of tufters were taken after the pack had been kennelled at Hacche Barton Farm. The five deer were soon set on foot. Three of them took the line to Whitechapel, the other two that to Bremridge Wood.

The Masters decided to lay on the latter, and, quickly unkennelling the pack, got the hounds on to the larger stag of the two, starting with what appeared to be a cold scent. The quarry, crossing the road near Nadrid Cross to Brembridge Wood, took up the river Bray, through Castle Hill Park, turned north over the railway near the viaduct, keeping to the left of the Punch Bowl, and made for Tordown, through Gunn. Here the stag turned south to Landkey, where he again changed his mind and worked back to Higher Dean, through Middle Dean, and was taken in the open under Chelfham Bridge. He proved to be a fine six-year-old stag.

Hounds were never once lifted, and hunted on the ploughed land with great perseverance, but with little scent. The run lasted an hour and 35 minutes, and, as hounds ran, covered a distance of 16 miles with a ten mile point.

This is the last meet of this pack for the season, which has been a most successful one, five stags and twelve hinds having been accounted for in 25 days' hunting.

Amongst those at the finish were the Masters, Mr F Day (Mayor of South Molton), Mrs Crocker, Miss Buckingham, Messrs R L Riccard, S Mortimore (2), J Merson (2), German (2), T W Smith, F S Yendell, G Richards, C Slader, Robins (2), and F Dobbs.

The Barnstaple Staghounds occasionally travelled on the Barnstaple Lynton Railway. A sketch by Terry Gable

September 4th 1902
Hunting
Barnstaple Staghounds

The Barnstaple Staghounds met at South Molton on Saturday. Among those present were Captain Paterson (Master), Miss Paterson, Mrs Higgins, Miss Bull, Mrs Froude-Bellew, the Mayor of South Molton (Mr Fred Day), Messrs C Slader (Hacche), John Mothersdale, D J C Bush, T Burnell (Stitchpool), Merson [2] (Brinsworthy), Stranger (North Molton), G Poole, F Dobbs, H J Bird, H Sanders, F German (Marsh), R Cook, R Webber, Lock, T Moor, H Rawle, J Elworthy, J Fewings, Thorne and Newton.

The Master arrived by train with 20 couples of hounds which, were looking very fit. Mr Charles Slader (Hacche), who is the harbourer for this district, reported a stag in Eldridge Wood, and a good stag with some other deer at Hacche. The pack was first kennelled at Eldridge. There was a quick find, and hounds were at once laid on. We crossed the valley to Bicknor and Limeslake on to Ley and Beasoncott, pointing for the Moor. But the scent was so bad that the Master decided to stop the hounds and return to Hacche and draw a fresh stag. We accordingly kennelled at Hacche, where we found a splendid stag with three on top, one one side and two on the other. After running up and down the coverts the stag broke away on the top of Halse Wood, going over Newpark to Lee, on to Nadrid and Rapscott, crossing the river into Blakewell, and up the valley through Reapham. After running up and down the whole length of these woods several times, he went down to Brayley Bridge, Embercombe, and up over Park Wood, passing close to Filleigh Station, up the valley towards Buckland, down the valley again, over the top to Higher Beer and Leary Bottom – where we saw the stag just in front of the hounds. Scent, however, was not good enough to press him. When near Swimbridge, he turned right-handed up the valley, and on striking the road at the top, he ran along it for about a mile to Stone Cross. The scent was now improving, and the hounds evidenced their determination not to be beaten. The stag turned left handed and pointed for Chelfham, but when near Stoke Rivers, although the hounds were still going at a rattling pace, the hunt had to be discontinued through darkness setting in. It had been a very hard day for horses and hounds. The part of the field which remained then adjourned to Beckett Farm, and after accepting Mrs Jones's hospitality turned their horses' heads towards home.

The residents in the neighbourhood of South Molton will be pleased to know that the Barnstaple Staghounds throughout the season will regularly hunt the district including Bremridge and Hacche Woods as far as the river Mole.

Barnstaple Staghounds
Kill at Saunton
18th September 1902

There was a good field at Heddon Mills, Braunton on Saturday, to meet the Masters (Capt Paterson and Mr Arundell Clarke) despite the threatening weather. Among those present, in addition to Charlie Tucker, the whip, were Lady Holland, Lieut E Chichester, RN, Miss Paterson, Mrs F H Toller, Miss Arthur, Miss Smoldon, Messrs W E Arthur, T W Smith, C Pearce, P Avery, J Berry, W Hallett, M De las Casas, M Impey, R Lake, Stanbury, J Braunton, W Ellett Braunton, W L Ashton, and Masters Dick Lake and J Jenkins, with a number of carriages.

A stag had been well harboured by Harry Hitchcock at the back of Spreacombe House, and no sooner had the tufters been thrown in than he slipped out from the woods and lay down in the gorse in full view of the field. He was quickly roused, and the tufters being called off and the pack laid on, he ran to Pickwell Down, where a slight check occurred. While the Masters were making some good casts the deer was viewed by Mr Berry. He ran as far as Pickwell Gorse, and again lay down. The hounds immediately roused him, and ran him straight on towards the sea between Croyde and Saunton, practically at Down End. He went over the cliffs and took to the sea without hesitation.

Later the stag came back to land and was taken. A large number of excursionists at Saunton, attracted by the hunt, saw the kill, the stag being a fine six-year-old. The run was through some of the prettiest hunting country in the West of England, the views of Lundy Island, the Bristol Channel, and the North Devon Coast being very fine.

October 2nd, 1902

Mr Arundell Clarke, joint Master of Barnstaple Staghounds, had a very narrow escape on Saturday week, when the hunted stag took to the sea near the Foreland, Countisbury. As Mr Clarke was watching the hounds his horse shied at a coach descending the hill and jumped the low wall bounding the road on the cliff side. The animal rolled over, but at once regained its footing and stood quite still. Mr Clarke threw himself off, but slipped and actually rolled some distance down the cliff. He saved himself by clutching to some bushes, regaining the top of the cliff with difficulty. It was a miraculous escape.

October 16th 1902
Hunting
Barnstaple Staghounds
Kill near Braunton

The Masters, Mr Arundell Clarke and Captain Paterson, arrived punctually at 11 o'clock on Saturday at Chelfham Mills, where a large field of over 100 were awaiting them. The hounds were looking in splendid condition, and none the worse for their hard work in the two famous runs of the 4th and the 7th inst. Harry Hitchcock, the harbourer, reported that the neighbouring woods were full of young deer, which had been doing considerable damage to the farmer's crops. A large stag, however, had been harboured in Youlston Wood, the property of Sir Edward Chichester. Captain Paterson kennelled the pack at the mill, and took in 2 1/2 couples of tufters, drawing down from the top, but in spite of careful drawing only a young male deer and two hinds were set on foot. Into the mill again, and six couples of fresh tufters were drawn, and again Youlston Wood was thoroughly searched with no better result; so on to Sepscott Wood, where hounds opened at once with splendid music, and our deer, a four-year-old one-horned stag, was viewed crossing to Youlston Wood, closely followed by the tufters. On he went through Youlston Wood at a great pace, Cot Wood, Woolley Wood, back through Cot Wood, over the Warren, across Shirwell, where Charles Tucker the whip was waiting with the pack, which fairly raced our deer across Youlston Park, through Youlston Wood, Sepscott Wood, Mill Wood, where he broke cover at Kingdon Gardens, down by Brightly Cott, through Pudner, Hartpiece, Blakewell, up the valley to Sloley, Muddiford, Bittadon, the deer taking the water the whole of the valley; then back to Westdown, Dudland, West Stowford Barton, Fullabrooke, to Button Hill, where he was fresh found, fairly raced through the wood, and killed in Mr Yeo's field, two miles form Braunton, where his calves were feeding, to the great excitement of the owner. This was the end of one of the finest hunts of the season. The pack was laid on at 1.30 pm, and killed by moonlight (at 6.45 pm), and a bull's-eye lantern, kindly lent by a policeman. There is no doubt that this magnificent run even puts in the shade the fast run from Lockbarrow on Tuesday the 7th. Scent was catchy at times. Our deer thoroughly tested the hunting qualities of this new pack of hounds so successfully got together by the Masters this season. Very few of the field finished, but I noticed amongst the few Mrs Toller, Miss Smalldon (who were both presented with slots by the Master), the Masters, Mr Smallridge, and a hard-riding farmer from the Bratton Valley. This pack has only hunted ten days this season, two of which were blank, and in spite of these they have accounted for seven deer. An eighth deer went to sea at Lynton and owing to darkness setting in could not be taken.

FERRYMAN

Sketch depicting a scene from the above 1902 hunt where the Barnstaple Staghounds took their stag in the moonlight assisted by a policeman's bulls-eye lantern.
© Terry Gable

October 30th 1902
Barnstaple Staghounds

Barnstaple Staghounds met at Chelfham Mills on Saturday in lovely autumn weather. There was a large assembly of horsemen, carriages and cyclists to meet the joint Masters (Mr Arundell Clarke and Captain Paterson). Harry Hitchcock reported that there were two good stags lying in Smithapark Wood, the property of Mr Comer Clarke, and the pack was accordingly taken on to Smithapark and kennelled there. Captain Paterson proceeded with the tufters into the wood. After tufting for some time several hinds were roused, most of them running down the valley towards Youlston Wood. Later it was discovered that the two stags which had been harboured had shifted on to Tidycombe, where we could not follow them. Stags are very restless at this time of the year, and are constantly on the move. Captain Paterson, however, in the hope of finding a warrantable deer, continued to tuft on down the valley through Coombe Wood and Heale Wood and on to Youlston Wood, where a heavy deer had been slotted in the morning. Failing, however, to rouse a stag, and as it was getting on to three o'clock in the afternoon, Capt Paterson decided to draw for a hind, and so give the field a gallop. A hind was known to be lying in the warren and on it being drawn hounds soon had her on foot and ran at a tremendous pace, giving us a fine gallop over Youlston Old Park, and on to Sepscott Wood and Coxleigh Wood to Kingdon Gardens, close to Barnstaple. Here she came down to the river Yeo, but again turned up the valley and into the wood, frequently coming down stream to the soil. She retraced the whole of the valley back to Woolley Wood. At times we thought we should take her, but several deer being now to foot, and as darkness was coming on, the pack was collected and taken back to kennels at Brinsworthy.

This run was advertised "to finish the season" but another meet is contemplated for Thursday at Heddon Mills.

An advert for the White Hart Hotel, Bratton Fleming, in 1902. This was a regular meet for the Barnstaple Staghounds.

125

Archibald Hamilton's book on the red deer of Exmoor, 1907, shows the numbers of autumn deer taken by four packs including the Barnstaple Staghounds.

"The red deer herd was probably at its strongest numerically in or about 1902, and four packs of hounds, hard at work trying to diminish their numbers, succeeded in killing fifty five stags. Appended is the record of their heads, which is very well worth study as it is doubtful if any forest in the north, killing a similar number, could show such a return. Subsequent years have shown excellent heads, but 1902 stands easily first. Of the thirty five deer killed by the Devon and Somerset, one was a three year old that was lame, two were four year olds, and one, the last deer taken, was of doubtful age, carrying brow, tray and uprights, but with a wide spread, while his mouth showed him to be at least five years old and probably more. In the following table, B stands for brow, B.B for brow and bay, T for tray, and the figures for the points on the top of each antler.

Devon and Somerset Staghounds

July 28	B.T. 1-1	
	(A lame three-year-old.)	
Aug 1	B.B.T. 3-2	
Aug 4	B.B.T. 2-2	
Aug 6	B.T. 3-2	
Aug 8	B.T. 2 B.B.T. 3.	
	(The opening meet of the regular season.)	
Aug 11	B.B.T. 2-2	
Aug 13	B.B.T. 3-2	
Aug 22	B.B.T. 2-1	
	(An old deer probably going back.)	
Sept 1	B.T. 2-1 (A four-year-old.)	
Sept 6	B.B.T. 6-4	
	(A very massive, level head, the finest killed for many years.)	
Sept 12	B.B.T. 3-4	
Sept 12	B.B.T. 3-2	
	B.T. 2-2	

Sept 20	B.T. 2-2	
Sept 22	B.T. 4	B.B.T. 3
Sept 24	B.T. 3	B.B.T. 4
Sept 25	B.B.T. 4-3	
Sept 27	B.T. 2-2	
Sept 29	B.B.T. 2-2	
Oct 1	B.B.T. 3-3	
	B.T. 3-2	
Oct 4	B.T. 3-2	
Oct 6	B.T. 7-3	
	(A very curious head)	
Oct 10	B.B.T. 2	B.T. 2
Oct 11	B.T. 3	B.B.T. 2
Oct 13	B.B.T. 3-3	
	B.T. 3-3	
Oct 15	B.T. 4-5	
Oct 18	B.B.T. 3-3	
Oct 22	B.B.T. 3	B.T. 3
Oct 24	B.T. 2	B.B.T. 2
	B.T. 1-1	
	(Probably five years or upwards.)	

Sir J H H Amory's Staghounds

Sept 18 B.B.T. 3 B.T. 3
Sept 26 B.B.T. 2-2
Oct 4 B.B.T. 2 B.T. 2
Oct 8 B.T. 4 B.B. 2 and 2
offers
Oct 11 B.B.T. 2 B.T. 2

Oct 14 B.B.T. 4-3
Oct 21 B.T. 2 (on offside, a
short deformed antler
on near side.)

Barnstaple Staghounds

Sept 13 B.B.T. 2-2
Sept 24 B.B.T 3-3
Oct 4 B.B.T. 3-3
Oct 7 B.B.T. 2-2
B.B. 1-1
(The Larkbarrow day.)

Oct 11 An old stag with a
head deformed from
an injury.
Oct 25 B.B.T. 2-2

The Quantock Staghounds

Aug 18 B.B.T. 4-4 (A
particularly fine head.)
Aug 21 B.B.T. 3 B.T. 2
Aug 23 B.B.T. 6 B.T. 5
Sept 2 B.T. B.B.T. 1

Sept 5 B.B.T. 3-3
Sept 8 B.T. -2
Sept 18 B.T. 2 B.T.1
Oct 2 B.B.T. 5-4
Oct 11 B.B. 3-3 (From Slowley.)

Cycling and Hunting
15th January 1903

It must be confessed that there is some basis for the protests which are being made in many quarters concerning the presence of cyclists and motorists at meets of hounds. They have, of course, as much right to be there as any of the other spectators, and we would not suggest, says a writer in the *Daily Telegraph*, that they should be debarred from enjoying the exhilarating spectacle; but they are often an unintentional annoyance to the followers of the hunt, usually from ignorance of the ways of horses, hounds and stag. They should bear in mind that hunting is essentially a horseman's sport, and that their presence alone is sometimes sufficient to spoil the pleasure of the hunt. When a large number of horses in the pink of condition are assembled it is a drawback to the enjoyment of the riders if they have to take care that their excited mounts do not damage or become frightened by bicycles or motor-cars. This is not a case where it may be argued that horses ought to be made used to motors and cyclists. Hunting is for horse-riders alone, and he must be very selfish who commits any action by which the enjoyment of its followers is marred.

Cycling Today

100 years ago there were many cyclists who followed the hunt, but today it is very rare to see any at all. However, if you look closely you will see Peter Benn (Terrierman to the Culmstock Minkhounds), John Smith and daughter Kate, and myself occasionally peddling away with the Tiverton Staghounds.

Right: Richard Lethbridge (the author) out hunting with the Tiverton Staghounds on his bicycle.

Right: John Smith and daughter Kate on their bicycles with the Tiverton Staghounds
© Richard Lethbridge

Left: Peter Benn getting his bearings while hunting with the Tiverton Staghounds 2003.
© Richard Lethbridge

February 12th 1903
Barnstaple Staghounds

Capt Paterson, one of the Masters of Barnstaple Staghounds, has written stating his intention to resign at the close of the season. Capt Paterson who is the adjutant of the Royal North Devon Imperial Yeomanry has hunted the pack conjointly with Mr Arundell Clarke the remaining master for the past 2 seasons.

Barnstaple Staghounds in the Tiverton Country

The following meets indicate that the Barnstaple Staghounds ventured into the Tiverton Staghound country meeting down in the Chulmleigh end. I also found the following article of Sir John Amory's Staghounds (now the Tiverton Staghounds), being transported for the first time in a van.

Sir John Amory's Staghounds
November 5th 1904

Chawleigh was the meet on Wednesday, and owing to the distance from Tiverton (seventeen miles), Sir John Amory's Staghounds were conveyed thither in a light van, wired each end and drawn by a steam motor known as the Little Giant. The journey occupied three hours. Hounds found in Leigh Wood and scent was never better. The deer was eventually killed at Down Wood near Stuckeridge. The furthest point was sixteen miles and the pace was so fast all through this fine run that many well mounted followers were left.

March 12th 1903
Barnstaple Staghounds

The Barnstaple Staghounds met by invitation yesterday at Eggesford, the joint masters (Capt Arundell Clarke and Capt Paterson) being present. Deer were far too plentiful for a satisfactory hunt, and there was no kill.

March 12th 1903
Barnstaple Staghounds

These hounds met at Chawleigh on Tuesday. A stag was soon found at Cheldon Bottoms and gave the field a splendid run, taking a course to Lapford then back to Worlington and thence to Tiverton where a kill was effected. Captain Paterson and Mr Arundell Clarke the joint Masters were supported by a large company.

26th March 1903
Barnstaple Staghounds at Eggesford

Barnstaple Staghounds met on Tuesday at the Fox and Hounds Hotel, Eggesford, when there was a large field out, including Captain Paterson and Mr Arundell Clarke (joint masters), Misses M and V Arthur, the Hon J Wallop, Major Dunning, Messrs W Penhale, A F Seldon, W Arthur, A Arnold, T Bater, H Bater, A W Luxton, C Mortimer, J Tavener, J Tripe, W Parkhouse, F Webber, W Dart, C Littleworth, G R Francics, and W Cole.

Captain Paterson hunted the hounds, and kenneled the pack at Chawleigh Barton. He threw the tufters into Foxes Cover, where a four-year-old stag was immediately aroused. It went away by Castle Down, over Chenson Farm, to Church Path, where, veering left-handed, it passed on by Fiddlecot, up to Labbets, and across to Chawleigh, where the pack was laid on. The stag ran down over Mr Phillips' farm to East Leigh, and then went up to Cheldon Valley and away by Affeton, to West Worlington, on by Witheridge, thence to Bradford Pond, and straight on to Baples Hill, where it turned to the right and went away by Oakford and on close to Tiverton. Scent was poor.

Previous to starting, the hounds were photographed outside the Fox and Hounds Hotel.

April 2nd 1903
Hunting
Barnstaple Staghounds last run
Hounds Sold

Barnstaple Staghounds met on Friday at Chawleigh and found at Lamma Cleave. The stag took the field to Lamma Cleave and Upcott and then back to Lamma Cleave, and through the Southcote Woods and on to Hill Down, where it was lost. The pack was then laid on to a deer at Stone Mill, which ran up the Cheldon Valley to Affeton Lutworthy, and on to Cotten Head, where the same deer was fresh found. It ran back to the Affeton Valley again, and on to Coxleigh Wood, and over the hill towards Lapford and down to Foxes Cover to Nymet Bridge, where the deer went to water and was lost. The field got on a fresh deer at Lapford Wood, and ran over the hill to Chawleigh Barton, the hounds being ultimately stopped.

The field included, in addition to the Masters (Captain Paterson and Mr Arundell Clarke), Major Dunning, Miss Paterson, Miss Curson, Messrs A W Luxton, W E Arthur, R Whyte, Carter, Littleworth, Tripe and Cobley. This was the last day of the hunt, as the hounds will go to Mr E A V Stanley, the Master of the Quantock Staghounds, who has bought them.

Mr E A V Stanley, Master of the Quantock Staghounds in 1903, who bought the Barnstaple Staghounds. Photo from the book *Devon and Somerset Staghounds* by ET Macdermot, 1936

April 2nd 1903

The dispersal of Barnstaple Staghounds has caused great regret in sporting circles in North Devon. Some weeks ago Captain Paterson – who will probably be leaving the district during the summer, his period of service as Adjutant of the Royal North Devon Imperial Yeomanry then expiring – resigned the mastership of the hunt, and as no one came forward to join him, Mr Arundell Clarke, the joint Master, felt bound to retire also. This led to the breaking up the pack, which has been sold, most of the hounds having been secured by Mr E A V Stanley, Master of the Quantocks. Mr Stanley lost, by a most unfortunate accident, many of his best hounds early in the season, but with this and other less recent purchases, he should have fully restored his pack to their previous high state of efficiency. Some of the couples will go to the New Forest, in Hampshire. Such an unexpected sequel to a highly successful season – twenty deer having been taken – has caused much disappointment, but deer are so plentiful in the Barnstaple district that local sportsmen hope that staghunting will be resumed next season. There would be no difficulty in securing another pack. Besides if no regular pack of hounds is organised, it is probable staghunting will be carried on in connection with the Barnstaple and North Devon Harriers who a few years ago were as Catholic in their objects of chase as any pack could be, may once more show their versatility by hunting a deer occasionally. It is not, of course, a very easy thing to organise another pack, especially at a centre like Barnstaple, when the hindrances to successful hunting are in one direction so severe. There is however, a nucleus in the staghounds which have been for sometime at Sowden Kennels. These with the addition of some fresh blood would make a first rate pack. A section of the dogs at Sowden have been hunted as the Barnstaple and North Devon Harriers and have done good work. The Staghounds, although taken out sometimes, are waiting for legitimate employment. Their future fate must now seen be settled for they will in turn be sold. At present it does not seem probably that Mr A L Christie will take the Mastership as had been suggested.

Mr Christie & The Mastership

Replying to the invitation that had been extended to him to take the Mastership of the Staghounds in the Barnstaple district. Mr A L Christie writes as follows to Mr W L Ashton. "I'm sure it is very good of my Barnstaple friends and owners of the covers and land to the North of Barnstaple to offer me the Mastership of the hounds. I fear it is impossible for me to accept it. There are various difficulties in my way today. Had I been able to see my way to fall in with your wishes, nothing would have given me greater pleasure.

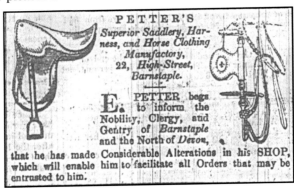

The Barnstaple Staghounds, early 1900s
Standing far right is Bill Ashton

The
Hon Mark Rolle's Hounds
POINT TO POINT RACES

WILL BE HELD
IN CONNECTION WITH THE ABOVE, ON

WEDNESDAY APRIL10TH

Further Particulars will follow later

JOHN HOLLAND

*Hon Sec to the Point-to-Point Meeting,
Monkleigh, Torrington*

Hon Mark Rolle's Point to Point races, 1901

CHAPTER 6

THE LOST STAGHOUND

May 13th 1909
Staghounds exempted
Interesting case at Barnstaple

An unusual case came before Barnstaple Borough Bench on Thursday, when *William Laurence Ashton* (Huntsman of the Barnstaple Staghounds and living in High Street, Barnstaple) was charged with having, on the 4th May, allowed a dog to be in the High Street without a collar with the owner's name thereon. The adjudicating magistrates were Messrs H Barrett (presiding), W F Gardiner, and A Bradford. The defendant, who was represented by Mr A F Seldon, pleased not guilty.

P C Gooding stated that on the 4th inst at 11 am, he saw a hound in the High Street without a collar. Witness took the animal to the Police Station, where, by the direction of the Chief Constable, he then took it to Mr Ashton's to see if it belonged to him. Mr Ashton admitted that he owned the hound, and said he had been exercising it. Cross-examined by Mr Seldon: Witness did not know whether the hound belonged to the Barnstaple Staghounds pack.

Mr B Chester, Master of the Barnstaple Staghounds, called by Mr Seldon, stated that the hound in question was a member of the pack and had been hunting regularly throughout the season.

Mr Seldon, addressing the Bench for the defence, recalled that the order relating to dogs wearing collars was made at Barnstaple in November last. The regulation which authorities were entitled to make with regard to the wearing of collars by

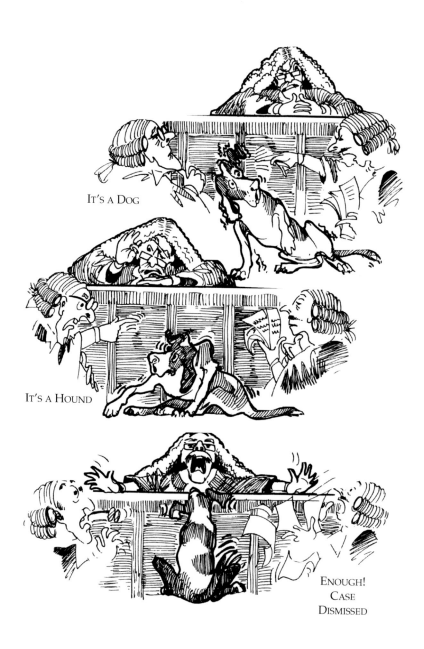

IT'S A DOG

IT'S A HOUND

ENOUGH!
CASE
DISMISSED

136

dogs were, however, restricted, ie, "these regulations shall not apply to any pack of hounds, or any dog while being used for sporting purposes, or for the capture or destruction of vermin, or for the driving or tending of cattle or sheep." They claimed in this case that the hound in question belonged to the pack of the Barnstaple Staghounds; indeed, he had so proved by Mr Chester that it was a member of the pack of hounds. No doubt the Chief Constable thought that the regulations only applied to a pack of hounds as a pack; but a similar case had been before the High Court, where it had been decided that a single hound belonging to a pack came within the exemption. Mr Seldon detailed the case to which he referred, which was sent up from Lincolnshire. Here a police superintendent summoned a farmer, who was walking a young hound until it became old enough to go into the pack. It was there considered by the Superintendent that a dog or hound did not come within the exemption because it had not been entered in the pack and was not used in the pack. The Magistrates dismissed the summons, and the Superintendent appealed to the High Court, which unanimously decided that inasmuch as this hound or puppy, and was intended for the use of the pack it came within the exemption. Similar cases had occurred in different parts of the country, there being a case, for example, in South Molton last year. In that case a puppy was being walked without having a collar, and the bench dismissed it. In other cases two Magistrates had decided that where a hound was a member of a pack it did not come within the regulations.

Mr Barrett: In the case before the Bench the animal was not being walked.

Mr Seldon said that this did not matter; it was a member of the pack. He admitted that if Mr Ashton gave to a friend a puppy for the purpose of keeping it as a pet, and it was never intended to be used for hunting, then it would not come within the exceptions.

The Chief Constable (Mr R S Eddy) remarked that the dog, or at least one hound, had been wandering about the town for days on and off.

Mr Seldon further said that this did not affect the question. He admitted that as the result of the exemption more or less of a nuisance might be created in some cases, but he repeated that this did not affect the question. Mr Ashton would of course take every precaution to prevent hounds wandering about. He added that if a hound had been wandering about it had done no harm.

The Chief Constable: But it might have done harm.

Mr Seldon further said that it frequently happened when a pack was being hunted that a hound got away and returned home singly, and if such an animal was found not wearing a collar, and there was a conviction, every Master of Hounds in the country would be liable.

The Chief Constable observed that if this particular hound had been hunted the same day or the previous day he would not have taken any notice of the matter.

Mr Seldon was understood to reply that it did not matter whether the hound had been hunting or not if they happened to be found.

The Chief Constable said that if this animal was allowed to go about the town any pack could do so. He thought that the phrase "while being used for sporting purposes" precluded owners of hounds allowing individual dogs to be at large without a collar.

Mr Seldon pointed out that Lord Darling dealt fully with this aspect of the matter in the High Court, and that such hounds were exempt.

Mr Gardiner: It does not necessarily apply to a "pack" of hounds.

Mr Seldon admitted that he thought that in such cases as that before the Bench individual hounds should wear collars, but they could not go against the decision of the High Court.

The Bench dismissed the case.

Denis Fowler of Newport Pottery, Barnstaple, who, with his wife Wendy, traded from 1971 until retirement in 2004. © Richard Lethbridge

This plate was made by Denis at the Newport Pottery. House signs and plaques made by Denis can be seen all over North Devon. These, together with all the personal commemorative pieces he has made will become collector's items in years to come

CHAPTER 7

CHERITON OTTER HOUNDS

Barnstaple also played host to the Cheriton Otter Hounds, with the hounds kennelled, at different times, at Brynsworthy near Fremington, Pilton House, Barnstaple Road Repository, and back to Pilton again in 1919. They also had frequent meetings and hunt balls at different venues around the town. In 1925 Mr W H Rogers wrote a book on the Cheriton Otter Hounds, there follows a few extracts from the text regarding Barnstaple.

Records of the Cheriton Otter Hounds

Coming to Barnstaple itself, we find running through the town one of the numerous Yeos distinguished from its namesakes by the prefix of Pilton. The main stream rises in Berry Down and comes by way of Arlington and Loxhore Cot to Chelfham, where the big viaduct of the Lynton Railway forms a striking feature of the landscape, thence along the valley of the aforesaid railway through Pilton to the tide. Pilton Bridge has for some years past been the opening meet, and is generally very well attended, a fine here being the rule rather than the exception.

Mr Arthur Blake Heinemann

Mr Heinemann was Master of the Cheriton Otter Hounds from 1902-1905, and is worthy of a mention because, while Peter Ormrod was Master of the Exmoor Foxhounds and hunting his staghounds on the moor, Mr Heinemann hunted the pack two days a week while Mr Ormrod was ill and afterwards whipped-in to him in 1905, occasionally hunting them. He killed the last stag of that season with nine and a half couples, at East Watersfoot by himself. In that year he killed this stag, a brace of foxes with the Exmoor, a brace of otters with his own pack, the Cheriton, and a brace of Badgers with his own breed of terriers, a combination of the Rev "Jack" Russells and all the best Devonshire strains of working terriers. Mr Heinemann could blow two horns at one time and one season the compliment was

Mr Arthur Blake Heinemann, Master of the Cheriton Otterhounds who also hunted Peter Ormrod's Staghounds while on Exmoor

paid him of asking him to blow the horn by the Masters of a pack of Staghounds, a pack of Foxhounds and a pack of Otterhounds. In 1905, when Peter Ormrod left Exmoor, he gave Mr Heinemann the pick of his private pack of staghounds at five guineas a couple. The pack was full of Old Southern and Welsh blood and Mr Heinemann acquired Banker and Bouncer and Labourer. In 1903 he had bought Rector from Mr Ormrod; half blood-hound, half Old Southern hound, unentered to anything, for two guineas. All his first season Rector followed him like a dog, his nose always in his hand, until on the very last day he heard a great bellow and a booming voice, and there was Rector swimming, his otter in mid Taw. Next season Rector became a marking hound forthwith and never looked back. Sultan had a beautiful cathedral-bell note, but Rector bellowed like a bull. He was all black and tan with great flews and was a very big hound indeed.

14th May 1896
Mr Cheriton's Otter Hounds at Barnstaple

The meet of Mr Cheriton's Otter Hounds on Saturday was at Pilton Bridge, Barnstaple, in order to hunt the river Yeo. The weather was superbly fine, and there was a large gathering. Fourteen couples of hounds were kennelled at Bishopstawton the previous night, and were, therefore, fresh in the morning, after their short trot into Barnstaple. Among those who made up the field were Mr Joe Cheriton (Master), Mr Walrond (Whip), Mr Leach (Huntsman) Major Winter, Major Hogg, Mrs Eyton, Mrs Harper, Miss Laburn, Miss Lovell, the Misses Harper, Mrs Brown, the Misses Brown, Miss Russell, Mrs Davis, Miss Ashton, Colonel Perse, Messrs Fletcher, C Hamlyn, Chichester, J and H Hutchings, W Dallyn, B Hill, P Harris, W Richards, S Denning, Bennet, German, T R Seldon, R Harper, C Thomas, W L Ashton, W J Lord, R M Hayman, J Harper, J R Harper, C Brailey, Pyke-Nott, G H Gould, W H Speke, Thornton, Hawker, Dyer, Pugsley, M H Totter A E Russell, Benfield, J Russell, W C B Davis, F B Manning, F W Petter, and W L Pike. The hounds first spoke to a weak drag near Pitt Farm but without result, the quarry having evidently left some time previously. Progress was made towards Snapper, and here again the hounds threw their tongues beautifully, but failed to find. It was not until Chelfham Mill was nearly reached that the hounds spoke in full and long continued earnest to an otter, their rich musical notes resounding from hill to hill down the valley. The otter was unquestionably here, and the hounds did capital work up and down stream, but the number of drains running from the embankment gave him exceptional facilities for evading his pursuers. Mining operations were carried on, and it was most interesting to watch in connection therewith the great working qualities of the two splendid terriers "Spot" and "Teaser". After nearly three hours energetic working it was found that the otter was so safely housed in one of the numerous drains as to be quite inaccessible, and the hounds had to be called off without a kill. The meet was the largest known in the neighbourhood, quite 200 persons being present. – OTTER

18th January 1900
Mr Cheriton's Otter Hounds

These hounds had their first long exercising morning on Saturday, leaving Brynsworthy Kennels, Barnstaple, under the command of Mr F Chubb (huntsman), assisted by Browning, at about 9am. On arriving at Instow, the Deputy Master (Master George Winter) met them. They had a swim in the river and a roll on the sands, and after that, went through Instow, Westleigh, and Hemmacott, returning to kennels about 1 o'clock, thus having a good four hours of it. Hounds have wintered exceedingly well so far, and are looking keen and a very fit. Major Winter receives excellent reports of otters being about, and he looks forward, it is said, confidently to a good season for 1900. He would have been another of the Devon Masters of Hounds going to the front in South Africa had not the age limit precluded him.

CHERITON OTTER HOUNDS

THE 87TH

Annual General Meeting

will be held at 3 p m. in the

Royal & Fortescue Hotel,

BARNSTAPLE, on

Friday, November 27th.

3925

25th September 1902
Meet of the Cheriton Otterhounds in Barnstaple Square

The meet on Saturday was in the square, influenced by capital weather and the prospect of good sport, a large number of followers put in an appearance. The Master, Mr A Heinemann and the whip arrived soon after 9 o'clock with 15 1/2 couple of hounds, looking in extremely fit condition after their long seasons work. Among the members of the hunt and others present were Mr R D and Miss Heinemann (brother and sister of the Master), Major G Winter (late Master), Messrs R D Wade (whip of the Culmstock hunt), W T A Radford (Lapford), C E Everett and two sons, Murry George, J Holcombe, C Squire, R Matts, J Dewar, M Impey, M H Toller, G W Lindsley, and

H H Williams, Mrs J H Smyth, the Misses Aylmer, Pitts Tucker, De Merrick, De Guerin, Lindsley, Trencher, Berry, and F Charrington. The Master took hounds through the marshes as far as Bishops Tawton thence to the Landkey stream for about 3/4 of a mile. Finding no signs, the Master returned to the main river (the Taw) and hounds went to a little beyond Chapelton Bridge. It was then thought advisable to go back to Chapelton Bridge and try up to Langridge ford but no trail was struck and hounds were called off.

16th April 1903
Hunting
Cheriton Otter Hounds

This famous pack commenced the season on Tuesday with a bye-meet at the Golden Lion Hotel, Barnstaple. The fine weather brought together a good attendance, although the cold wind and the fact that the water is still far from warm were not favourable for sport. The Master (Mr Arthur Heinemann) was in charge of the hounds, and those who met him included the Misses Aylmer, Miss Russell, Miss Pitts-Tucker, Misses Cartwright, Miss Lindsley, Miss Dumeresque, Mrs Pyke-Nott, Major Winter (ex-Master), Messrs Pyke-Nott, F Hortin, C D Turrell, C Everett, G W Lindsley, H Williams, M Impey, Gotto, Rogers, Court-Granville, Scogie, Middleton, Cartwright, Conybeare, Hendy, and others. The hounds were taken to Chapelton Station, and thence the Chapelton stream was drawn upwards for two or three miles. Nothing being found, Mr Heinemann brought the hounds back by road to Chapelton, and put them in at Newbridge. The river was worked down as far as Spadey Gut, under Tawstock, but no sign was seen of an otter, and the water being very cold, the pack was called off about three o'clock.

CHERITON OTTER HOUNDS

PILTON KENNELS BARNSTAPLE.

Joint Masters:
W. H. ROGERS, Esq., J.P.
Orleigh Court, Bideford.
Major Hon. R. T. GRAHAM-MURRAY
write a card, St, ... St.
S.W. 1

Please address reply to:-

Hon. Secretary and Treasurer:
Lt.-Col. J. C. BASSETT
Wayafiete, Northam

A letterhead from when the Cheriton Otterhounds were at Pilton

14th May 1903
Cheriton Otter Hounds

A bye-meet was held at the Kennels, Pilton House, Barnstaple, on Saturday. The Master (Mr Arthur Heinemann) had out twelve-and-a-half couple hounds and four terriers. The field included Mrs Heinemann, Mr Blew (acting whip), Mr and Mrs German, Miss James, Miss Lovell, Mr G Mrs and Miss Lindsley, Miss Rowe, Mr and Mrs Pyke Nott, Misses Russell (2), Messrs W F Rowe, M Impey, Williams and others. The hounds were taken to Bradiford and down to the railway culvert before being put to water. They worked up the river as far as Westaway, where an otter was seen on Friday, but the mill leat and the main stream were drawn without any luck. Hounds then continued up stream as far as Blackaford, but there was no find, and they were then called off at 2 o'clock.

21st January 1904
Cheriton Otter Hounds Sold

Lack of adequate support for the Master of the Cheriton Otter Hounds (Mr A Heinemann) resulted in the pack being advertised for sale. They were offered on Friday afternoon at Williams' Horse Repository, Barnstaple, by Mr T Sanders (Messrs Sanders and Son, Barnstaple). There was a good attendance of sports-men and otter hunters from different parts, including Messrs A Heinemann, J Rose (Master of the Essex Hunt), Stanley Blew, Murray George, G W Lindsley, Turrall, Wade, S Heard, M Impey, J Williton, E R Berry-Torr, and Major G Winter (a former deputy-master of the hunt).

The Auctioneer stated that Mr Heinemann would vacate the country in favour of any purchaser of the whole pack who would guarantee to hunt the entire country. He would also guarantee a subscription of £25 for two years, 1904 and 1905, on condition that the hounds were fed on the same food as he had used for the past three years, and that the hounds were looked after by his present kennelman. If there was no purchaser of the entire pack, the hounds were be sold singly. Pending the result of the sale, Mr Heinemann had not vacated or resigned the country, and continued to hold the concession of the waters as granted to him by every owner of water on his succeeding Mr Wm Cheriton in 1902. There was no committee in existence. A new Master had been advertised for without result, and Mr Heinemann had offered to meet Mr Joe Cheriton in every way if he would hunt the country again, but the latter decline to do so. The reasons for the Master giving up were want of adequate support, and unexpected notice to quit kennels.

The pack was first offered as a whole, and Mr Turrall bid £100 for the 23 hounds. The Auctioneer observed that £60 was guaranteed already, and Mr Heinemann had not brought the pack there to test their worth, he wished to sell. Bidding was carried to £135 were it stopped. This, said the auctioneer was a shockingly bad price, and Mr Heinemann remarked, with a smile, that he gave £50 for 7 1/2 couples; he certainly would not sell at that price.

The hounds were thereupon submitted singly, the first five offered being pure otter hounds. "Sinbad," d, aged, good in his work in every way, fine voice and one of the original pack, fetched 15s only, Mr Rose purchasing. "Sultan," d, aged, good drawer, beautiful voice, went to Mr Blew for £2 15s, Mr Heinemann humourously remarking that his skin was worth 15s. "Ploughboy," d, aged, good swimmer, beautiful voice, Mr Rose £1. "Cheerful," b, 5 years, good swimmer and drawer, fine voice, Mr Blew, £5. "Gaylass," b, 4 years, same qualities, Mr Blew £5 10s. "Sailor," d, 2 years, half otterhound half foxhound, entered this season, fine voice, good killer, Mr Blew, £6 15s. The next twelve are staghounds, "Monarch," d, 6 years, wonderful finder, marker and killer, good voice, Mr Turrall started at £10 and bought at £15. "Content," d, 6 years, good marker, draws well, good killer, been with Mr Heinemann three years, Mr Turrell, £10. "Senator," d, 5 years, entered this season, works well, Mr Blew, £1 15s. "Harlequin," d, 4 years, good all-round, marks well, good killer, Mr Blew, £8. "Fencer," d, 4 years, very good marker and swimmer, works hard, started in £10, purchased by Mr Turrall for £17. "Vampire," d, 4 years, good finder, very resolute. This hound, said Mr Heinemann, could speak for himself – (laughter) – he had been one season with Mr Amory and two with himself was perfectly sound and done good killing;he would be invaluable as a yard dog. (Laughter.) Mr Blew purchased for £7. "Valesman," d, 4 years, good voice, draws well, splendid nose and tongue, started in £2, Mr Blew, £3 5s. "Viceroy," d, 3 years, careful drawer, best voice, started in £5. Mr Turrall, £8. "Contest," d, 2 years, good worker, very active, from the Royal pack, Mr Blew £3 15s. "Merryman," d, 2 years, good all-round and killer, hard worker, Mr Blew, £8 10s. "Monarch II," d, 2 years, good all-round, hard worker, Mr Blew £8 10s. "Pilot," d, 5 years, good voice, good all-round, Mr Blew £2 10s. The next eight are foxhounds. "Render," d, 4 years, good drawer, killer and marker, Mr Blew, £3 5s. "Granhy," d, 4 years, good drawer, good voice, Mr Blew, £3 5s. "Fencer II," d, 4 years, same qualities, Mr Blew, £2. "Damper," d, 4 years, fine voice, and wonderful trail hound and finder, started by Mr Fletcher Harris in £10, secured by Mr Turrall in £20. "Hamlet II," d, 3 years, good all-round and voice, Mr Blew, £3 5s. "Belmont," d, 2 years, hard-working, steady, from the East Essex kennels, Mr Blew, £3 15s. "Bendigo," d, 2 years, hard-working, Mr Blew, £2. "Scrutiny," b, 4 years, wonderful on trail and to swim the foil – "Would breed a pack." said Mr Heinemann. (Laughter) – Mr Turrall, £18. "Hamlet I," d, aged, Welsh hound, fine marker, good voice, good trail hound, seen 200 otters killed, Mr Rose, £3. "Ranter," d, 5 years, Welsh hound, very smart, all round, fine voice, Mr Turrall, £5.

This pack, it will be seen, is still retained in the country, only one and a half couple going to other parts. The present Master still wishes to find successor, and the hon secretary (Mr C D Turrall of Northam) will be glad to negotiate with any gentleman desirous of hunting the country. Failing this, every effort will be made to retain Mr Heinemann for another season.

The Cheriton Otterhounds at Newbridge, circa 1905.
Courtesy of Tom Bartlett's Postcard Collection

147

The 1906 Cheriton Otterhound season sees the hunt at Pilton House:

From Baily's Hunting Directory:

CHERITON

Hunt Uniform – White "bowler" hat or blue peaked cap, dark blue coat and waistcoat, white breeches, dark blue stockings. Gold button. (The Master and Deputy Master wear yellow waistcoats.)

Kennels – Pilton House, Barnstaple
Telegraph Office – Barnstaple
Railway Station – Barnstaple (near)
Days of Meeting – Monday, Thursday and Saturday, and sometimes a fourth day.

The pack hunts the following rivers: Taw, Torridge, Teign, Mole, Bray, Creedy, Little Dart, Dalch, Yeo. The waters, generally speaking, afford good hunting, but are liable to sudden floods. The Taw is somewhat muddy; the Torridge very rapid. Otters are fairly numerous; ten brace may be killed in a good season. The hounds are the property of the Master. Non-subscribers are capped. Minimum subscription from visitors £1 1s.

The Cheriton pack was established in 1846 by Mr Wm Cheriton, of Ellicombe, Morchard Road, N Devon; Mr Cheriton hunted hare and otter with the same pack, and on one occasion killed two hares and three otters on the same day. Early in the seventies Mr Cheriton found it necessary to retire from active Mastership, and the pack was maintained by subscription under Lieut Arthur Connop RN as Deputy Master. Mr J A Budgett succeeded Mr Connop in 1887; he was succeeded in 1889 by Mr Cecil Archer, who held office till 1894. Mr J A Budgett then resumed office as Deputy Master, renting from Mr Cheriton the hounds, which he kennelled at South Molton Road Station. The uniform of the Hunt is now blue coat, COH on button, white "bowler" hat, white breeches, and heather mixture stockings with anklets. Mr Budgett bred pure otterhounds and also, with drafts from the Devon and Somerset Kennels, cross-bred hounds with great dash and lovely music. Mr Budgett died in 1895; and was succeeded by Major Geo Winter (Cameronians) as Hon Secretary and Field Master to Mr J Cheriton who retired in 1899. Major Winter then took office, with J Chubb (from the Stevenstone) as huntsman, young Chubb and the Rev R D Wade as whippers-in. In 1900 Major Winter resigned, and save for a few days in the Crediton district the country remained unhunted during the season. In 1902 Mr Arthur Blake Heinemann bought the pack from Mr Cheriton, and he added the hounds he had brought with him from the Essex country. In 1905 Mr Loraine Bell hunted the country; in 1906 Mr Welsh hunted it with the hounds he hunted in co Cork in 1905.

Master – (1905) Henry Welch Thornton Esq, Beaupaire Park, Hants.

Deputy Master – C F Andrews.

Hon Secretary – C D Turrall, Esq, Northam.

Huntsman – The Master.

Whipper-in and *Kennel Huntsman* – Tom James and Frank O'Boyle.

Ten couples of pure otterhounds, Welsh hounds and staghounds.

13th August 1903
Cheriton Otter Hounds

This popular pack had a moonlight meet on Monday, the rendezvous being Venn Quarry at eleven o'clock. A field of over 200 met the Master (Mr Heinemann). The stream was tried to Landkey and back to Bishops Tawton, but unfortunately there was no find.

17th October 1907
Hunting
Cheriton Otter Hounds

The annual meeting of the Cheriton Otter Hounds was held at the Golden Lion Hotel, Barnstaple, yesterday, under the presidency of Mr Rogers.

The Master (Mr W Littleworth, of Eggesford) stated that during the season they had 22 finds and killed 14 otters. In addition, Mr D Davies hunted the district with his pack four days, and killed four otters, making the total number of kills 18. He had not been able to show the sport he should have liked, because he had had a new pack of hounds, strange to the game, while the water had been very high. Towards the end of the season, however, the hounds had done very much better. Mr Littleworth offered to again hunt the country, provided the hounds were placed in his hands, to do as he thought best in his efforts to make the pack a perfect one, which he thought with a little perseverance could be done. He would hand over the pack at the end of the season to the country to do what they liked with. He expressed cordial thanks to the Master of the hounds and others for the assistance they had rendered in enabling him to get the pack together.

Mr Littleworth's offer to again hunt the country was cordially accepted, while the Master was warmly thanked for his services.

Mr Oldfield, who was re-elected Honorary Secretary, reported that the hunt had been well supported during the past season by subscribers, a sum of £208 having been subscribed.

After some conversation as to the working of the country, a field committee was appointed to assist the Master on field days, in regard to visitors who were not conversant with the rules of the hunt.

22nd June 1916
Cheriton Otter Hunt
Meet at Barnstaple. A Kill.

Cheriton Otter Hunt, the popular Master of which is Mr H R Taylor, met at Pilton Bridge, Barnstaple, on Monday. Hounds, put to water above the weir, hit off a trail at once, which improved until Kingdon Gardens were reached, where hounds marked under an old tree stump. After considerable terrier and bar work, an otter was bolted, but was unfortunately headed, and got back into the same holt, from which it was impossible to dislodge him. Hounds drew on up stream, found again on the island, and pushed their otter with rare dash down the leat, where about one-and-a-half hours' pretty hunting took place. Eventually the otter landed and crossed to the main river. With plenty of music they then pressed him hard up and down through the withy bed, back into the leat and to the overflow of the leat, after two hours' brilliant hunting. It was a dog otter of 21lbs. Among the field, in addition to the Master, were Mr Rogers, Mr and Mrs Springfield, and the Master of the Crowhurst Otter Hounds (Mr Varndell), who rendered considerable assistance.

To-day (Thursday), the hounds will meet at Dart Bridge at 9.30, whilst Saturday's meet at 9.30 will be at South Molton Road.

21st August 1924
Cheriton Otter Hunt
Annual Ball at Barnstaple Last Night

A brilliant function was once more the annual Ball held under the auspices of the Cheriton Otter Hunt in the Albert Hall, Barnstaple, last evening. Drawn from a wide district, over 150 were present, those attending including Mr W H Rogers of Orleigh Court, Bideford (the Master), Mrs Rogers and Miss Bridget Rogers and family, Col Bassett (Hon Secretary) and Mrs

Bassett, Lady Hehir and party, Capt and Mrs W B Incledon Webber, Capt and Mrs Scott and party (Crediton), Capt Paton, Capt and Mrs Cavan, Capt Fanshawe Royle, Dr and Mrs Dixey, Major and Mrs Mundy, Mrs Godfrey Mundy, Mrs and Miss Dennis, and Miss Seldon (Bideford).

The Ball was organised by a ladies committee under the direction of Mrs Rogers, who is to be warmly congratulated on the striking success attending their efforts. The dresses of the ladies were both charming and handsome, and special appreciation was expressed in regard to the decorations of the Hall in blue and white (the Hunt colours), whilst masks and rudders displayed along the front of the platform were distinguishing features. The floor was in splendid condition for the dancing, and music was supplied by the Blue Lagoon Band (a fine combination) from London. The very choice refreshments were served by Mr A G Bromley, of Bromley's Cafes Ltd, and elicited the highest encomiums.

27th August 1925
Cheriton Otter Hunt Ball at Barnstaple

A company of about 250, representing the most prominent families in the district, assembled at Bromley's Cafe, Barnstaple, on Thursday evening, on the occasion of the Cheriton Hunt Ball, which proved a brilliant success. The event had been capably organised by the Master (Mr W H Rogers of Orleigh Court, Bideford), and Mrs Rogers, with the assistance of a Committee, and the hon secretarial arrangements were in the able hands of Lieut Col J C Bassett, of Fairhaven, Westward Ho!. The ballroom had been very appropriately decorated by Mrs Rogers, the Hunt colours (blue and white) being an outstanding feature. From the electric light globes hung streamers of these colours, while hoops placed at intervals along the panelled walls, decorated with ribbon of similar hue and evergreens, formed a framework for otter masks. Other trophies of the chase depended from the hoops. Supper was in the restaurant, bands of blue and white and vases of cornflower and gypsophila being used in the decoration of the tables. The floor was in excellent condition, and a splendid selection of music was rendered by the Blue Lagoon Band (London), now engaged at the Torquay Medical Baths.

The Master, and Mrs Rogers, were accompanied by a large house party from Orleigh Court, and amongst others present were Lieut Col Bassett, of Westward Ho! (Hon Secretary and Treasurer of the Hunt), with Mrs Bassett and Party, Mrs Fairburn and party, Miss Channer, Capt Babbington, Capt

Cavan, Mrs and Miss Scott, Mr Lovering, Mrs Chichester, Cmdr and Mrs Wilson, Mr Browining, Mrs and Misses Templer, Mrs Howart and Party, Major Croft, Mr Patterson, Capt Lawford, Mr Saunders, Mr Phelps, Miss Pilkington, and party, Capt and Mrs Slatter and party, Col and Mrs Williamson and party, Mr Anstey and party, Mr N Swift and party, Capt J C Fanshaw-Royle and party, Mr and Mrs Turner and Party, Capt and Mrs Needham and party, Mrs Magniac and party, Miss Stokes, Miss Frazer and party, Sir E Petric, Bart, and Lady Petric, Lady and Sir Patric Hehir and party, Lady Gayton and party, Mrs Chritchley-Salmonson and party, Mrs Nickels and party, Miss Hallows and party, Mr Heaman, Miss Williams, Mrs and Miss Bathgate, Mr Wigram, Mr Hibbert, Capt and Miss Caven and party, Lady Pearce and party, Mrs Watts and party, Mrs Guy Watts, Miss Dodd, Miss Varwell, Miss Bazeley, Mr Elliott, Miss Francis, Mr and Mrs Lefroy and party, Mrs Furgusson, Miss Williams, Col and Mrs Gracey and party, Capt and Mrs Incledon Webber and party, Capt and Mrs Lawford and party, Mrs Meyer and party, the Hon Graham Murray and party, Col and Mrs Maskell and party, Miss Parker, Miss Patterson, Misses Tewson, Mr Ponsonby and party, Miss Bruce and party, Mr Heaman and party, Miss Nelson and party, Mr Furse, Capt Anderson, Col and Mrs Scott, Mr Leakey, Mr D'Egville, Miss Marsh, Mr B Walters, Miss Talbot, Mrs and Miss Dennis and party etc.

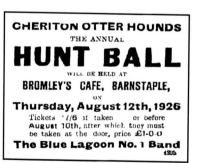

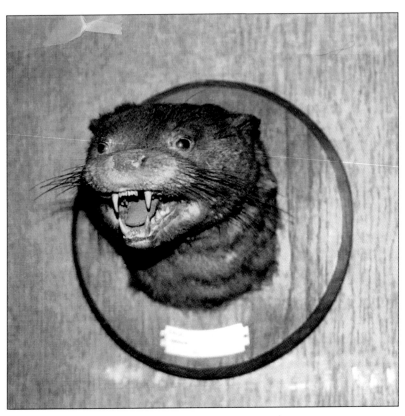

Photographs © Richard Lethbridge
with thanks to Henry Barrett

CHERITON OTTER HOUNDS
UMBERLEIGH WEIR POOL
· JUNE 17TH 1930 ·

The Cheriton Hunt of Today
Notes courtesy of Henry Barrett

The Cheriton Otter hounds managed to continue hunting through World War II, with occasional meets within walking distance of the succession of kennels situated near the river Torridge. However, by the end of the 1945 season, the hunt finances were in a low state and there was difficulty in finding new kennels. The hunt committee therefore took the momentous decision to dispose of the remaining three couple of hounds, and these were sold to the Culmstock Otter Hounds in June 1946 for £30. The committee resoved to keep the country open by inviting existing packs to hunt the Cheriton waters as often as possible, until such time as conditions permitted the acquisition of new hounds. Initially the Culmstock Otter Hounds were invited, and they were soon joined by the Dartmoor Otter Hounds in 1952. The Hawkstone were invited during the seasons 1950 to 1975. Other packs from further afield come occasionally over the years. The otter was made a protected species in 1978, so the Cheriton hunt committee switched to hunting the mink and have arranged invitation meets up to the present day on the North-flowing Cheriton rivers, whilst lending the South-flowing rivers to the Devon and Cornwall Mink Hunt on an annual basis. The Culmstock Mink Hounds and the Devon and Cornwall Mink Hounds have been the regular guest packs but other mink hunts have participated from time to time. The Cheriton committee elected annually by the subscribers, continues to exist with the hon secretary and treasurer Mr H L Barrett, arranging the meets. He has held this office since 1969.

The Cheriton Hunt 2002-2003 Season
from the Baily's Hunting Directory

CHERITON HUNT
Uniform: Dark blue waistcoat and stockings, white breeches, grey bowler hat or dark blue double-peaked cap. Evening Dress: Royal blue coat, with white cloth collar and blue silk facings, white waistcoat.
Chairman and Hon Sec: (1993) H L Barrett, Netherleigh, Torrs Park, Ilfracombe, N Devon EX34 8AZ. Tel 01271 862634.

Meet: Tuesdays, Wednesdays and Saturdays. No hounds are kept at present.

Subscription: £3 (minimum). Cap £2 for non-subscribers.

The rivers hunted for mink are the Bovey, Bray, Creedy, Kenn, Taw, Teign and Torridge. Best centres: Eggesford and Hatherleigh.

The Hunt was founded in 1846 to hunt otter by William Cheriton of Ellicombe, Down St Mary. Although no hounds are registered, for several years the Hawkstone Otter Hounds hunted the country by invitation; and when the pack ceased operations, the Culmstock and Dartmoor packs were invited to hunt in a similar manner from the 1976 season, while the southern waters were loaned to the Dartmoor Otter Hounds on a yearly basis. The otter having achieved protective status in January 1978, the Cheriton turned to hunting mink by inviting the Culmstock and the Devon and Cornwall packs to hunt their waters. The Pynes Mink Hounds also participated in the seasons 1983-85.

The Cheriton Otterhounds, 1916, outside what is known today as the Bridge House Veterinary Hospital in Pilton. With the Master, Mr H Taylor, far right, is Mr W L Barrett. (secretary) Photo courtesy of Henry Barrett

A cartoon
depicting
Henry Barrett

Henry Barrett, treasurer secretary
and chairman of the Cheriton Hunt
in 1996. Seen here capping from the
Fox and Hounds meet at Eggesford.

156

CHAPTER 8

WILLIAM LAWRENCE ASHTON
ONE-TIME HUNTSMAN OF THE BARNSTAPLE STAGHOUNDS

The name of W L Ashton is featured throughout this book. He was an all round hunter when the Barnstaple and North Devon Harriers were established in 1893 becoming Secretary and later on hunting them and also became Secretary of the Barnstaple Staghounds and enjoyed three successive years as huntsman to them. Although some people say he was also the Master of the Barnstaple Staghounds, I have found no reference to this fact, but found on occasions he acted as Master. Mr Ashton once bought the hounds and they became his property for a season in 1903 at a time when there was a danger of the pack going out of the country. In 1904 the committee bought the hounds from him.

Mr W L Ashton,
Huntsman of the Barnstaple
Staghounds

Mr Ashton was a grocer by trade with his shop being

in the high street. In a book of the Devon and Somerset Staghounds written by ET Macdermot in 1936, W L Ashton is described as a 'veritable jorrocks', who was not above taking orders for his goods at meets and in intervals of the chase.

I was later able to find members from both sides of W L Ashton's family. They have been proud to tell me of their connections with the Barnstaple Staghounds through their descendent William Lawrence Ashton. Unfortunately they were unable to give much new information about him, but they all have hunt trophies which belonged to him which provide a valuable contribution to the history of the hunt. These trophies, together with the cuttings I have collected, help build a better picture of William Ashton.

William Lawrence Ashton died on July 8th 1915. His obituary is a source of much information:

"To the deep regret of a very wide circle of friends, Mr William Lawrence Ashton, senior member of the firm of Messrs W L Ashton and Sons, grocers of Ludgate House (64, High Street), passed away on Thursday at the age of 62.

The deceased was a native of West Putford; a son of the late Mr Samuel Clement Ashton, a well known agriculturist. Mr W L Ashton learnt his trade and was for some time with the late Mr John Watts, grocer of Boutport Street.

Mr William Ashton's grocery shop in Barnstaple High Street
Harry Ashton is on the left

Thirty-four years ago he commenced business on his own account, and was conspicuously successful, the Ludgate House grocery establishment enjoying a very wide connection. Mr Ashton was widely known as a sportsman, being a familiar figure in the hunting field in North Devon. For some time he was huntsman of the Barnstaple Staghounds. A great lover of horses, Mr Ashton believed in keeping the best, his mounts generally being much admired. He was a fine judge of horses, the deceased was a man of most general and kindly disposition. The deepest sympathy is expressed to his widow Polly and two sons and four daughters – Messrs Lawrence William Ashton, Harry Jordan Ashton, Mrs Parker (South Molton), and Misses Ethel, May and Winnie Ashton."

Mr Ashton's grocer shop in Barnstaple High Street.
William and May Ashton standing outside

William Lawrence Ashton with his dog, Toby, in Joy Street, Barnstaple

Left: The silver cup which was presented in 1904 to William Ashton, huntsman of the Barnstaple Staghounds by the Master, Lieut Chichester

Right: Glenda Tucker proudly shows her great grandfather's (William Ashton) staghound memorabilia, alongside her faithful dog Darkie.

Left: William Ashton's Barnstaple Staghound collection. The stag slot is quite remarkable with its silver cap with the antlers on top

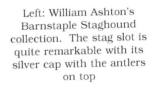

Right: Glenda Tucker blows "the going home" on William Ashton's hunting horn in memory of her great grandfather. William Ashton now hunts in heaven with the Barnstaple Styxhounds.

© S A Hesman (Scenic Prints)

Henry Barrett, Chairman and Secretary of the Cheriton Hunt today from a meet of the Culmstock Minkhounds at the London Inn, Morchard Bishop

© M J Shepherd

Lynton Station.
Photo courtesy of Tom Bartlett's postcard collection

A wheatear sits on the sign to the Hunters Inn, Heddons Mouth.
At one time, this was a regular meet of the Barnstaple Staghounds.

© Johnny Kingdom

© Johnny Kingdom

Photographs from Barnstaple Fair 2003.
Years ago, the fair stag hunt became one of the main attractions of fair week.

Above The Mayor and Mayoress, Mr and Mrs Chris Haywood at the opening of Barnstaple Fair, September 2003

Above: Left to right, George Lovering (Mayor Beadle), Mayoress Sue Haywood, Mayor Chris Haywood, and Chris Hammett, (Senior Beadle)

The Mayor and Mayoress enjoying a ride at Barnstaple fair 2003.

John Norrish, huntsman of the Tiverton Staghounds,
one of the three remaining packs of staghounds in the Westcountry today.
Photo © Richard Lethbridge 2001.

© S A Hesman (Scenic Prints)

December 27th 1900
Runaway Horses at Barnstaple

Two horses ran away in High Street, Barnstaple, during Saturday evening. One bolted from outside the shop of its owner (Mr W L Ashton, grocer), with the porter on its back, and on reaching the north end of High Street it fell, throwing its rider several yards. The other horse (with a railway delivery van attached) ran in the opposite direction from outside the shop of Messrs Richards and Co grocers, Mr Stanley Lile (a member of Barnstaple Football Club), pluckily jumping to the animal's head and stopping it outside High Cross. Some excitement was caused among the numerous pedestrians in the street, several of whom ran into shops in order to avoid being knocked down; but unfortunately no damage was caused by the runaways. Owing to both the reins breaking, a pony attached to a governess car with three occupants, also bolted from the vicinity of the North Walk on Saturday evening. It went at a gallop through the Strand and across the Square, when it turned up Litchdon-street. In swerving near the Albert clock, it went perilously near the kerbing and it looked as if an ugly accident was imminent; but just as it was entering the narrowest point of the street, Mr S T Babb grabbed its head collar and succeeded in bringing it to a standstill.

161

I found the following notice, published a year after William Ashton's death.

March 9th 1916

The license held by W L Ashton, grocer of High Street Barnstaple, was transferred to his widow, Mrs Polly Ashton, at the adjourned annual licensing meeting held at Barnstaple Guildhall on Thursday. Mr A F Seldon made the application.

There follows a report of an accident William Ashton had while hunting the staghounds in 1903.

September 3rd 1903
Hunting
Barnstaple Staghounds
Accident to the Huntsman

It having been heard that the deer had been doing a great deal of damage at Heddon Mills, the hounds met there on Tuesday. The weather was fine, and there was a fair attendance, including Mr W E Arthur (acting master), Mr W L Ashton (huntsman), and Morgan (whip). Several deer were reported to be lying in Stoneyard Wood, and tufting had not been started more than 10 minutes before a fine deer was seen. All that was possible was done to prevent him going into forbidden covers. He made his point straight to Featherbrook and the pack was soon laid on. From Featherbrook he went to Halsinger Down and Burlands, where the huntsman met with an accident. His horse probably put one of its feet into a rabbit hole and turned a somersault. Mr Ashton escaped with a shaking and a few scratches. The horse was badly stunned. The deer went across the Ilfracombe road, and over Huish, where it turned to the right, hounds pressing hard, to Whitefield, on to Bowden's Corner, Eastdown, and then into the Arlington covers, where the hounds had to be called off, this being the second deer lost this season in the same way.

162

In 1904 William Ashton was presented with a hunting crop at Hunters Inn, Heddons Mouth. In August of the same year, he was presented with a handsome silver cup by Lieutenant Chichester (Master of the Barnstaple Staghounds) in recognition of his services to North Devon hunting, and most especially in appreciation of the excellent manner in which he hunted the Barnstaple Staghounds at that time.

Barnstaple Staghounds, March 17th 1904
An interesting presentation.

These hounds met at Hunters Inn, Heddons Mouth on Saturday. There was a large field. Before the tufters were taken out, Major Penn-Curzon (acting Master) presented Mr W L Ashton (Huntsman) with a hunting crop. The Master (Mr E Chichester) had previously presented him with a horn in appreciation of the sport he had shown. Mr Ashton acknowledged the gift, and spoke of the pleasure it had given him to carry the whip under Major Curzon's Mastership. Harbourer Litson had a deer harboured in Helewood where the tufters soon had a fine stag on foot. He first made a short turn towards Wooda Bay and Wooda Bay Common, and then ran straight towards the sea. He then made for the cliffs between Wooda Bay and Hunters Inn where he stood at bay, he then climbed up over the cliffs and ran across the Wooda Bay Station as though for the moor but retracing his steps he turned down through the cliffs again where he was killed. He was a fine six year old deer, with brow, bay, and tray and two on top, and gave four hours sport.

The late Arthur Parker showing hunt memorabilia from his grandfather, W L Ashton

163

Illness of Mr W L Ashton
9th January 1913
Barum Tradesman's
Seizure Following a Day
with the Hounds

The many friends of Mr W L Ashton, principal of the well known firm of Messrs W L Ashton and Son, grocers, of High street, Barnstaple, will regret to learn of his serious illness.

As is well-known, Mr Ashton is an enthusiastic follower of the hounds, and on Saturday attended the meet of the Instow Harriers at Hollacombe Moor. Whilst returning in company with Mr M Squire, of Barnstaple, near where the bridge spans the River Taw at Bishopstawton, Mr Ashton was suddenly taken ill, and fell from his horse. Realising that something serious was the matter, Mr Squire called for assistance, but the place where the accident happened being some distance from the village some considerably time elapsed before help arrived. When assistance did come, Mr Squire, finding it ws too late to telegraph, rode to Barnstaple for medical aid. In the meantime Captain Clive, of King's Cottage Bishopstawton, kindly directed Mr Ashton's removal to his residence. He was there attended by Drs Harper and Gibbs, and an examination revealed that he was suffering from a slight seizure. Subsequently Mr Ashton was conveyed to his home.

The sufferer is, of course, still under medical treatment, and it will be some time before he is able to get about again. We are glad to state that yesterday his medical attendants were pleased with the progress he was making towards recovery. Mrs Ashton and family desire to return thanks for the numerous expressions of sympathy and kind enquiries and regret they are unable to answer them all personally.

July 3rd 1913
Meet of the Cheriton Otterhounds
Mr W L Ashton watching proceedings.

From a meet of the Cheriton Otterhounds at Pilton Bridge, it was reported that Mr W L Ashton, now unfortunately indisposed, watched the proceedings from an open carriage.

The above advert, from 1936, shows that Mr W L Ashton's family was still trading in the High Street at that time, selling their very appropriate Stag Blend Tea.

Cartoon of William Ashton, Huntsman of the Barnstaple Staghounds
© Norman Hood

CHAPTER 9

MISS ROSALIE CHICHESTER AND HER OPPOSITION TO HUNTING ON HER ARLINGTON COURT PROPERTY NEAR BARNSTAPLE

The Chichester family at Hall (Bishops Tawton), Youlston Old Park (Shirwell) and Arlington Court, were, like all landed gentry at the end of the 19th and beginning of the 20th century, very much into hunting, shooting and fishing. So it must have been a shock to the family when Miss Rosalie Chichester of Arlington Court took an opposing role to hunting; so much so that she eventually banned any hounds from her property.

This chapter concentrates on the times that Sir John Amory's Staghounds, the Barnstaple Staghounds, Peter Ormrod's Staghounds, the Tiverton Staghounds and the Cheriton Otter Hounds trespassed on her Arlington Court property and the consequences for doing so.

There follows a report of an incident in 1897 when Sir John Amory's Staghounds actually killed a stag in the grounds of Arlington Court.

Another Stag hunt near Barnstaple
Kill at Arlington

Sir John Amory's Staghounds on Tuesday had another run in the Exmoor country, meeting at Chelfham, a few miles from

166

Barnstaple. There was a very good field considering the weather, and a successful day's sport resulted. The master, Mr Ian Amory, was accompanied by Messrs De Las Casas. Mr Comer Clarke announced that he had several deer lying in his woods at Smythapark, and the hounds were consequently taken on to Mr Clarke's. They were no sooner in the wood than a fine stag was on foot and a bevy of hinds. Indeed, the woods appeared to be teeming with deer. The tufters scattered, some taking after hinds and a few sticking to the stag, which it was decided to follow. He held a course up the valley somewhat in the same direction as on Saturday, running parallel with the new Lynton and Barnstaple Railway, which unfortunately the deer seemed very reluctant to cross.

After a bit he stuck to the left over Tidycombe, crossed the coach road leading to Lynton, and then made his way into Lady Chichester's woods at Arlington, running up to Eastdown. Underneath Eastdown House he turned sharply back and came down the water to Woolley Wood, just opposite Loxhore Cot. The pack was then fetched up from Chelfham Mills, and some fresh tufters thrown into the wood, when the stag – speedily re-found – again pointed upstream. the pack raced him through the woods at a tremendous pace up to the large fishing pond in the Arlington grounds. He then took to the water, the area of which is five or six acres, and which is very deep. The deer proved to be a bold swimmer. Consequently a boat was manned, Mr W Smith, of Eastdown, at the oars, and Lady Chichester's keeper with a lasso, and eventually the deer was brought to land, where he was speedily despatched. He proved to be a fine stag, with brow and bay and tray, with two on top on each side, probably a five-year-old.

The Devon and Somerset Staghounds also came under close scrutiny from Miss Chichester. The following meet took place on September 22nd 1898.

Forbidden to hunt the Arlington Covers

The Devon and Somerset Staghounds met on Saturday at the friendship inn near Bratton Fleming. It had been the custom to hold a meet in North Devon on the Saturday after Barnstaple Fair and the field is usually a large one. It was estimated that quite 500 persons were present on Saturday. Amongst them were the Master (Mr R Sanders), Mrs Sanders, Mr C H Basset and a host of others, including a large contingent of staghunting people from Porlock and Minehead nearly all the farmers of the

neighbourhood and many persons from Barnstaple, Lynton and South Molton. Expectation ran high, but all hopes of a good day's sport were blighted on the Master receiving a sealed letter from Miss Chichester of Arlington Court, delivered by her coachman, saying that the Loxhore Covers on the Arlington Estate were not to be hunted. This was most disappointing to the field, for Fred Goss, the Harbourer, had been successful in harbouring two magnificent stags in Mr Kent's warren. But in consequence of Miss Chichester's letter, the Master decided to take the hounds to the High Bray Covers, some five miles off, for it would have been an impossibility to hunt the two harboured stags at Loxhore, because immediately they were found they would make for the forbidden grounds. On arriving at High Bray, the pack was kennelled at Mr Robins' Lydecott, when it was reported that a heavy stag had been seen early that morning, but as there had been no expectation of the pack coming into this district no proper harbouring had been done. The Master decided that those who had come long distances should not go away without seeing some sport. A young stag was soon found underneath the farm. After beating up and down the cover for a short time he broke away over the top, pointing for Exmoor. Turning left handed into East Down wood and then onto Kidworthy where, adopting the old tactics of these deer, he beat up a hind which drew the tufters off the line. The heat was oppressive, and consequently scent was indifferent. After being stopped from the hind, hounds were able to re-find the stag, although the whole of the covers on that side of the country were again drawn. This ended in disappointing fashion what might have proved a good day's sport. A correspondent writes: It is to be feared that the refusal on that part of Miss Chichester to not allow hounds to draw or run through the Arlington Covers must result in the abandonment of a large portion of country hitherto hunted by the Devon and Somerset Staghounds.

The Cheriton Otter Hounds were also subject to Miss Chichester's ban. There follows a report of a meet at Pilton Bridge in 1899.

Cheriton Otter Hounds at Barnstaple
August 24th 1899

The meet in connection with the Cheriton Otter Hounds on Saturday was at Pilton Bridge, Barnstaple. Among those present at the start were the Master (Major Winter), Messrs J Moor and Incledon Webber (acting as whips), Messrs C Everett, J Impey, C Furneaux, W J Lake, T S Lake, Piggott, Rogers, A E Russell, W Daw, E Berry, and L Bissett, Mr & Mrs Colin May, Mrs Everett, Misses Wasteneys, Brown, Tamlyn, Russell and Berry, and many others afterwards joined in at different points. Evidence of the recent work of an otter in the Yeo was apprent, and a trail was soon struck. The hounds hunted beautifully as far as chelfham Bridge, where the otter had turned towards Loxhore, eventually entering the Arlington property. Here the hounds were called off, in deference to previously expressed wishes of the owner of the property, Miss Chichester. The run lasted five hours and the sport regarded as capital.

Right: The lake below Arlington Court, where many a stag took its last stand before Miss Chichester banned the Barnstaple Staghounds from her property. In the foreground is a memorial urn which marks the place where Miss Rosalie Chichester's ashes lie.

© Richard Lethbridge

© Terry Gable

SHALL STAGHUNTING AT BARNSTAPLE CEASE?

Miss Chichester's Objections and Threats Cause the Meets to be Abandoned.

The Owner of Arlington Court Refuses "to Express any Opinion on the Matter."

22 March 1900

Owing to action taken by Miss Chichester, of Arlington Court, the meets of Sir John Amory's Staghounds arranged for Friday and Saturday in the Barnstaple district were abandoned. Two years ago it became known that Miss Chichester wished to provide a "sanctuary" for wild deer on her estate, notice being given that hunting would not be allowed on any part of the demesne. This embargo stopped the meets for a time, as the Arlington coverts are situated in the heart of the staghunting district on the Barnstaple side of Exmoor.

But the sport is so popular in the locality that it was decided to have meets and trust to the hunted stag keeping outside the prescribed area. Several splendid runs were enjoyed, and in the hope that fortune would be again favourable, four meets were arranged for last week. Unfortunately, both on Tuesday and Wednesday the quarry entered Arlington grounds, the stag hunted on Tuesday being actually brought to bay and killed in the Arlington lake. Miss Chichester promptly communicated with her solicitors, who on Thursday gave Mr Ian Amory, the Master of Sir John Amory's Staghounds, notice that unless he gave an undertaking that the Arlington estate should not be trespassed upon an injunction would be applied for. This practically left Mr Amory no alternative, and so he cancelled the remaining fixtures. He was unable to give a public intimation to this effect, and consequently large numbers of persons made their way on Friday to the rendezvous – only to find there was no meet. Many ladies and gentlemen came to Barnstaple from Tiverton, Bideford and elsewhere with horses in the hope of participating in the sport. And so it is scarcely surprising that the incident has caused great irritation in hunting circles throughout the district. Experts consider that so long as Miss Chichester takes this stand there is no hope of Barnstaple becoming a recognised staghunting centre.

Miss Chichester's Position

In view of the general feeling of annoyance and regret which Miss Chichester's action has called forth, we thought it advisable and courteous to afford that lady the hospitality of our columns for the purpose of making some explanation. The lady "had no opinions to express." *Voila tout!* Miss Chichester is a daughter of the late Sir Bruce Chichester, and the present owner of Arlington Court. her extensive covers in the Loxhore valley are the centre of the staghunting district on the Barnstaple side of Exmoor. ...

... This year, in deference to the wished and feelings of the large number of her neighbours who take a keen delight in the chase, better things were confidently anticipated. The unpleasant experience last week, however, removes this hope, and must seriously affect any future chance of sportsmen pursuing staghunting in the Barnstaple country. ...

... On Wednesday the Hunt galloped – actually galloped – across her lawn, in full view of the house, and through the Park, leaving the gates open behind. This audacity was just a little too much, and all the Chichester blood rising in indignation at the direct violation and defiance of *the* Miss Chichester's wishes, both expressed and written, the necessity for asserting her authority was deemed to have come. On the awful facts in all their hottor being reported to Miss Chichester, her legal representatives in London were at once commicated with:

From a Huntsman's Point of View

A *North Devon Herald* representative saw a prominent attendant at the Meets with a view to obtain the Hunt side of the question. He pointed out that Miss Chichester permits a horse show to be held annually at the Court, at which prizes and cups for a young hunters' class, among others, are offered. "What is the use of encouraging the breeding of young hunters," he asked, "if they can be put to no use?" It is well-known that the young farmers who ride to hounds are thus brought into close touch with likely purchasers, and more than one sale was negotiated as a result of the meets last week. "Although," continued *The Herald's* informant, "the majority of those who attend the meets are local ladies and gentlemen, and therefore one could have thought, as near neighbours, worthy of Miss Chichester's consideration, there are a fair sprinkling of strangers to the district whose advent must mean the spending of considerable sums of money in the district. Last week three gentlemen came down from London in order to be present, while another rode 25 miles from Hartland, on Friday morning only to find that Mr Ian Amory had been forced to abandon the meet. The oats, hay, straw &c required for the horses, the enhanced price of hunters occasioned by a ready market, to say nothing of the business accruing through the demands on the posting establishments of the town, mean the spending of some hundreds of pounds in the district. Miss Chichester's action cannot fail to send down the rent roll, and further depress the already none too prosperous industry of agriculture, increasing the difficulty experienced by the tenants and farmers of getting rid of their produce at a fair price."

"What would be the position in West Somerset," asked the gentleman referred to "if staghunting was abandoned? The land would not be half its present value. Miss Chichester is the only objecting landowner in the district, and but for her action probably the district would be regularly hunted."

Deer are rapidly increasing in the neighbourhood, and if hunting has to be abandoned, they will have to be shot, which will result in much greater suffering, as numbers of the wounded and maimed deer will creep away to die in the covers days or weeks after. Neither of the deer killed last week was roused in Miss Chichester's property, but only crossed it when hunted.

A letter to the editor of the North Devon Journal:

16 March 1900
Staghunting near Barnstaple

Dear Sir – Will you kindly allow me through your columns to say how sorry I am not able to hunt today at Chelfham Bridge and tomorrow at Loxhore Cott.

I have received a telegram yesterday evening – too late to make the news generally known – saying that Miss Chichester definitely forbade either hounds or horsemen to cross any part of her Arlington property, and requiring me – under threat of an immediate application for an injunction – to give an undertaking that her wishes in this matter should be observed.

Under these conditions, hunting the Barnstaple country becomes an impossibility, and no alternative was left me but – most reluctantly – to abandon the meets.

I am, Sir yours truly
Ian H Amory (Master of Sir John Amory's Staghounds)
Hensleigh, Tiverton, Devon

In October 1900, Peter Ormrod's Staghounds also got into trouble with Miss Chichester, when Peter Ormrod received two summonses.

October 18th 1900
STAGHUNTING IN NORTH DEVON

MR PETER ORMROD RECEIVES TWO SUMMONSES

Miss Chichester Complains of Trespass at Arlington, and Invokes all the Terrors of the Law

(Special to "The North Devon Herald")

The expected has happened – expected, that is to say, by us, although scoffed at and denied by everyone else. The season of staghunting in North Devon, so far as the Barnstaple district is concerned, has come to a natural but somewhat stormy ending. The termination of the season has been distinguished by the agents of Miss Chichester, of Arlington Court, serving two summonses for trespass upon Mr Ormrod, and that gentleman, as was threatened against Mr Ian Amory, seems likely to be forced into litigation in order to maintain a sport, which – above all things – should be voluntary and free from threats of prosecution. Miss Chichester has, however, not quite triumphed after all, nor has she yet secured the object which she has carefully and consistently set herself of suppressing the sport – the legitimate sport – pursued by hundreds of North Devonians. Unfortunately, however, the lady's action renders rather ridiculous the numerous prophecies of her sponsors, who assured us that if the hounds came into the Arlington Covers now and again no action would be taken, unless the hunt followed; and, again, that the lady would not proceed to such severe measures as to issue a summons against the Master except under extreme provocation; and yet, again, that the hunt could very well be carried on without it being in the least degree necessary to encroach upon the Arlington preserves.

HOPES THAT WERE BASELESS

Some assurances went so far as to state that anterior to Mr Peter Ormrod's hounds being brought to Barnstaple Miss Chichester had been seen and won round by a well-known and poular gentleman of the neighbourhood, to whom – so it was alleged – the lady had given a sort of half-promise that no notice would be taken of any little trespass, provided that her grounds were kept free from encroachments by the members of the hunt itself. We candidly confessed at the time that we placed little or no credence upon any such understanding having been given, since it would have completely upset all the previous theories formed of Miss Chichester's action in opposing the hunt, and which – as we always understood – were based entirely upon humanitarian grounds, and not upon any posible financial loss which her property might sustain by damage. The latest action of the owner of Arlington clearly proves that our scepticism was well grounded, and that those who were so ready to reassure themselves and others upon the safety of their proceedings were entirely misled. So far as the particular trespass now complained about is concerned, we understand that this merely consisted in two or three of the hounds running into the Arlington Covers, where the stag had sought shelter, and that one or two of the members of the hunt trespassed upon some fields which they did not know belonged to the owner of Arlington. The "trespass," therefore, has been purely a technical one, but it is still in the eyes of the law a trespass. The mere fact of snatching at this trumpery occurence as a basis for an injunction will demonstrate completely how little Miss Chichester was won over to the side of the hunt, and how relentlessly she had determined to do all in her power to bring it to a conclusion. The only cause for surprise in our minds is that the step was not taken before, since the hounds have now been out for some weeks past and have been zealously watched with a view to eventual proceedings. Under these circumstances it may be taken for granted that Mr Ormrod will not fight the case which Miss Chichester is said to have commenced against him, and all that he can do is to submit quietly to whatever fine may be imposed – it may be safely concluded that he will not be sent to prison – and then come back again next year – as we believe he thoroughly intends to do – and endeavour to keep clear of any property belonging to the owner of Arlington Court. The season for staghunting would have ended in any case on Tuesday next, but it is to be regretted that it should have closed in an atmosphere of writs and injunctions.

STAGHUNTING NEAR BARNSTAPLE
(A letter to the editor of the *North Devon Journal*)

Sir – I should be glad if you would contradict the misleading statement of your correspondent that my solicitors have withdrawn legal proceedings against Mr Ormrod. The matter is still in their hands. They considered if Mr Ormrod gave a written statement that he would not allow the hounds to enter the Arlington coverts it would be sufficient. I have not heard whether he has done so, but scarcely think it is likely, as the hounds were again in these coverts on Tuesday, though this fact was omitted by your correspondent. My solicitors have instructions to take proceedings against any pack of hounds entering this estate, as I cannot allow such cruel and debasing "sport" on the Arlington property.

Yours truly,
Rosalie C Chichester
Arlington Court, Barnstaple, March 28th 1901.

24th August 1901

Supporters of staghunting in the Barnstaple district have had another disappointment this week, difficulty having again arisen in connection with the Arlington property. It will be remembered that Sir John Amory's Staghounds ceased to arrange fixtures in the Barnstaple district a couple of years ago because Miss Chichester declined to allow the Hunt to enter the Arlington estate, which is situated in the centre of the district. but when Barnstaple Staghounds were organised last summer there was a distinct understanding that Miss Chichester's wishes should be respected, and the Committee went to the expense of erecting a wire barrier round the boundary of a considerable portion of the estate. Every endeavour seems to have been made to keep the hounds out of the prescribed territory, but apparently a trespass has been committed, for Miss Chichester has taken steps with a view to obtain an injunction against the Masters (Captain Paterson and Mr Arundell Clarke). In consequence of this the meet arranged at Hunter's Inn for Tuesday last was abandoned, while other fixtures have been postponed pending the result of the proceedings.

Barnstaple Staghounds
Miss Chichester's Action to be Resisted
A Defence Fund at Last to be Started
31st October 1901

The following circular letter is being sent out to all Masters of Hounds in the country and to the leading supporters of hunting the stag in North Devon:

Westaway, Barnstaple, October 1901
Dear Sir,   I venture to bring to your notice, as one I know to be interested in hunting, a matter which has arisen in this district, and seriously affects the existence of hunting throughout the country.

It is possibly within your knowledge that the Barnstaple Staghounds hunt the Wild Red Deer in that part of the stag hunting country which lies between Barnstaple and Exmoor, such country having been lent to this pack by the Master of the Devon and Somerset Staghounds.

A portion of the Barnstaple district consists of the Arlington Estate, owned by Miss Chichester, who objects to hunting of every kind, and with a view to doing all in their power to meet her wishes the committee of the Hunt lately erected, at considerable expense, a substantial wire fence round a boundary of the Arlington Estate so as to prevent the deer going into it, and the plan has worked with some success, although possibly hounds may have occasionally followed a deer on to Miss Chichester's land, but neither Masters, servant, nor Field have at any time trespassed, and hounds have always been called off as quickly as possible.

On the 19th inst however, a writ was issued by Miss Chichester against the Masters, asking for an injunction to restrain them, their servants and people hunting with them and hounds, from trespassing on any of her lands.

The Masters feel that, if they allow such an injunction to go, it would mean the cessation of all hunting in this neighbourhood, and might certainly be used by any small owner in the middle of a hunting district as a precedent for stopping hunting in his district. They have, therefore, decided to enter an appearance, and a public meeting has been called at Barnstaple for Friday, the 8th November, to consider the matter, and ascertain the support likely to be accorded to them in their defence of the action.

It is felt that there are many Masters and followers of hounds who would appreciate the seriousness to hunting of an adverse verdict being given in this case, and would, therefore, be glad to avail themselves of an opportunity of expressing their views and according their support.

May I, therefore, ask you, if possible, to attend the meeting at the Barnstaple Guildhall of Friday, the 8th prox at 4pm or in the event of your being unable to do so, any reply you may have to make, and any promise of support which you could give, would be read and much appreciated – I am, yours faithfully,

C H BASSET, Chairman of Committee.

PS: Will you kindly reply to the Honourary Secretary in the enclosed envelope.

[In publishing the above communication we think it desirable to call attention to the fact that, at a public meeting held at the Guildhall, Barnstaple, some twelve months back, in connection with the presentation of a testimonial to Mr Peter Ormrod, the Master of the Staghounds, one of the subscribers – Mr Percy F Marks, of Combe Court, Marwood – proposed the very same resolution which is to be submitted for consideration and approval on the 8th prox. Had Mr Marks' proposition been then accepted and a Defence Fund been formed, the present regrettable suspension of the hunt in this district would have been avoided, inasmuch as sufficient funds would have been in hand to enable the Masters to deal with any interference upon the part of objecting landowners. Mr C H Basset mildly chided Mr Marks for introducing such an idea as a "Defence Fund". It is worthy of note that the same suggestion is now approved of and advocated. – Ed. *North Devon Herald.*]

Staghunting.

AN action having been commenced by Miss Chichester, of Arlington, against the Masters of the Barnstaple Staghounds, praying for an Injunction, which, if granted, will put a stop to Hunting in this-District,

A PUBLIC MEETING

Will be held on FRIDAY, 8th. November, 1901, at the Guildhall, Barnstaple, at 4 p.m., to consider what steps shall be taken in defence of a Sport which materially affects the welfare of the whole district. All interested in Hunting are invited to attend.   C. H BASSET,
[5615]   Chairman of Committee.

November 8th 1901
Miss Chichester and Barnstaple Staghounds
important public meeting

Mr C H Basset JP and former Master of the Devon and Somerset Staghounds, who takes a prominent lead in connection with Barnstaple Staghounds convened a meeting of followers and supporters of staghunting at Barnstaple on Friday. Mr Basset was loudly applauded and said they all knew that an action had been commenced by Miss Chichester of Arlington Court against Capt Paterson and Mr Arundell Clarke, (Masters of the Barnstaple Staghounds) praying for an injunction which, if granted would stop staghunting in that district (cries of "Never"). This meeting had been held to consider what steps should be taken in defence of the sport.

Mr W Penhale, the hon secretary, then announced a number of letters from all parts of England including one from the Duke of Norfolk, Marquis of Exeter, and Lord Fitzharding, expressing the hope that the hunt would be maintained. The Baroness Le Clement de Taintegnies wrote that she had many pleasant recollections of staghunting in the west country. She regarded it as the premier sport of England, and promised to do anything she could in support of their cause. Among others who wrote similar letters were Lord Tredegar, Mr W D G Singer (Liverpool), Colonel Garratt (Master of the East Devon Hounds), Mr Carlton Cross (Master of Hounds), Dr Longstaff (Putney Heath), Messrs A J Curinck (Chessington), C W M Kemp, (MFH, Tunbridge), J Hargreaves (Master of Hounds) and F Hamlyn, High Sheriff of the county. In the latter part of Mr Bissett's Mastership of the Devon and Somerset Staghounds the Bray coverts came into prominence, since which time deer had spread until they had come down close to Barnstaple, and the coverts now were well stocked. It was, therefore, most important that they should go on hunting (loud applause).

Each successive Master had had the active support and assistance of almost every landowner and farmer in the district. There was one significant exception, a Mr Chichester in the early part of last century showing such hostility to staghunting that it was followed by a good many deer being shot and there would assuredly be a similar result if Miss Chichester succeeded in her present action. If the injunction was granted, staghunting in the Barnstaple district must cease, and the inevitable result must follow that stags would be shot. That, as they knew, was very much more cruel that hunting the stag ("hear hear"). Mr J G Hamling, deputy Mayor, present at the meeting, yielded to no one in this love of the animal world, but he was certainly of the opinion that if staghunting was stopped and the deer increased, the necessity for shooting them would create an amount of suffering among them which would be most appaling. A great many of them were not practised with the gun, and unless the deer was hit in a vital part, it was in the habit of creeping away into the thickest part of a wood, where it was unable to get food, and after prolonged suffering would die of starvation (applause). Mr E J Soares MP said they had read a great deal in the papers from time to time of the subject of cruelty in regard to sport in general, but he thought they ought not to let it go down to posterity that they were absolutely indifferent and callous, and were prepared to torture any inoffensive animal in order to gratify their own selfish instincts. He did not think that this was the case at all. They all regretfully admitted that there was a certain amount of suffering incidental to hunting and every other sport, but every true sportsman did everything he could to minimise it and to make it as little as he possibly could (applause). Every true sportsman did all he could in the way of looking for a wounded bird, and so it was in hunting, for when a stag had to be killed it was always dispatched in the most expeditious

179

manner possible. He pointed out that that excellent society the RSPCA said in its rules that it did not intend to interfere with legitimate field sports, and they had it that hunting, shooting and fishing did not come within the category of cruel amusements. Putting aside the moral aspect of the question, they must remember that hunting did an immense amount of good to a neighbourhood. It brought many people to a district, and benefited the farmer, tradesman and the merchant. He referred to the extension of the imperial hotel at Barnstaple, which was being effected, he hoped, for the purpose of accommodating intending staghunting visitors. For all these reasons he trusted that the Barnstaple pack would continue to flourish of good in various ways.

Staghunting Near Barnstaple
Chichester v Clarke
23rd January 1902
Case in the Chancery Division

In this action the plaintiff was Miss Rosalie Caroline Chichester, of Arlington Court, Barnstaple, and the defendants were Mr Arundell Clarke and Captain Ewing Paterson, Masters of the Barnstaple Staghounds. The plaintiff moved for an injunction until the trial of the action or further order restraining the defendants, and each of them and each of their huntsmen, servants and agents, from entering or causing or permitting any hound or any pack of hounds, belonging to or hunted by them, or any person hunting with such pack of hounds, to enter in pursuit of, for the purpose of hunting stag or otherwise, upon any part of the lands and hereditaments of the plaintiff, situate near Barnstaple, and known as the Arlington Court Estate, and from otherwise trespassing upon any part of the said estate – Mr Astbury, KC, and Mr R J Parker for plaintiff, and Mr Henry Terrell, KC, and Mr R Roope Reeve for defendants – When the motion came on Saturday morning Counsel stated that subject to the approval of the Court the parties had arranged that the following order should be taken:

"The defendants undertaking by Counsel that they, the hunt, servants, and so far as the Masters can control them, the field, when hunting shall not enter on any part of the plaintiff's land and that they will do their best to prevent any of their hounds from entering any part of the plaintiff's lands. Stay further proceedings in the action, except so far as necessary to enforce the undertaking. No order as to costs." – The order was accordingly made. – *Times*.

Another Account

This was an action by the daughter of Lady Chichester to restrain an alleged trespass upon large estates near Barnstaple by the defendants as Masters of the Barnstaple Stag Hunt. The matter came before Mr Justice Buckley in the Chancery Division of the High Court of Justice on Saturday, upon a motion, the parties having arranged an order.

Mr Astbury, KC, who represented the plaintiff, said that his client had strong views as to the humanity of hunting, and also thought that her property had been interfered with, but the defendants had met her with extreme fairness, and had agreed to continue an undertaking they had already given not to go on the plaintiff's land, to prevent the hunt servants from doing so so far as they had control over them, and to prevent as far as possible, the hounds entering the plaintiff's land; upon that undertaking stay all proceedings in the action, except so far as might be necessary, for enforcing the undertaking.

Mr Terrell, KC, for the defendants, said that his clients were Masters of the Barnstaple Stag Hunt. He wished to know if hounds did stray on the plaintiff's land, whether the hunt servants were to go on and whip them off. Mr Astbury said that he understood that the huntsmen blew a horn and the dogs came back. (Laughter.)

Mr Justice Buckley: Hounds like other people are sometimes obstinate.

Mr Astubry said he would prefer the undertaking in the form agreed on, and upon that his Lordship made an order staying further proceedings.

23rd January 1902

The difficulty which resulted in the suspension of staghunting in the Barnstaple district in the height of the season has been adjusted. In the Chancery Division on Saturday an order by consent was made under which the authorities of the Barnstaple Hunt continue the undertaking they had previously given that Miss Chichester's property at Arlington should not be trespassed upon, so far as it was in their power to secure this. The Hunt therefore stands just where it did. For at the outset the promoters and supporters of the Hunt determined to respect to the full Miss Chichester's rights and her desire to make the Arlington coverts a sanctuary for the red deer, actually going so far as to erect long stretches of wire netting in order to reduce the risk of trespass to the minimum. It is a common-sense conclusion. Miss Chichester continues, in pursuance of a policy dictated by feelings that do her honour, to offer sanctuary to the red deer, and lovers of staghunting will continue to enjoy their sport. This conclusion of the matter has given lively satisfaction in local hunting circles.

Barnstaple Staghounds Resume Hunting
30th January 1902
A Double Kill

After a lapse of over three months – necessitated by the action brought by Miss Chichester against the joint Masters – Barnstaple Staghounds resumed hunting on Monday, the meet being at Chelfham. The weather was boisterous, with heavy rain at intervals; but despite this, there was an attendance of nearly 100, several of those mounted being ladies. The pack was kennelled at the Mills, but before the tufters were taken to cover, Mr A F Seldon, solicitor, Barnstaple, acting for Mr E J Pitts Tucker, (the legal adviser of the Masters in recent proceedings) on behalf of the Joint Masters Captain Paterson and Mr Arundell Clarke, addressed the "field". He mentioned the arrangement which had been arrived at with Miss Chichester, and requested everyone not to trespass or allow any trespassing on any of the Arlington property. Captain Paterson then took a strong draft of tufters into Youlston Wood, but the covers from Loxhore Cott to Kingdon Gardens a distance of nearly six miles, were literally alive with deer of all ages and descriptions, affording a time sight to the followers of the Hunt and to the pedestrians, as deer were constantly coming into view. Soon after the tufters entered the cover, a hind was set on foot and ran on to Coxleigh Wood, where she turned short back through New Barn and Long Timber to Cot Down. Just about this time no less than eight deer came down to the wire fencing round Arlington Estate recently placed by the hunt, and endeavoured to jump it, but all failed to get over. The hunted hind turned into the valley opposite Bratton Cross, when the pack was brought by Captain Clarke and laid on. The hounds ran the deer smartly down the valley to New Barn. With so many deer on foot matters were complicated, but, turning back with a stag also in front of them, they chased the hind at a fast pace back to Cot Down, where she was taken. The stag soon afterwards, in trying to negotiate the fence was also captured, and dispatched by Mr C H Basset. In the meantime another very fine hind came down the water, followed by a por-tion of the pack and most of the field. this hind traversed the valley to opposite Shirwell Mills. She ran down to Sepcott Wood, then turned up stream to just opposite the five-mile post on the Lynton-road, where she was viewed soiling in the water. The pack being called up, they again raced her down the valley to Kingdon Gardens, where deer were so numerous that the pack became considerably divided. As the day was now growing late, the Master collected the hounds, and the field returned home.

(To the Editor of the NORTH DEVON JOURNAL)
February 25th 1904

"SHOOTING" VERSUS "HUNTING" DEER

Sir – Having read a lot of twaddle lately in the papers anent the hunting of red deer in this district which has been described as inhuman and cruel, and as the owner of Arlington has suggested to me through her Man of Law that the alternative of shooting them should be resorted to, with a view of keeping them down. I should like to mention an incident which occurred yesterday, which will help to show that a great deal more pain and agony is likely to be suffered by these animals if the indiscriminate use of firearms is adopted against them, than if hunted in an orthodox manner by hounds, as in the latter case the deer either gets away unhurt, or, if he is brought to bay, usually has a quick despatch by a knife used by a skillful hand.

What happened yesterday was this. A fine hind was discovered in a very distressed condition near the Eastdown Rectory, evidently badly wounded in one hind leg, and when a well known sporting gentleman was acquainted of this he came out and put the poor animal out of pain. The wound, which I have this day inspected, had evidently been caused by a bullet, which had shattered the bone at the hock joint. In what locality the animal had been fired at is unknown, but it had come direct from the Arlington property, which was proved by her slot.

Personally speaking, I don't hunt, but I like to see everyone enjoying his own line of sport, and for that reason I have allowed my Yeo Valley coverts to be drawn by the staghounds *ad lib* for the last four years. Apart from the sporting point of view I recognised that the tenants on my estate must be protected from the depredations of the deer, and that the latter must be kept down for the tenants' sakes, especially when it is remembered that they have to find £800 per annum for the Dowager Lady of Arlington Court.

Were there no hounds in the district I am afraid that the use of firearms would have to be resorted to in order to reduce the number of deer, and so protect the crops, which method would, I am sure, only lead to many scenes such as the one which was witnessed at Eastdown yesterday. – Yours truly,
EDWARD CHICHESTER Rear-Admiral.
Youlston, 19th February 1904.

In 1910, staghunting was still on the agenda regarding Miss Chichester and Arlington Court with a special meeting to discuss this and hunting the deer in the Barnstaple country for the coming season.

Staghunting in the Barnstaple district.
Meeting at Barnstaple, November 3rd 1910

A public meeting was held at Barnstaple Guildhall on Friday afternoon to consider the question of hunting in the Barnstaple country this season with Mr E R Berry Torr (secretary of the Instow Beagles) being voted to the chair on the proposition. The chairman read a letter that had been addressed to the meeting through Mr T S Watkinson, agent for Miss Chichester:

"Sir, I have been instructed by Miss Chichester to say, on her behalf, that the Arlington estate will be closed as heretofore against staghunting, and that Miss Chichester will allow no one to hunt over her grounds. I am bringing this before you in order that in making whatever arrangements you may think fit, no misunderstanding may arise hereafter. I am, sir, your obedient servant, T S Watkinson, agent for Miss Chichester."

The chairman said he knew that in regard to the letter he had read, he believed that they would be wise in acknowledging Miss Chichester's wishes. They might be able to hunt the country outside her coverts, but, if so, they should make strenuous attempts to try and prevent hounds entering her coverts. The greatest courtesy to that lady would be to adhere to her wishes. If deer increased some people might be tempted to use illegitimate means of destroying them, and he felt that Miss Chichester would do her utmost to prevent that kind of destruction of deer. He thought it would be right for a damage fund to be opened. He was educated under two great sportsmen, the late Rev Jack Russell and the late Hon Mark Rolle, and he could tell them that neither one of those worthies were of the opinion that there was anything wrong in hunting. In fact, it created a common bind of union between them. The more they hunted the deer, the more were they convinced that it was wrong and cruel to shoot and kill them in other ways. He (the speaker) fully concurred with what the chairman had said on the Arlington question. Miss Chichester was of the opinion that hunting was cruel, and ought not to be indulged in. Everyone had a right to his own opinion and those who agreed with hunting would, he believed, find it quite possible to hunt the Barnstaple neighbourhood and keep out of Arlington coverts altogether.

Arlington Court, once owned by Miss Chichester.
The property was handed to the National Trust in 1949 in her legacy.

Carriage rides are given to the public while visiting Arlington Court today.

Photos © Richard Lethbridge

There follows an extract from Richard Stapledon's book *Exmoor Elegance and Rhythm* which contains an account of a day in 1920 when he joined the Tiverton Staghounds from a meet at South Molton Station and later entered Miss Chichester's Arlington Court.

About 1920 I boxed two horses down in the special and had a great day with the Tiverton Staghounds. We drew White Hill, just south of the South Molton–Barnstaple road, and found about 12.30 p.m.

The stag crossed the main road where the pack was laid on. And now the line taken was Shallow Ford, up the Bray and under the viaduct, out left-handed by Brayley Barton, south of East and West Buckland, Gunn, Middle Dean and down the valley between Goodleigh and Stoke Rivers, up the water, swinging left to Loxhore, thence to the Arlington preserves. Miss Chichester's estate was sanctuary for deer and the few of us still left with hounds knew it: but the stag had somehow found his way through the boundary fence and hounds were now entering the very holy of holies – the gardens of Arlington Court itself!

The big wooden drive gate was chained and locked. Percy Yandle (huntsman of the Tiverton Staghounds) came to it first: when he was seen to be grinding his teeth one knew perfectly well that he was in one of his wild moods! He flung himself off his horse and attacked the gate: he could make no impression by charging it with his shoulder or by kicking it with his top boots. "Come on, you fellers," he shouted. "Us 'ave got to get drew yere." And with that four or five heavyweights set to work – the hinges gave way to the onslaught and the gate rolled over, held by the chain and lock alone.

"Now," said Percy, "us must all keep close together 'cos there's sure to be trouble."

We heard pandemonium a short way ahead – the worst had happened, hounds were baying the stag in the pond right in front of the very house itself! However, the clatter and noise of our arrival broke things up and we left the precincts and the stony stare of Miss Chichester herself as fast as we could. The end came half-a-mile further on and we then jogged back to Barnstaple, whither the special train had been summoned from South Molton. The point was 10 miles over an unusual line. We were well aware of how naughty we had all been and fully expected the solicitor's letter which arrived in due course.

Captain Amory, who had taken over duties as Secretary, was not at all pleased with us. However, it was not very long before he found his expressive grin again and said, "Well, I suppose boys will be boys; but no more of it!"

186

The pond in front of Arlington Court where the hounds were baying the stag. The background shows the church of St James, Arlington. © Richard Lethbridge

It is interesting to note that Miss Rosalie Chichester's father Sir Bruce Chichester had his own pack of hounds which were kennelled at Arlington Court, known as Sir Bruce Chichester's Foxhounds. There follows some runs of these hounds.

2nd November 1871

Opening day with Sir Bruce Chichester's Foxhounds

On Thursday last the opening meet of these foxhounds took place at Arlington Court, where, with the hospitality always so conspicuous in Sir Bruce and Lady Chichester, a most substantial breakfast was provided for all-comers, and, despite the inclemency of the weather, a goodly muster assembled to greet the worthy master on his opening day. Breakfast over, the hounds appeared, looking in first-rate condition, and quite equal to the task of giving a good account of their foxes. The worthy master was soon amongst them, and proceeded to draw Woolley Wood, when, in a very few minutes, a fox was found, and being unmistakably warned that "delay would be dangerous," he went off at a rapid pace through Woolley Wood to Hammett's Grove, over Woolley Down, through Woolley Farm to Garmond's Down, where, being headed by a man in the road, he turned short back to Woolley Wood, passed The Lake, went straight through the Park to the Home Farm, thence through the water meadows to

187

Eastdown Wood, when a long check occurred, and for a time, he baffled his pursuers. By this time the field was considerably scattered, and "Where are they gone" was heard in all directions; and no wonder, for the short turn back through Woolley Wood had upset the calculations of the knowing ones, and the pace the hounds kept up did make them hard to find. A long cast forward was made without hitting off his line, when suddenly he was viewed, having evidently laid down in a hedgerow. The hounds were quickly on his track, and this time he led them through Brockham Plantation up to Woolley Down, through Cot Wood, passed Loxhore Cot (where he was viewed by an excitable old lady) through the small enclosures to Loxhore Tower, where he must have been again headed by a man at work in a field, for, turning through Deerpark Wood, he went through Woolley Cleaves, Hammett's Grove, and Woolley Wood to the Lake, where, a heavy shower coming on, the scent entirely failed, so he was left to his own reflections. Deerpark Wood was then drawn, but no fox was found, and, as it was very wet and getting late, the hounds were taken home. Thus ended the opening day, greatly to the satisfaction of all who were present, amongst whom we noticed, Lady and Miss Chichester, of Youlston, Mr Beach, MP, (Master of the Vine), and Mrs Beach, Mr Williams MP, Mr Lee, Captain and Mrs Moore, Mrs J Chichester, Mrs Markham, Mr and Mrs Brudenell Bruce, Mr and Mrs Pinckney, Captain Newton Chichester, Captain A Baker, Rev J Arthur, Captain and Mrs Riddell, Mr and Mrs Roe, Rev H Fursdon, Drs T Law, J Harper, and W Cooke, Messrs I Bencraft, Gregory, Parminter, Rock, Thorne, Tamlyn, J Baker, Dovell, Vicary, Tucker, Yeo, Southcombe, &c, &c, &c. In conclusion, we heartily hope that Sir Bruce will receive on all sides that support he so richly deserves, and have a most successful season; also that his hounds may keep strong, and his horses healthy. That he may have good sport and foxes aplenty, is the sincere wish of, yours faithfully, A LOVER OF FOXHUNTING.

8th February 1872

Sir Bruce Chichester's Foxhounds met at Heasley Mill on Tuesday week, and drew Long Wood, but could do very little. They then went on to South Wood and found directly. The fox went away, pointing for North Molton, but was headed back by Heasley Mill, into Long Wood, where there was a long check, but a forward cast to North Radworthy, put the hounds right again, as they hit the line off directly, and went away as if tied to him, through Radworthy Wood and across to Lydcott, and over the bottom to Span Wood. They did not dwell in covert a moment –

away pointing for Bera Wood. Two fields from the Poltimore Arms, the fox turned short to the right, as if he meant to try back for Buttery Brake, but leaving that to his right, he went straight over Exmoor, where the fog was so thick one could not see ten yards ahead. However, the hounds went on and killed their fox close to Cornham Brake, near Simonsbath. Time, one hour forty-five minutes.

189

CHAPTER 10

THE BARNSTAPLE AND NORTH DEVON RACES
AND THE BARNSTAPLE HORSE AND HOUND SHOW

B arnstaple led the field in the early Point-to-Point races which were known as the Barnstaple and North Devon Races. The earliest account of this event I found is dated 1831, and there follows articles from the papers. I also found a report of what turned out to be the first Bratton Down Race (1877), where today the Dulverton West Foxhounds, the Exmoor Foxhounds and the Tiverton Staghounds hold their race meetings.

THE BARNSTAPLE AND NORTH DEVON
RACES

The Hunt Stakes Race at the Barnstaple and North Devon Races at Pitt Marsh in 1867

Hurdle Race, over Twenty Flights of Hurdles, 3 Miles. A sweep-stakes of Two Sovereigns each, half forfeit, with £20 added. Entrance 10s. For Horses that have been regularly and fairly hunted with any established Pack of Fox or Stag Hounds in Devonshire, Cornwall, Dorsetshire, and Somersetshire during the Season 1866 and 1867, and that have not been liable to Race Horse duties. Four years old, 10st 7lbs; five years old, 11st; six years and aged, 11st 3lbs. The second horse to save his Stake. Winners of one Race to carry 5lbs extra, of two Races to carry 10lbs extra. Thoroughbred Horses 7lbs extra. A Certificate that the Horse has been regularly and fairly hunted, under the hand of the Master of the Fox or Stag Hounds, must be produced before it can be entered for the Stakes.

STEWARDS:

The Right Hon LORD CLINTON
The Rt Hon SIR S H NORTHCOTE, Bart, MP
SIR ARTHUR CHICHESTER, Bart
The Hon MARK ROLLE
FREDERICK WILLIAMS, Esq, MP
SIR GEORGE STUCLEY, Bart, MP
THOMAS CAVE, Esq, MP
SIR BRUCE CHICHESTER, Bart
CHARLES CHICHESTER, Esq
G E KINGSON, Esq, Judge
Mr JOHN SELDON, Hon Secretary
Mr T D GREGORY, Starter
CHARLES WILLIAMS, Esq, Clerk of the Course

EXCURSION TRAINS will run over the North Devon Line, at Cheap Fares.

September 8th 1870
Barnstaple and North Devon Races

The Barnstaple and North Devon Races were held on Monday, at Pitt Marsh, and met with very equivocal success. The racing, on the whole, was very good, but the weather was most unpropi-tious, and, no doubt partly owing to the threatening appearance of the sky in the morning, the attendance was less than usual. In the middle of the afternoon the rain descended in torrents, and fell with more or less power during the greater part of the time the racing lasted. The result was not only great discomfort

191

to the spectators, for whom the awning over the grandstand was but a mockery of a protection, and who, in less than half an hour, presented the appearance of a large assemblage of drowned rats, but also the rendering of the course, which was in excellent condition in the morning, marshy, slippery, and unsafe for the horses. Some of the races were run in the midst of the pelting rain, which made the colours difficult to distinguish, the white being in all cases turned to an unpleasant-looking slate. It is always said to be "an ill wind that blows nobody good," and, if the remark be equally applicable to rain, Monday's showers were a proof of its truth. The wet might incommode the visitors, and endanger the limbs of both horses and jockeys, but it certainly benefited the booth-proprietors, as it drove all who could obtain an inch of standing-room to the friendly shelter of their canvas and the anti-catarrh properties of their liquors. Though the number of these refreshment-booths was great, there seemed to be room for even more, for not one could be seen which was not quite full of people clamouring for the drinks – good or bad, stimulating or poisonous, as the case might be – which the pro-prietor could supply. On the other hand the exhibition-booths, with the exception of that devoted to the illustration of the "noble art of self-defence," did not seem to be doing much business. Whether it was that the country-men were fearful that the canvas was not watertight or suspicious of being "done", certain it is that the invitations to "walk up and witness this most astounding performance for the charge of only one penny" were mostly unheeded. "Aunt Sally" seemed to be entirely without patrons, and but few consented to "try their strength" by strik-ing something resembling the buffer of a railway engine, notwith-standing the repeated asservations that "Tom Sawyers, Tom King, and ever so many others well known within the ropes" had achieved their successes in the art of mauling their fellow creatures by using this means of practice. Card sharpers and thimble-riggers were conspicuous by their asbsence; of roulette-tables there were but few, if any; the police (under the able direc-tion of Capt Hilliker) had but few pick-pockets or drunken men to occupy their time; formosas were few in number; but there were more bookmakers than could have been anticipated. The number of people present showed a marked falling off from that at former meetings, partly owing, no doubt, to the races coming off so much later in the year than usual, and partly to the unfavourable weather. The excursion trains which ran to the temporary station – with a perfectly sublime unpunctuality, and a disregard of published times wonderful to witness – had, however, as many people as they could well carry on each of their numerous journeys. Barnstaple, Bideford, Exeter, and even

Plymouth were represented, and crowds of yokels poured in from the adjacent district. All seemed to enjoy themselves pretty well, despite the "damper" thrown on the festivities by the rain, and the solemn texts from Holy Writ borne on banners among the crowd by well-meaning but mistaken men, who forgot that the introduction of such subjects on such an uncongenial occasion tended rather to bring them into ridicule than to impress them upon the minds of their readers. The enjoyment, too, seemed to be generally of an innocent character, very little money changing hands in betting transactions. A young man named Henry Galliford, fractured his collar bone in a fall he received when resisting the police, who, in consequence of his disorderly conduct, had directed him to leave the spot. One of the horses, Thornettle, threw her rider, but without injuring him. Another, Her X L N C was clumsily ridden, when not racing, against the sharp projecting end of a horizontal piece of rough wood which formed part of a barrier on the paddock side of the straight. The point tore up her breast in a frightful manner, and the unfortunate animal was immediately taken off the course, bleeding profusely. These were the only accidents which came to our knowledge, with the exception of a policeman's falling from the shock of a concussion with a horse which was leaping a hurdle. As, however, he was not hurt, the feeling raised was rather a tendency to "chaff the bobby", than to pity his misfortune. But two protests were made during the meeting, and one of these was withdrawn. The stewards of the races were Sir Stafford Northcote Bart MP, Sir F M Williams Bart MP, Mr Thomas Cave MP, Mr C H Williams MP, Mr Charles Chichester, and Capt Newton Chichester. Mr T P Seldon worked hard as honourary secretary, Mr Rhodes Bankes was a most efficient clerk of the course and clerk of the scales, being ably assisted in the latter department by Mr Pridham, Mr G E Kingdon officiated as judge and Mr Gibbings as starter. The races were started with fair punctuality.

Hunt Stakes Hurdle Race, over six flights of hurdles, two miles; a sweepstakes of two sovs each, half forfeit, with 20 sovs added.

Capt N Chichester's b m Primula 5 yrs, 11st 7lb	(Mr Riddell)	1
Mr Matthew's Tufter, 5 yrs, 11st, 7lb	(Owner)	2
Mr Davey's br, g, Jerusalem, 5 yrs, 11st, 7lb	(Tucker)	0
Mr Courtney's b g Top Sawyer, 4 yrs, 11st	(Luxton)	0
Mr G Davey's b h Harry Brailsford, aged 12st 7lb	(Owner)	0

The Rho Doubtful, and Bowstring were scratched. Betting – 5 to 4 and 2 to 1 bar 1. Primula had the winning game all through the run, and won in a canter. In her first leap, she caused a great deal of amusement by flooring a policeman who was in her way without hurting him. Jerusalem came behind Primula at first, but gave way to Harry Brailsford, and subsequently to Tufter and Top Sawyer. Harry Brailsford soon fell back again, but the other two had for some time a neck and neck run for second. Tufter got the advantage and lost it in refusing a hurdle. He took up the running again, though, passed the rest and came in second, distancing Top Sawyer and the others.

Barnstaple and North Devon Races
August 31st 1871

On Monday last these annual races were held on Youlston Old Park. From an early hour in the morning until about noon, well-filled vehicles left this town for the course, the distance between the two being about four miles, whilst many pleasure-seekers travelled thither on foot, either unable or unwilling to pay the somewhat heavy charge for conveyance there. The attendance on the race ground was comparatively limited. There could not have been more than a thousand persons present, a fact which can only be attributed to the inconvenience attending a migration from the town to the park, the whole distance being a continuity of hills, up which, on a hot summer's day, it was by no means pleasant to climb. Last year the races were held at Pitt Marsh, where there was a much larger assemblage, although then there was "rain, rain, nothing but rain" all day long. Monday, on the contrary, was one of the finest days we have had during the summer. Scarcely a cloud obscured the sky, and the sun shone with unwonted brilliance and splendour. Still, the elevated position of the course, and a gentle breeze that blew, imparted to the atmosphere a coolness which was evidently appreciated. The spectators also seemed to take very little interest in the races. They would "come in at the death", inquire which horse had won, and then, having satisfied their spasmodic curiosity, wander off again to more congenial amusements. There were refreshment booths on the ground which seemed to do a fair stroke of business, but the usual adjuncts of a race-course – "Aunt Sally", shooting galleries &c – although represented, were by no means "the features" they usually constitute. The grand stand was erected on a spot commanding as good a view of the course as could be obtained, which, however, was only little more than half the distance. A handbill, signed by Mr R D Gould, borough surveyor, was posted in conspicuous positions on the structure, certifying that it was constructed firmly and substantially; but, notwithstanding this assurance to the more nervous, that there was no fear of a "smash", the stand was by no means crowded. The course cannot be called first class – for it was over very undulating ground, and abounded with sharp curves. The turf was in excellent condition – no rain having fallen for several days which might have rendered it soft and slippery. The races were, on the whole, better than have been expected, the horses generally were well matched, and the jockeys evidently did their best. There was, however, some clumsy riding. The races of Monday were remarkable for the almost total lack of incidents to enliven the scene or keep up the excitement. Except that a horse was hurt in a race, and that there were two or three "scrimmages" between the police and the more reckless of the mob, who persisted in running across the course at the moment the horses were coming in, there was nothing that came to our notice worth recording. Still, all seemed to enjoy themselves, and the day's proceedings were, we may say, successful, as in previous years. The following were the stewards, The Hon Mark Rolle, Sir Stafford Northcote Bart MP, Sir F Williams Bart MP, Thomas Cave Esq MP, Charles H Williams Esq MP, Charles Chichester Esq, and Gage Hodge Esq, Mr W Manning ably acted as secretary, and Rhodes Bankes Esq as clerk of the course.

Open Hunt Stakes, hurdle race, over eight flights of hurdles. Two miles. A sweepstakes of £2 each, half forfeit to the find, with £20 added.

Mr J R Riddell's Rouble, 4 yrs, 11st 7lb	(English)	1
Mr H Lake's Special, 4 yrs, 11st	(Owner)	2
Mr Martin's Sauterne, aged, 12st 12lb	(Hitchens)	0

A capital start was effected, from a point a quarter of a mile from the grand stand. Just after passing that structure Sauterne, which led ahead finely, bolted, but was brought to just as the other horses came by, and it again went forward. All the horses took the hurdles well, neither of them having made a single hitch, except that, when she came to the last hurdle, Special kicked the furze, by which she probably lost a step. At the three-quarter mile point Sauterne unfortunately bolted for the second time, and fell back into a irretrievable position in the rear. It now became an equal contest between Special and Rouble, and many were the conjectures as to which animal was to be the lucky one. Both held their places well, but, in rounding a curve about half a mile from the grand stand, Rouble took advantage of the opportunity to field his antagonist, and swept ahead finely, winning as he pleased. Special followed up about five lengths in the rear.

Barnstaple and North Devon Races
23rd May 1872

Barnstaple and North Devon Races, "long looked for," have "come at last," and are over. They were held on Tuesday, by the kind permission of Robert Chichester Esq, of Hall, at Pitt Marsh in the parish of Bishop's Tawton, which was both a suitable spot, and with respect to the adjacent scenery an interesting one. They went off most successfully, the admirable arrangements made being carried out in a most satisfactory manner, the entries of good animals being large, and the running stiffly contracted. As a day for spectators it was all that could be desired and more than many expected, the racing being especially good, the course near to the town, trains (of unusual length) setting them down at Chappletown siding, within a few minutes' walk of the course, and what was perhaps of more consequence to the mass of simply sightseers and pleasure-seekers, the weather, in opposition to the vaccinations of elderly dames, and the still more ominous fall of a rather smart shower at mid-morning, being "just the thing" – most agreeable – neither too hot nor too cold, so that for a wonder there were not amid the very large concourse of people, the customary grumbles and expressions of desire that the weather was other than it happened to be. Besides the gaily-attired masses of a sporting air discharged from the heavily-laden trains, vast numbers of holiday seekers, embracing members of the highest families in the county down to the truant school-boy, arrived in vehicles ranging too from the aristocrat's carriage down to the pony cart, by saddle, and by the proverbial "Jinx's Pony," otherwise on foot. The traps, as usual, served as stands, and from their occupants, as well as from those not favoured to stand so high in the world, the customary "feeding scenes," drolleries, and little amusing incidents, which must be seen to be duly appreciated, emanated. Barnstaple race course, as compared with others, is upheld as a rather model one – one on which the betting is on a very moderate scale, and where the running is genuine; at all events that for 1872 was said to be. No serious disturbance occurred; in fact, but for one or two "skuffles" between pugilistically-inclined youths having taken place, causing the interference of the posse of policemen, who in their turn were somewhat hustled, perhaps more for roguery and with the view of enlivening the scene than anything else; and for such little incident as the starter's man mounting his master's nag and in leaping the hurdle in front of the grandstand getting over before the horse did; the intervals between the races would have been comparatively dull. Of course, a troup of "black men", "rubbing the hair of the horse against the bowels of the cat" (commonly termed violin playing) thumping at a tambourine, and drawing music from bones &c, were there; and of course tents to accommodate those desirous or constrained to refresh the "inner man" were not wanting. Although a good stroke was apparently done threat, it was gratifying to notice an entire absence of persons who failed to walk about or from the gound in an upright manner – in fact, sobriety and good humour seemed to be the order of the day. The ground was entirely taken by Messrs John Seldon and Wm Manning, and they received the admission fees, stand taking &c. Under the stand they had their luncheon and refreshment rooms, whilst they let parts of the ground to other persons who followed suit with regard to supplying eatables and drinkables on a smaller scale. Besides those stalls for the sale of confectionery, cups of tea &c, &c, occupied positions.

Hunt Stakes, over with flights of hurdles. Two miles. A sweepstake of £2 each, half forfeit, with £20 added. For *bona fide* hunters that have been regularly hunted with any established pack of fox or stag hounds in Devon, Somerset and Cornwall, in 1871, or 1872, and have not been in a training stable in 1872.

Mr Brown's b g Venice, 13 st	(Hitchings)	1
Mr R Stone's Hannah, 12st	(Shepherd)	0
Mr Pedrick's b g Haverfield, 12st	(French)	0
Mr J R Riddell's ch g Spectre, 11st 7lb	(Owner)	0
Capt N Chichester's br g Badajos, 12st	(Owner)	0
Mr E Woolmington's v c Marlo, 11st 7lb	(Owner)	0
Mr I Bencraft's Discord did not run.		

This was, perhaps, as exciting a race as any, once on after several false starts. Spectre led boldly, and would doubtless have won easily but for some person (it is said wilfully) riding in front and fouling him, securing a fall to his rider. He, however, quickly remounted, and after riding back for some distance to "punch the other's head" once more resumed the race, and although hopelessly in the rear picked up amazingly, the animal showing its capabilities to perfection, and winning both lusty and deserved cheers. On the throw Haverfield, which had escorted the remaining four, drew somewhat ahead, but they took the straight pretty well together, Haverfield, Hannah and Mario almost side by side, and Venice pulling up, leaving Badajos behind. On again taking the straight and passing the stand, they ran in just the same order, Spectre now hotly pursuing Badajos. Halfway round Baverfield bolted, and was out. The race now became intensely exciting, four only standing any chance of place. They ran some distance, and passed the stand as follows: Mario and Venice a dead heat; Hannah about ten lengths behind; and a similar space separated her from Badajos.

Mr Brown (owner of Venice) raised an objection to Mario holding a place, his rider not having drawn his weight. Mr Woolmington then discovered that he had not his bridle; but Mario having left the paddock with it, Mr Brown held that it could then be brought. After a warm dispute, the stewards (Sir A Chichester, Sir Bruce Chichester, Mr Sheriff Johnson, and Charles Chichester Esq) were called in, and they, after a short colloquy, decided that the objectives must stand good. Mario was therefore disqualified, and the objector's gelding, Venice, took first place. Hannah claimed the second, but the question of placed horses remained in abeyance.

Barnstaple
HORSE SHOW
TO BE HELD IN THE GROUNDS OF PILTON HOUSE
(By the kind permission of C H Williams Esq)
ON WEDNESDAY 30TH JUNE 1875

The following PRIZES open to all England will be offered for competition:

HUNTERS

		£	s	d
14 – stone	Best Gelding or Mare calculated to carry 14 and upwards not under 4 years old	5	5	0
	2nd Best Gelding or Mare	2	2	0
15 –	Best Gelding or Mare for light weight hunters not under 4 years old	5	5	0
	2nd Best Gelding or Mare	2	2	0
16 –	Best Gelding or Mare not exceeding 6 years old bona fide the property of farmers	3	3	0
	2nd Best Gelding or Mare	2	2	0
	3rd Best Gelding or Mare	1	1	0

12th April 1877
THE HORSE RACE AT PITT MARSH

Some time ago, Barnstaple, we believe, boasted an annual race meeting, and the fact that a great deal of local interest is still taken in the national pastime was abundantly proved on Saturday last. On that day, a race took place at Pitt Marsh, between two animals, belonging respectively to Mr Mugford, wine and spirit merchant, and Mr Adams, Bear Street. The event had been talked of for a long time. Every person acquainted with local matters of interest knew that the race was to be for £10 a side, that it was to take place on the afternoon mentioned, that Mr Adam's cob (which was to have the advantage of being ridden by Mr "Jack" Hayman) was supposed to be able to outstay its opponent, and that the betting had run high. Thus it came to pass that, with the object of seeing these two horses run against each other, nearly everybody who could give or get a "lift" was to be seen going up Newport and through Bishopstawton, on Saturday afternoon last. The weather was fine and the drive a very pleasant one. On reaching the course, there was but little delay in effecting a start. Both horses were duly examined and criticised, and were then cantered round the course. It was expected that Mr Mugford's horse would have been mounted by a local rider, but a "jockey from Taunton" was finally engaged. P C Jones of Barnstaple, officiated as clerk of the course, promptly cleared a space for the horses which would have accommodated a field for a dozen, and the race began. Hayman, on Mr Adams's horse, at once took the lead, by a length or more, and, in this order, the two went twice round the course, the "jockey from Taunton" riding in a way which, to say the least of it, was somewhat eccentric. On commencing the third and last round, the pony drew out and won with ease, without Hayman, who had been riding admirably, once calling up on her. The local "jock" was loudly cheered, while some very hard things were said of the gentleman from Taunton. Refreshments were supplied on the ground, and shortly after the race, the highly-excited lovers of sport rode, drove or tramped home.

BARNSTAPLE & NORTH DEVON
RACES—

WILL BE HELD ON

BANK HOLIDAY, MONDAY,
AUGUST 3rd,

ON a COURSE adjoining the BRAUNTON ROAD, about Half a Mile from BARNSTAPLE, when the following will be competed for .

£10.— RACE FOR PONIES not exceeding 13 hands 3 inches. 7lb allowed for every inch below, with penalties.

£20.—RACE FOR GALLOWAYS not exceeding 14 hands 3 inches. 7lb allowed for every inch below, with penalties.

£25. OPEN FLAT RACE, weight for age, with penalties.

£25.—OPEN STEEPLECHASE, weight for age, with penalties.

£25.—OPEN HURDLE RACE, weight for age, with penalties

£20. — FARMERS' and TRADESMEN'S STEEPLE CHASE, for Horses that have never won a Steeplechase of £10, weight for age

£20.—DEVON and SOMERSET HUNT STEEPLE. CHASE A Silver Cup, value £20, added to a Sweepstake of £2 2s Minimum weight 11 stone.

£10. BEATEN HANDICAP.

All entries to be made in writing to the HON. SECRETARY before 8 o'clock on the evening of Friday, 31st July. The stability of the Grand Stand will be certified by Mr. R. D Gould, Borough Surveyor.

Further particulars on application to
JOHN D. YOUNG, Honorary Secretary.

BARNSTAPLE AND NORTH DEVON
RACES

WILL TAKE PLACE ON

THURSDAY, SEPT 18, 1902,
(Being Second Day of the Fair),

On the Old Course, at Brindsworthy,
About one Mile from the Town.

Stewards :—A. L. Christie, Esq. ; Admiral Sir Ed. Chichester ; J. A. Foster, Esq. A. E. Arnold, Esq., J.P.

The following Events will take place :—

£6 OPEN PONY RACE —2.30 P.M

POLO PONY RACE.—3 P.M.

£12 LICENSED VICTUALLERS' OPEN STEEPLECHASE.—3.30 P.M.

£12 OPEN FLAT RACE.—4 P.M.

£8 OPEN GALLOWAY RACE —4.30 P.M.

£12 OPEN HURDLE RACE.—5 P.M.

CONSOLATION RACE.—5.30 P.M

A BAND will be in attendance. Entries close on Tuesday, 16th Sept.—For particulars, apply to
EDWARD MUGFORD
[7357]   Boutport St., Hon. Sec.

THE BARNSTAPLE & NORTH DEVON RACES
IN ACCOUNT WITH JOHN D. YOUNG (HON. Sec.) 1884

Dr.	£ s. D.		Cr.	£ s. D.
To Balance in Banker's hands....	4 1 11		By Rent of Raceground............	20 0 0
Subscriptions Received	90 5 0		,, Paid Stakes......	104 0 0
Tolls, Entrance Gate	58 0 0		,, ,, County Police	3 17 7
,, ,, Grand Stand	37 10 0		,, North Devon Hussar Band	5 10 0
,, ,, Sale of Cards	9 10 0		,, Printing and Stationery	12 11 0
,, ,, Refreshment Booths	20 0 0		,, Bill Posting	1 9 0
,, Paddock	13 0		,, Manual and Horse Labour.......... ..	10 6 5
	126 13 0		,, Erecting Grand Stand, &c..	50 0 0
,, Entrance Fees	34 0		,, Flags, Posts, use of Numbers & Cab hire	1 16 6
,, Sale of Hurdles	1 6 0		,, Telegrams, Bill and Postage Stamps, } Cheque Books, Wrappers and Sundries }	2 8 6
			,, Hurdles	9 16 0
			,, Balance	40 19
	£255 11			£255 8 11

The above Balance of £40 19s 11d is subject to a sum of £30 for unpaid stakes in the Farmers' and Tradesmen's and Licensed Victuallers' Races, and estimated cost of £5 for Iron Hurdles and alteration to fences; the Receipts therefore exceed the expenditure by £5 19s. 11d.
I have examined the above account, and find it correct.

JAMES BOSSON, Auditor.

THE FIRST BRATTON DOWN RACES 1877

On Monday last, for the first time, a race meeting was held at Bratton Fleming. The new venture partly owes it origin to a match which was run some time since at Pitt Marsh, so much interest being taken in that event that it became evident that local races would be largely supported if someone could be found to set the thing a-going. Eventually, Mr John Baker, of the Grange, Bratton – a gentleman known and liked by everybody hereabout – took the matter in hand, and a Committee was formed comprising the following gentlemen: Messrs J D Young and Son, Mr G Davey jun, Mr T P Seldon, Mr Mugford, and Mr Baker jun. Subscriptions were readily obtained, Sir Bruce Chichester giving a five-guinea cup, and the very decent prizes offered ensured a fair number of entries. A Bank holiday was rather a "risky" day upon which to start such an undertaking, as so many other attractions are offered, but, generally speaking, people who care for horse racing at all like it "out and out", and, in point of attendance, the meeting proved a great success. In the morning, the weather was very fine, and a stream of vehicles of all descriptions – from Mr Pridham's well-horsed coaches to those uncomfortable market "butts" – poured up Bear Street on the road to the Down, which had been selected as the course. The only objection to this place is that it is difficult of access. In other respects it is all that can be desired, and the magnificent view from the hill – of green valleys, golden corn fields, and abrupt torrs, sweeping right away to the horizon on all sides – would alone have repaid a visit. All this, of course, lent a greater charm to the business in hand. The grandstand was erected on the highest part of the ground, with the paddock in front, and the weighing tent behind – all rather rough, but answering their purpose. In a large tent adjoining, luncheon and refreshments were served. On the other side of the grandstand a number of stalls for the sale of confectionery were erected. Here, too, the gentleman who, for one penny, allows any customer the privilege of attempting to throw a ring over a knife handle – the man with the lifting machine – and the fellow who invites one to hit a dummy man violently in the stomach, "to try yer strength" – had taken up a position. The last two caterers for the public were furiously patronised by the rustic youth. The more aristocratic portion of the assembly occupied vehicles, and enjoyed their champagne and cold chicken, on the other side of the way. Throughout the whole day, the proceedings were of a most order-ly character, the course being kept clear by only four of the Barnstaple Borough Police, under the direction of Superintendent Songhurst and Sergeant Eddy. Mr John Baker was "here, there and everywhere", and all members of the Committee worked hard. The delicate business of looking after the weighing was entrusted to Messrs Young and Son, and of the manner in which they did the work it need only be said that there was dispute. Mr Seldon was starter, and C H Williams Esq, had kindly consented to act as judge. Mr Hancock, town crier of Barnstaple, was crier of the course.

The weather was rather rough at the commencement of the racing, but the clouds cleared off after an hour or two, and the afternoon was delightfully fine. Nothing occurred which was in the slightest degree calculated to mar the day's enjoyment until nearly the close of the programme, when a somewhat serious accident happened. In the first heat of the hack stakes, Tally Ho! on nearing the distance post, fell and broke its neck, the jockey Lugg, who had won several races during the day, being very heavily thrown. Horse and man lay so still for a moment or two after the fall, as seen from the grandstand, that it was evident something serious had occurred. A crowd of people hurried to the spot. Lugg was on his back, stunned by the fall, with blood flowing from a wound on the head. Fortunately Dr Harper was on the ground, and was quickly in attendance, the police having great difficulty in keeping off the people. Water was fetched, and, in a short time, the poor fellow came round, and was lifted to his feet. He was afterwards taken home in a trap, and by the latest accounts he is in a fair way towards recovery. Mr Saxon shewed great concern in regard to the injuries sustained by the man, and the loss to himself, in the value of the horse, must be very considerable. The ground where the horse fell was very soft, and, in the Hunter's Race, Mr Carter's Creeping Jane went down near the same spot.

Hunters Race – for 10 sovereigns; weight for age: 4 years old – 10st 7lbs; 5 years old – 11st 8lbs; 6 years and aged – 12st 7lbs. Two miles and a half, over 10 flights of hurdles. Winners at any previous race of the value of £10, once, 7lbs extra; twice, 14lbs extra; thrice, 21lbs extra.

Mr F Courtenay's Black Bess	(Rawle)	1
Mr Carter's Creeping Jane	(Elworthy)	2
Mr J H Wagner's Caper-Felto	(Horne)	3

Mr W Skinner's Redland and Mr J Baker's Peter and Skylark were also entered, but did not start. Black Bess, a well-known horse, was the favourite. Mr Wagner's horse, however, made the running until the last round, when Rawle passed him opposite the grandstand, amidst much cheering, and thence forward had it all his own way. Creeping Jane was behind throughout, and, coming over the hill over the soft ground, she fell down. The rider was not hurt, and he quickly remounted. Meanwhile, Horne, on Caper Felto, who had held a long lead, could not get his horse to take the last flight of hurdles, and Creeping Jane, coming up gamely after the tumble, took second place. A protest was entered against Black Bess on the ground that she carried a penalty of 7lbs instead of 21lbs.

A recent advertisement for the Bratton Down Races
© Richard Lethbridge

Shirley's Dream Comes True at Bratton
Point-to-point

Glorious sunshine, a beautiful course in wonderful surroundings, an excellent field ... Bratton Down provided the perfect back-drop for the penultimate meeting of 2004 Point-to-point with the Tiverton Staghounds

And for one Tiverton couple the day was very special ... the long wait for a winner was over!

The opening Members' race saw seven runners and riders go to the post. But Rodney and Shirley Grant's Irish horse Harnage later took the spoils by 25 lengths under Caroline Prouse.

Later delighted Shirely revealed: "We've been trying for 17 years to win this race ... and we are over the moon!"

The owners also celebrated a double with Spinnning Silver in the Open Maiden race giving rider Mervyn Woodward his first winner this season. And keeping it local, Bampton-based Ashley Farrant raised his score to 54 for the season, riding a double for David Pipe, securing the 2004 jockey's title.

Neil Harris and Will Biddick both rode winners at the meeting, with no less than 50 horses running in six very competitive races.

RESULTS
Tiverton Staghounds at Bratton Down

Hunt Members, seven ran: 1 HARNAGE (IRE), Miss C Prouse, 4-1;   2 Stepasideboy, G Weatherley, 4-1;   3 Magical Fun (IRE), Miss T Hayes, 12-1.

Shirley & Rodney Grant with their horse Harnage who was ridden by Caroline Prouse, and the Hunt Members Race. Their other horse, Spinning Silver won the Open Maiden, ridden by Mervyn Woodward.
Photo courtesy of Tiverton Gazette, © Sarah Hibbert.

Intermediate, eight ran: 1 CIMMAROON (IRE), A Farrant, 11-10F; 2 HOLD ON HARRY, L Heard, 3-1; 3 SHERBOURNE GUEST (IRE), J Kwiatkpwski, 25-1.

Mixed Open, nine ran: 1 LET'S FLY (FR), W Biddick; 5-1; 2 COLQUHON, A Farrant, 4-6F; 3 WEND'S DAY (IRE), M Hooper, 7-2.

Confined, five ran: 1 I AM SAID 1 (IRE), A Farrant, 1-4F; 2 MILLYHENRY, Miss C Tizzard 10-1; 3 KHAYAL (USA), Miss R Green 7-1.

Restricted, eight ran: 1 PORTO (IRE), N Harris, 9-2; 2 RIVER DANTE (IRE), S Kidston, 5-2; 3 NICE APPROACH (IRE), Miss V Murphy, 12-1.

Open Maiden, 11 ran: 1 SPINNING SILVER, M Woodward, 14-1; 2 THE FOOTSY, G Barfott-Saunt, 10-1; 3 QUEEN'S HOUSE, Miss R Green, 6-1.

Torrington Farmers Point-to-point

At the Torrington Farmers Point-to-point the following week, Rodney and Shirley Grant's horse Harnage, ridden by Caroline Prouse, won again over seven rivals in the restricted race.

The Barnstaple Horse and Hound Show

Barnstaple also led the field in the hound shows; the first recorded one I found being in 1881. In 1900 Barnstaple was the host of the Devon County Show which featured a hound show – the results follow. The Devon and Somerset Staghounds paraded at this show and the hounds were kenneled for the night at Barnstaple at the expense of the committee

---

Barnstaple Horse and Hound Show

The annual meeting for 1881 will be held by kind permission of C H Basset in the grounds of Pilton House on Wednesday the 6th of July.
For prize sheets and entry forms apply to:
Jas H Seldon, secretary,
Boutport Street, Barnstaple.
April 30th 1881.

The Hound Show
May 24th 1900
at the Devon County Show, Barnstaple

This was an entirely new feature, due to the energy and influence of Mr C H Basset, and proved a thorough success. Needless to say in such a sporting district the judging and exhibits came in for keen scrutiny. The competition was open to kennels in the West Country – Devon, Cornwall and West Somerset. The packs represented the Stevenstone (Hon Mark Rolle, Master), West Somerset (Mr Wilfred Marshall), Mr Eathurst's, the Dartmoor (Mr William Coryton). East Devon (Lieutenant-Colonel J A T Garratt), and South Devon (Messrs Singer and Vicary), the judges being Mr Sam Morgan (from Lord Galway's Serlby Kennels), Mr John Isaac (from the Pytchley), and Mr William Dale (from the Badminton). Prizes were provided by the local committee and two specials were offered. following were the results:

Best couple of unentered dog-hounds, whelped since January 1899 – 1 and 2, Mr Bathurst's.

Two couple unentered dog-hound 1s, not under 24ins. – 1, The Dartmoor; 2, Mr Bathursts's.

Best stallion hound, not under his 3rd or over his 4th season, and certificated to be the sire of living puppies – 1 and 2, The Dartmoor.

Best stallion hound not under his 3rd or over his 7th season, bred in a West Country Kennel and certified to be the sire of living puppies – 1, The West Somerset; 2, The Dartmoor.

Best couple of unentered bitches, whelped since January 1899 – 1, Mr Bathurst's; 2, The Dartmoor.

Best couple of unentered bitches, no under 22 ins, and not over 7th season, to have been bred in a West Country Kennel – 1, The West Somerset; 2, The East Devon.

Best brood bitch, must have produced living puppies or in whelp – 1, The East Devon; 2, Mr Bathurst's

Cup for the best stallion hound in the show – "Eagleman," of the South Devon Hunt.

Cup for the best bitch – "Treason," of the East Devon Hunt.

Hon Mark Rolle's Point to Point races, 1901

CHAPTER 11

THE BARNSTAPLE HARRIERS AND
THE BARNSTAPLE AND NORTH DEVON HARRIERS

The Barnstaple Harriers were first mentioned in the *Journal* in the 1870s, their quarry being the hare. I found no reports of runs, or where the kennels were. Beyond the 1870s, no reports are recorded, indicating they might have disbanded. This may well have been the case for in 1893 a pack was established with a fresh name, the Barnstaple and North Devon Harriers. A few gentlemen bought the Ilfracombe Harriers, and the new pack was born.

The Barnstaple and
North Devon Harriers
hunt button

The Barnstaple Harriers

Dear Sir – I, as well as a good many others of your readers, read your hunting intelligence with pleasure, and the splendid runs of the Devon and Somerset Staghounds are generally reported. I have often observed the Barnstaple Harriers' announcement of meets, but never of any runs. How is this? Surely the runs of the Barum hounds ought to be duly reported in Barum papers. As such, however, is not the case, I will give a little information of the runs that have taken place in this neighbourhood during the past ten days. As your paper announced, the hounds were to meet at Parracombe, on October 23rd, Blackmore Gate October 25th, Parracombe again on the 27th. The hounds arrived on friday evening, 22nd October, and were kennelled in the stables of the Fox and Goose and remained till the 28th.

The meet on Saturday (being a wet day) was exceedingly small. Martinhoe Common was the hunting ground, where they remained from 10.30 until between five and six in the evening. They turned up several hares, and had a gallop or two, but returned without killing anything. "Show sport another day," being the motto adopted.

Monday's meet at Blackmore Gate was better attended: the hunting scene today was Rowley Down and Challacombe Common. They turned up one hare, which the hounds killed near Ridge, and without waiting for the cook took French leave and gobbled it up then and there. Several hares were turned up and soon lost. The hounds took scent on Challacombe Common, and ran away towards Chapman Burrows, when it was discovered the hunted animal was a *fox*, and thus after a *wild goose chase* they returned to the *Fox and Goose* without any hares.

Wednesday 27th, Martinhoe Common again. Meet small, only one gentleman. They killed, and this time (thanks to having a lawyer with them) they saved the hare. They turned up a fox on Parracombe Common. Reynard went away across Holhardy ridge, to Highley Combe, over Chapman Burrows, to Sharland brake; and in spite of all the master and his whips did to restrain, the hounds followed, but of course did not catch, and thus ended the three days' sports. "Killed two hares. Saved one hare," being the entry.

Now, Sir, in these enlightened days of progress and reform, when everything is superior to our forefathers, how is it that harehounds, instead of progressing towards perfection, are degenerating to nothing? Those of your readers who remember the hunting days of Parson Hole, of Georgeham, or more recently Mr Gilbert, of Barnstaple, well know that such an occurrence as hounds eating the hare never took place then; yet it occurs *frequently now*: in fact, it is reported the hounds eat eight out of ten they catch. Surely there must be something wrong either with the hounds or huntsmen. Hares are very plenty, and if the hounds were worth anything they could obtain first rate sport; but the yeomen here don't see the sport in the hounds eating all; and one large farmer, I understand, locked his gates on Wednesday, thus causing considerable annoyance to the hunters, who were obliged to go round instead obediently,

Parracombe, November 1st 1875.   SPORTSMAN

16th December 1875
Barnstaple v Southmolton Harriers

Dear Sir – In answer to "Nimrod," when he accuses me of writing disparagingly of the Barnstaple Harriers, and says, "the least a Nimrod can do is to speak well of their performances, or say nothing at all," he evidently overlooks the fact – that it was merely an account of the three days' run in this neighbourhood, and if it was not flattering it was at least truthful. Truth is not always complimentary, I know; but because it is not I do not see the reason why we must not speak the truth. Also, by pointing out their little imperfections some alteration can be made to bring the pack nearer to perfection; while, if the accounts were always favourable, might not the "master" get a little bit conceited, and consider his hounds a paragon? "Nimrod" will not deny when I say the Barnstaple Harriers are badly trained and badly managed or worked in the field, being much too wild and under scarcely any control.

"Nimrod" has taken my meaning too literally with regard to Mr Gilbert's hounds. Of course, now and then , when something occurs, such as the bad state of the ground or a long run, the hunters may be some distance behind.

I am glad to see such a good account of the South Molton Harriers. They must be perfectly under control, and thus while affording excellent sport.

Yours obediently,
Parracombe   SPORTSMAN

The Barnstaple Harriers

Dear Sir – I fear very few of the yeoman will rejoice at Mr Wagner resuming the command of these harriers, especially if he serves other places the same as he has this neighbourhood. He crosses our lands without permission, often doing considerable damage; and should he ever by rare luck catch and save the hare we at least never have it. I will give you one instance only of their unsportsmanlike proceedings. Early last season they were hunting over Rowley Barton, a large farm occupied by Mr R Gammon. In crossing Rowley Down they broke several hurdles and left open gates so that upwards of 300 sheep got into a twelve acre turnip field. The damage done can be better estimated than described. Mr Gammin demanded £5 for damages. Mr Wagner refused. The next time the hounds were here Mr Gammin ordered them off; but, thanks to the Rev John Russell's intervention, the affair was amicably settled. Mr Wagner was to pay the £5 for compensation, in consideration of which Mr Gammin gave them permission to hunt over Rowley. The £5 not being forthcoming, Mr Gammin applied for it, but Mr Wagner refused to pay because the Combe Martin Harriers had been over Rowley. Mr Gammin pays nearly £20 a year for the game on Rowley, principally for his friends, as he seldom shoots or hunts himself; and the Barnstaple Harriers have hunted there for years without ever paying a penny. The Rev John Russell, both at the time and since, offered to subscribe towards the compensation, which, I think is a sufficient guarantee for the justice of this claim, as the reverend gentleman's judgment is as well known as his sporting abilities. Can you wonder then, if, on Mr Wagner hunting the Woolhanger neighbourhood, he finds the Parracombe gates locked against him, as he has found them before? It is a pity masters of hounds cannot retain the good will of the yeoman, for it is they and they alone, who have the control over their sports.

I am Sir, yours obediently,

ARTHUR SMYTH

Parracombe, May 7th 1877

[There must be some misunderstanding in this matter, for the master of the Barnstaple Harriers is not a gentleman to forfeit his word. We are told he understood the agreement to be that he was to pay £5 for the hunting of Rowley, but that finding other hounds permitted there, he considered the occupier had violated the contract, and so had absolved him from payment. – Ed]

<h1 align="center">March 11th 1893
The lead up to establishing the
Barnstaple and North Devon Harriers</h1>

A remarkable mishap has occurred to the Ilfracombe Harriers The Master (Mr Penhale) has become a debtor to the owner of the kennels at two pots for rent, and the owner being unable the same 20 couples were seized by the Sheriff of Devon, Mr H Barrett, together with three of the horses. It was hoped that a friendly "ring" would be formed to buy in the hounds at the auction, so as to keep the hunt going. This took place at the Lansdown hotel, Ilfracombe on Tuesday. Several farmers and others were present, but no bid was made for the hounds which were put up in one lot. Mr Morgan, auctioneer, then himself bid £5, quickly putting another £5 on top of it, and for £10 the hounds were knocked down to him. It is hoped that either a company of Ilfracombe or Barnstaple sportsmen will speedily arrange to get possession of the hounds, otherwise they will probably go to South Pembrokeshire.

April 1st 1893

The Ilfracombe Harriers which, as announced in these columns a fortnight ago, were sold by auction under a distress for rent of kennels have been purchased by a few Barnstaple gentleman with a view of establishing a hunt for that district.

The Barnstaple and North Devon Harriers' quarry was also the hare, but on occasion they hunted foxes and, before the Barnstaple Staghounds were established, the deer. They also hunted deer when the staghounds were out of action at different times. In 1901 when the Barnstaple Staghounds came into being, paper reports and the *Bailys Hunting Directory* indicate that the two packs of hounds were in the same kennels at Sowden. This seemed to be a joint affair for the papers and the *Bailys Hunt Directory* gives the Master and huntsmen hunting both packs jointly.

BARNSTAPLE

SHORT NOTICE.

A PUBLIC MEETING

WILL be held at the KING'S ARMS HOTEL, BARNSTAPLE, on

FRIDAY NEXT MARCH 24TH,

to take into consideration the desirability of establishing

A PACK OF HARRIERS

FOR THE DISTRICT.

The Mayor (James Brady, Esq.), has kindly consented to take the chair at 3 o'clock.

N.B.—It is hoped that all interested will make an effort to attend.

A Pack of Harriers for Barnstaple
March 28th 1893

PUBLIC MEETING

The Mayor (Mr James Brady) on Friday presided over a well attended public meeting at Barnstaple, called for the purpose of considering whether a pack of harriers should be established for Barnstaple. The Mayor said the Ilfracombe pack had been purchased by a few Barnstaple gentlemen with the view of hunting the North Devon country. Should it be definitely decided to establish a pack in Barnstaple, every gentleman in the town or neighbourhood would have the opportunity of taking part in what they fairly considered the greatest of all English pastimes. He referred to the loss to the district of the Eggesford hounds, and thought the present a favourable opportunity for establishing a pack of harriers. The whole of the company present unanimously agreed with the Mayor's observations, and the following committee was appointed to take the initiative: Major Winters, Messrs H Mugford, W L Ashton, M Squire, W Dennis, Smith, D Smaldon, Chugg, W Tarr, Copner, J Gaydon, A Rock, O Rock, J Alford, J Downing, W H Smith, J Tucker, Benfield, W Smith, Hellier and J R Chanter. A letter was read from a gentleman who it afterwards transpired was Mr Wilson Hoare, stating that he would hunt the country at his own expense, if cordially invited, three days a fortnight for a season, at the end of which he should he quite willing to give way to any other gentleman who desired to do likewise. The Chairman remarked that this was a very excellent offer. The Committee were instructed to obtain the landowners consent to run over their ground, and to present a report on their negotiations to a meeting to be held that day fortnight.

The Barnstaple and North Devon Harriers
April 14th 1893

The Barnstaple and North Devon Harriers are now an established pack. The hounds (late Ilfracombe), were taken to their new kennels at Brynsworthy about a mile and a half from the town on Monday afternoon. The kennels are on land occupied by Mr A Mugford, who very kindly provided refreshment for the friends of the hunt who put in an appearance. Among those present were Messrs G D Dennis, J Dollam, J R Riddell, Menderson, D Smalldon, J D Young, S Petter, J Marsh, H Waldon, M Squire, W L Ashton, C Youings, J Frederick, T Copp, J Dennis, Winter, H Littleworth, T Pearse, Vicary, Fleet and Benfield &c. After refreshments had been served, Mr Mugford proposed "Success to the Barnstaple and North Devon Harriers," expressing an opinion that the pack would become a very popular one. Mr T Horn replied. Mr J D Young proposed "The Committee and Secretary," which was responded to by Mr D Smalldon, Mr Mugford gave "The Labourers," and Mr J R Biddell acknowledged it, and in conclusion gave "The Farmers and Hare Preservers," which Mr T Copp replied to. The lunch was followed by some horse racing of an interesting character. The first was a steeplechase over part of the steeplechase course. Mr J D Young acted as judge, and Mr Mugford as starter. The results were:

Steeplechase – Mr T Horn's Bay Comus (Riddell). 1: Mr T Horn's Newton (Chowen), 2: Mr G Dennis Dolly Varden (Farmer), 3: Good jumping, Won by half a length.

Flat Race – Mr T Horn's Dick the Whip. 1: Mr T Horn's, 2: Mr J Micklin's (Ash), 3: Mr G Dennis (Farmer), 4: Mr T Horn (Riddell), 5: A good race, won by a head.

The Barnstaple and North Devon Harriers will
meet at 11am on Wednesday December 26th 1894
at Deptford Cross, High Bickington,
December 28th at Roborough
Monday December 30th at the Square, Barnstaple

Barnstaple and North Devon Harriers
October 3rd 1893

This newly-established pack met at Burrington Moor, where a large field assembled, including the Huntsman with 12½ couples of splendid looking hounds, Mrs Benfield, a few members of the Hunt, and nearly all the leading sportsmen of the district, numbering about 50 mounted. At a few minutes to eleven "See O!" was heard in a field adjoining the meet, and away goes the hare at full speed. The hounds were soon laid on and took up the pursuit in good earnest, but it was quickly seen that scent was nothing too good. The hounds, however, hunted her in good style across Aze Moor, Sugworthy, Deptford, Weekdown, where at least two fresh hares were on foot, but old "Rattler," nothing daunted, hit off the line, and hounds, flying to his music, struck to the hunted hare and ran her across the Dolton-road to Arson Moor, Furze, and Villavin, where she was lost. In the meantime another hare had been seen leaving Mr Coles'

213

field, and the hounds were laid on the line in Arson Moor, and away they went to Common Heads, Folly Goyle, Aze Moor, Deptford, Weekdown, Burrington Moor, Arson Moor, Common Head, and Halfsbury, where after an hour's splendid hunting she was lost for a time. Too much praise cannot be given to the Huntsman for the manner in which he stuck to his hare. At last "Remedy" was heard to whimper, out came puss dead beat from a patch of gorse, and soon the "who whoop" was given to as good a hare as ever hounds hunted. Halfsbury was then tried and in a turnip field another hare was found. Away they went at a rattling pace, "Tomboy," "Riot," and "Bridesmaid" leading away to Sugworthy Plantations, Parkins, East Villavin, and Burrington Moor, where she was killed not many yards from the meet. Thus ended a splendid day's sport which augurs well for the future of the Barnstaple and North Devon Harriers, who have now one of the finest countries to hunt over in the West, and fairly well stocked with hares. The hares were caught on the land of Mr Coles of Ashreigney, and Mr Turner, of Burrington, but they were given respectively to Mr M Squire and Mr W L Ashton of Barnstaple. One of the hares was represented to the the Mayor of Barnstaple (Mr Alderman James Brady), who presided at the first public meeting when the Hunt was formed, and the other to Capt Penry, the Chairman of the Committee.

Barnstaple and North Devon Harriers
(To the Editor of the North Devon Herald)

Sir – It has come to the notice of the Committee of the above pack that horse-flesh etc, for the kennels has been sent to Brynsworthy by mistake. The Committee wish it consequently to be made known, through your valuable paper, that the pack has been removed to their new kennels near the Great Western Railway Station, Barnstaple, where all kennel-flesh should be sent in the future, to ensure its being used for the purpose it is intended. – Yous truly,

W L Ashton, Hon Sec

Ludgate House, High Street, Barnstaple, June 28th 1898.

From the Baily's Hunting Directory
1898
Barnstaple and North Devon Harriers

Master – W H Speke, Esq, Barnstaple
Secretary – W L Ashton, Esq, Ludgate House, Barnstaple
Huntsman – The Master
Whipper-in – S Morgan
Twenty-seven couples of cross-bred hounds, 20 1/2 inches
Kennels – Sowden, Barnstaple
Telegraph Office and *Railway Station –* Barnstaple 1 mile distant.

Days of Meeting – Wednesday and Saturday
The Barnstaple and North Devon Harriers' territory lies in North Devon; it is a wild and rough country, consisting of one-half moorland, 35 per cent pasture, 10 per cent, and 5 per cent woodland. The Stevenstone, Exmoor and Eggesford Foxhounds hunt parts of the country. There is no wire. Hares are numerous in places, and very often a deer strayed from Exmoor affords a run.

A subscription pack. Any subscription is accepted; capping is not practised. The Master has no guarantee.

The Barnstaple and North Devon Harriers were established in 1893. Previously they had been kept at Ilfracombe for many years.

Masters of the Barnstaple and North Devon Harriers:
Major Winter   from 1893 to 1895
Mr R Wynn Eyton from 1895 to 1898
Mr W H Speke   from 1898

October 20th 1893
The Chase
with the Barnstaple and North Devon Harriers

On Saturday the Barnstaple and North Devon Harriers met at Cheribeer Cross. Although a wet gloomy morning the huntsman with his pack in the pink of condition arrived, and punctually at eleven, as the hounds were about to move off, a "halloa" was heard not 20 yards from the meet. It was with difficulty the pack could pick up the line, scent being anything but good. After a few fields had been crossed she was lost. The hounds were then trotted to Stafford Moor, when about 12 o'clock Puss jumps up in the open, and away dashed the pack in full cry over Venton Farm to Hollacombe Moor. Scent became somewhat cold, but the hounds stuck to their work in good style, running through Westacott Moors to Wood's, leaving Dolton Parsonage to the left

215

by Halfpenny Land, rattling through the Great Cudworthy as if heading for Iddlecott, then swinging to the right to Northcote, where 2½ couple of hounds went away on another line. The hare got away to a drain. Another hare was started on Beaford Moor. The scent was better and after an hour and forty minutes one of the finest hares that ever gave chase was killed. Amongst those at the finish was the Huntsman, Major Winter (Instow), J J Graydon (London), D Smoldon, W L Ashton, M Squire (Barnstaple), F H Tucker, E Stanbury, J W Friend, T Folland (Dolton), J Turner (Dowland), G Saunders (Wembworthy), B Headon, R and J Harris, J Hancock, J Carter, T Squire and W Callard (Ashreigney). The pack was then taken back to Cherrbeer-moor, where a third hare was found, which gave the field a good twenty minutes gallop to Kenton, Riddlecombe-moor, across Westacott. She was ultimately lost. It now began to rain and the field dispersed.

April 14th 1898

Puppies of the Barnstaple and North Devon Harriers were yesterday judged at the residence of the retiring Master Mr R W Eyton of Landkey. It has been customary for farmers and others of the district to walk the puppies during the winter, but owing to the muzzling order, this has only been found convenient in five cases during the past season, the other puppies being walked at the kennels. Messrs C H Basset and W Penhale, the judges, awarded first prize to "Admiral" (a very stylish animal of the foxhound type), second to "Marksman" (a pure harrier), and third to "Mimic" (which was not in such good condition as the others). Commended animals were "Mystery" (walked by Mr Squire of Ashreigney), "Matchless", "Merryman", and "Mindful" (the latter walked by Mr O J Lock). The entire pack was paraded after the judging and the improvement in the breed during the past few years was generally commented upon. Mr and Mrs Eyton entertained at luncheon the party, which consisted of the judges, Messrs D Smoldon, S N Adams, W H Speke (the new Master), Lock, D Squire, W L Ashton and Capt Laurie.

January 20th 1898
Barnstaple and North Devon Harriers

This pack met on Saturday at Prospect House, Landkey, the residence of the popular Master Mr R W Eyton. A large company assembled, both on horseback and on foot. Among them I noticed the Mayoress of Barnstaple (Mrs Chanter), Mrs Eyton, Mrs Hugh Toller, Miss Smolden, Miss Bissett, Miss Squire, the Rev and Mrs Barton (of Landkey), Mr W H Speke, Master Chanter, Messrs German, R J Stanbury, H Impey, D Smolden, M Squire, W L Ashton and son, G Webber, B Bissett, Thorne, Howle (2), Smallridge, Chugg, and others. After partaking of Mr & Mrs Eyton's kind hospitality, a move was made for Hurscott and Birch, which, however, proved blank, and then on towards Hutcherton Down. Here a fine hare was soon roused, and the

Master had his hounds on the line in a twinkling. Scent was not too good on the Down, but when over the fence into a clover field matters greatly improved, and away the beauties raced, on past Gunn, skirting Tree, the residence of that good preserver of hares, Mr H Chichester, across to Stoke Becsott, turning right handed away to Stone Cross over Stone Farm, swinging eastward on by Yard Cottages, and heading for Yard. The hare was in full view, and it was a splendid sight for the field, but she was not done yet. Although the pace was fast and furious, "Puss" still led us on up the valley close to Yard House, turning to the right, over the South side of Barnicott Farm to Mockham Down. Then she retreated to Barnacott, where she was killed after an enjoyable run of 40 minutes without a check. I cannot close my account of this day's run without referring to the splendid sport provided by this merry pack throughout the season. FOR'ARD AWAY.

March 16th 1899
Barnstaple and North Devon Harriers
hunting the fox

There was a very successful meet of this popular pack yesterday at Chelfham. A fox was found at Deane (Mr John Alford's), where the field is always rewarded with a find, and after a clinking run she just saved herself by going to earth at Bratton, in Mr Chichester's covers. Mr Speke decided to return to Goodleigh, and at Higher Deane a second fox was started. This one was killed close to Landkey village, after one of the best runs known in North Devon for some time. The time was 55 minutes. About a third of a large field was in at the finish. Miss Hibbert received the mask and Miss Raby the brush.

March 16th 1899
Annual Parade of Puppies

Walking the puppies in an annual event anticipated with much interest by friends of the Barnstaple and North Devon Harriers – friends who at the Kennels Ground, Sowden, on Tuesday afternoon, noted with much gratification a striking improvement in the stamp of the young animals paraded. Numerous couples reared for the Hunt by residents in the town and district were sent, but only 5½ couples were entered for competition. The general level of excellence was throughout so good that Messrs C H Basset, W Penhale, and R W Eyton (now Master of the Stevenstone Hounds, and formerly of the Barnstaple and North Devon Harriers), acting as judges, were occupied the greater part of the afternoon in "placing" the animals, "Sleepless", Capt Laurie's entry (the chief winner), possesses a very fine head, with good back and feet, and tested in the open proved to have a good turn of speed. The next animal (Mr R W Ellerton's "Merrymaid") was a very close second, her only fault being that she was a trifle short in the quarters. An animal shown by Mr S Adams, of Rumsam, acquired third. She is a typical harrier, but was rather shy, and did not, as the result, show off to the best advantage. The fourth, Mr W Lock's "Razor" of Croyde, was thought to be a trifle long in the back; it was, however, greatly admired for its other qualities. Although, perhaps, not showing quite so much quality as some if its rivals, Mr A F Seldon's "Mixture" (fifth) also excited very favourable notice. After the judging was concluded, the pack of Harriers was turned out, and they were evidently still very "fit" despite the fact that the season has far advanced. In addition to those who walked puppies, others present were Mrs Eyton, Mrs Chanter (the Mayoress) and her sister, Misses Chichester (Pilton House), Mrs A F Seldon, Messrs W H Speke (the genial Master), E J Soares, D Smoldon, G H Gould, W L Ashton &c &c. The Mayoress distributed the prizes. The first was a saddle, given by Mr Speke; second, bronze kettle and stand, presented by Mr T R Yeo; third set of carvers, given by committee; fourth, a bridle, present by the committee; and fifth a hunting crop, also given by committee. Prior to the judging, friends were generously entertained by the Master at his house in Victoria Road . The weather was beautifully fine, thus allowing visitors to follow the judging with additional pleasure. The several competitors were: Fable, walked by Mr S N Adams, Barnstaple; Mixture, Mrs A F Seldon, Raleigh, Barnstaple; Actress, Miss Chichester, Pilton; Magic, Mr Squire, Ashreigney; Mindful, Mr Gillard, Barnstaple; Merrymaid, Mr Ellerton, Barnstaple; Sleepless, Capt Laurie, Barnstaple; Rescue, Mr G H Gould, Goodleigh; Rachel, Mr Withicombe, Fremington; Major Mr Ridd, Bratton Fleming; Razor, Mr I J Lock, Croyde; Dainty, Mr D Smoldon, Barnstaple; and Rockwood and Rattler, two puppies walked at the kennels.

May 17th 1900
Letter from Captain Speke

Captain Speke, who is command in South Africa of the Devon Volunteer contingent, in a letter dated from Elandslaagte, Natal, to Mr W L Ashton, Barnstaple, Secretary of the Barnstaple and North Devon Harriers, of which Mr Speke was formerly Master, writes inquiring after the welfare of the Hunt, and giving his experience at the front. He says, "Now the season is all over do write and tell me what sort of sport you had to finish it. I fancy I must have gone away just about the right time as you must have had a lot of hard weather. Well here we are right at the front, with very little fighting to do. It all seems to have gone over the other side of the country. However, last week we had a bit of an excitement; the Boers began by bobbing a shell into our camp, and my tent now has plenty of ventilation, as they simply riddled it, but luckily I was not at home. They sent us a few more, and then we went out and drove them off. You would have enjoyed it; in fact I thought of you at the time. I have bought a pony and play a bit of polo, but the ponies are not very well suited to the game. I wish we had a pack of hounds here. The country would just suit you – miles and miles of grass, no fences and no bogs. There are a few hares and some small deer here ... Goodness only knows how much longer war will go on, but I hope I shall be able to get a bit of hunting next season. I don't mind spending the summer here. I heard from Mr Eyton, who is on the other side of the country. His letter took a fortnight to reach me. My two brothers are there with him."

We now come to 1900 when plans were being discussed regarding a pack of staghounds for the Barnstaple district. As mentioned before, the staghounds and the harriers amalgamated, with both packs of hounds being kennelled at Sowden. The report below gives us an insight into the prospect of having both packs in the same kennels.

July 19th 1900
Barnstaple and North Devon Harriers

Referring to the successful meet held at Barnstaple on Friday in support of starting and maintaining a pack of staghounds for the Barnstaple country, we are informed that a strong feeling exists that some steps might very well be taken just now to assure the continuation of the hitherto flourishing pack of harriers, which has been such a boon to sportsmen, besides of commercial value to the neighbourhood for some years. Formerly the Ilfracombe Harriers, they were purchased about seven years ago by the late Mr Tom Horn, of Barnstaple, from whom a Committee of sporting gentlemen took them off, and have since hunted the Barnstaple country with most creditable results. When it is remembered that the Mastership has been held by Mr R W Eyton and by Mr Speke, both of whom volunteered for service in South

Africa, it will be understood that nothing was wanting in good Mastership to keep up the popularity of the Hunt. After Mr Speke left, Mr E Arthur, of Marwood, accepted the Mastership, and finished the season in fine style. The pack has become thoroughly established and is well supported by the farmers who are making the very best preservers of hares the Hunt could desire. The hunt has been to considerable expense to lay down a number of imported hares in different parts including Goodleigh, High Bickington, Atherington, Swimbridge, Challacombe, Berrynarbour, Westdown, &c and the desire is only natural that nothing should occur which would be likely to jeopardise the existence of the hunt. Hints were given at the public meeting on Friday that the harriers might be considered but as the meeting was called to consider the advisability of starting a pack of staghounds the Chairman very properly ruled that they could not very well be drawn off the scent by the harriers.

It is now thought – writes a correspondent – that the appointed Staghunt Committee might well consider whether it would not be advisable to make some arrangement with the Harriers Committee whereby both hunts would benefit. The proposal is that much saving of expense would be effected were the Committee to amalgamate with the Harriers Committee so as to take over the management of the Harriers; or, even were the Staghunt Committee to undertake the double work it would be acceptable to the Harrier sportsmen and would be the means of preventing the hunt falling through. By this arrangement the Staghounds could be put out one day a week and the harriers another day. The saving would be in the management, as the hounds, although kept separately, could be at the same kennels: one kennelman would only be necessary, and one professional huntsman. In the matter of food, too, and in other ways, it is said that much expense would be saved. It is not at all an unusual thing for the same officials to hunt hare and deer in the same week. It should not be forgotten that the harriers have shown their good quality by hunting the deer successfully on several occasions in the Barnstaple district, affording capital runs. It would be more than a step in the direction of preserving the interests of sportsmen generally if the proposal made by the Committee of the Harriers Hunt was seriously considered. If adopted, it would in many instances, obviate the necessity of subscribing to both hunts, which impost would probably ere long result in failure. Now is the time for both Committees to discuss the situation. *Exeter Gazette*

In 1900 when Peter Ormrod came down to hunt the Barnstaple district with his staghounds, he also took on the duties of hunting the Barnstaple and North Devon Harriers while Capt Speke, who was Master at the time, was away fighting at the front. In a letter in the *Journal*, Peter Ormrod said that he hoped to hunt his staghounds twice a week and also the Harrier pack twice a week.

October 25th 1900
Hunting
Barnstaple and North Devon Harriers
Opening Meet

The above splendid pack of harriers met at High Bickington – one of the most popular harrier meets in the North of Devon – on Wednesday, when a large field turned out to meet the new Master (Mr Peter Ormrod) and whip, with 12 couples of hounds in the pink of condition. Shortly after the advertised time a move was made for Vauterhill and Yelland Moors, and very soon hare No 1 was set on foot, but scent was bad, and hounds could do but very little with her. Puss No 2 was found near Seckington, and, with improved scent, a very pretty spin of 30 minutes was provided, the beauties killed her down near the moors. No 3 was soon found by that dear old friend to hunting, Mr William Tucker, only a field or so away from where the 1st was killed; but scent seemed to have totally failed, at least for a time, and hounds were unable to make here away. The pack was ten taken to Deptford, where hare No 4 was soon set on foot and she gave us a pretty gallop of about ten minutes until she got on the roads, and hounds were unable to follow the line. Hare No 5 was found on Parsonage Farm and was accounted for, making the second kill for the day. Bad scent partially spoiled what otherside must have been a clinking day. Hares are fairly plentiful, and are safe in the hands of good sporting farmers of High Bickington and neighbourhood. Among those out besides the Master were Major Raby, Captain Laurie, Messrs W L Ashton and Son, R J Stanbury, M Squire and Son, J Kennedy, D Squire, Rafarel, and Lewis (Barnstaple), Baker (Chittlehamholt), Hellyer (3), Pedlar (3), Tucker (2), Folland, Cole (2), Slee, Harris, and F Hooper (High Bickington), Folland and Tanton (St Giles), Westacott (Beaford), Potter (Burrington), and many others.

> The Barnstaple and North Devon Harriers will meet on Wednesday December 26th 1900, leaving Bear Street, Barnstaple at 9am for Challacombe.

March 21st 1901

A meet of the Barnstaple and North Devon Harriers was fixed for yesterday at the Friendship Inn and Mr W L Ashton left Barnstaple in the early morning in charge of the pack. Mr Ashton got as far as Bratton Down when a blinding snow storm came on rendering it impossible to proceed further and the meet having therefore to be abandoned. In the district the snow lay to an average depth of nearly a foot, and in some parts it had drifted to a height of five or six feet.

December 26th 1901

Marriage of Captain Speke – Captain W H Speke (a relative of the famous African traveller of that name), who before going out to South Africa in command of the Devon contingent of Volunteers was Master of the Barnstaple and North Devon Harriers, has been married at St Stephen's Chuch, Kensington, to Miss Lilian Birch, daughter of the later Mr Birch, of Agden Hall, Cheshire. The ceremony was a quiet one, relations only being invited. White flowers and graceful palms were tastefully arranged in the chancel. The bride was given away by her step-father, Colonel Free, late RHA, and she was attended by her sister, Miss Free, while the bridge-groom was attended by his brother, Mr Hugh Speke, as best man. Relations and some friends were afterwards received by Colonel and Mrs Free at their house in Queen's Gate Terrace, but on the previous Thursday Mrs Free held a large reception at the South Kensington Hotel, 400 guests having been invited. Among the numerous presents was a silver tantalus given by the members of the Barnstaple Hunt.

April 24th 1902

Captain Speke, who commanded the Devon Service Company of Volunteers at the front, has just been presented by the farmers of High Bickington with a handsome kettle and stand. Captain speke is held in high esteem in North Devon, and especially by the farmers in the High Bickington country, over which he hunted for some years with Mr Eyton, and afterwards as sole master of the Barnstaple and North Devon Harriers. Some months ago he married, and took up his residence at Ilminster.

May 22nd 1902
Anthrax at Barnstaple

There has been an alarming outbreak of anthrax among the Barnstaple and North Devon Harriers kennelled at Sowden, near Barnstaple; but we are able to state authoratively that the disease is now well under control, and that there is no danger of it in any way spreading. A few days since it transpired that a week or so previously two of the harriers died suddenly, whilst five others were in turn taken ill. Mr W Penhale (the Hon Vet), and Mr A T Hutton, of Barnstaple, were promptly called in at an early stage, and the nature of the disease was soon recognised, a first-class bacteroilogist to whom a specimen of blood from one of the infected animals was sent also confirming the opinion which had been previously expressed. Steps were at once taken to deal with the dread disease, and the effectiveness of the measures adopted may be judged when it is stated that there have been no further deaths, the five animals alluded to having now completely recovered. The last serious outbreak in North Devon was at Great Shelfin, Ilfracombe, four or five years ago, when practically a herd of bullocks was exterminated. In the present case the disease was introduced through the carcase of an infected bullock (believed to have come from the Braunton district) having been unknowingly given to the pack. Solitary cases of anthrax among cattle are not infrequent – there was a case at Landkey a month or so ago – bullocks being very susceptible to the disease, which is generally imported in foreign maize and manure.

Barnstaple and North Devon Harriers
8th January 1903

A capital day's sport was enjoyed by a good field, which met Mr W L Ashton with this pack at Hollacombe Moor, Winkleigh, on Wednesday week. A hare, found on Narracott Farm, after giving a good run of about forty minutes, was killed on returning to the same farm. Another capital gallop, although of shorter duration, was afforded by a second hare, quickly found, which was taken close to Redland Farmhouse. Mr Ashton presided over a hunt dinner, held in the evening at the Winkleigh Hotel, and proposed "The preservers of hares and foxes," coupling with the toast the names of Messrs Tout, Potter, Westaway, Chammings, and others, and expressing thanks to the Master of the Eggesford Hounds for the kindness and courtesy he had shown towards the harriers. On Thursday the meet at Winkleigh village was very largely attended. A hare was found, but she ran in the woods, and the Master, thinking that the hounds had picked up the trail of a fox, called them off. Puss was not discovered afterwards.

Barnstaple and North Devon Harriers
5th February 1903

Barnstaple and North Devon Harriers met at the Friendship Inn on Saturday, Mr Ashton, with Morgan, the whip, bringing up 11½ couples of hounds. There was a good field, including Miss Curzon, Miss Taplin, Major Curzon, Messrs Freeman, F Taplin, J Stanbury, W Crang, W Smyth, Conybeare and Smallridge. A hare was found on Mr Smith's ground, Wistlandpound, which gave a smart gallop for three-quarters of an hour, and was then lost at Hileycombe. A second hare was found close by, and succeeded in keeping in front of the hounds for the remainder of the day. Scent was very bad, and the hounds could not pace her enough to kill her.

Barnstaple and North Devon Harriers
17th November 1904

The meet was at Bishopstawton in most unfavourable weather, and the hounds were hunted by Major Penn Curzon, his sporting daughter, Lorna, bravely acting as whip. Hounds were taken to Coddon Hill, where a hare was soon found. She ran round the hill a few times, affording a pretty sight for the foot people. Being pressed hard by the little bitches she was obliged to move off, and, crossing to the right over Overton, went straight for Hall covers. She had to retrace her steps, and went boldly up the hill towards Coddon, turning to the right into Downdrew. The rain being excessive about this time she was lost. On the way back to Coddon Hill a young hare was found, which gave a very smart half-hour's run round the hill, and was eventually killed.

The Barnstaple and North Devon Harriers
26th January 1905

The Barnstaple and North Devon Harriers met at Gunn yesterday. In the absence of the Master (Major Penn Curzon), and through Mr W L Ashton (the huntsman), being indisposed; the result of an accident when hunting, Mr C Pearce, the hon secretary, hunted the hounds. A capital field turned out, including some good sporting farmers and hare preservers, and they were rewarded by a thorough good day's sport. Three hares were found. The first was lost after a clinking good run, lasting about an hour-and-a-half. The second and third hares were killed after two very fast and exciting runs.

CHAPTER 12

FURTHER HUNT REPORTS OF
THE BARNSTAPLE STAGHOUNDS

I n chapter five we learnt that in 1903 the Barnstaple Staghounds were to be sold due to the resignation of Captain Paterson and Mr Arundell Clarke (joint Master) who felt bound to retire also. It was stated at the time that staghunting would probably be carried on in connection with the Barnstaple and North Devon Harriers. This was the case for the meet reported below, which took place on April 16th 1903.

Between 1903 and 1904, staghunting was still taking place with Lieut E G Chichester acting as temporary Master. A hunt meeting from 1904 has the heading "Barnstaple Staghounds and Harriers (the future of the hunt)", suggesting the staghounds had regrouped with some new hounds.

This chapter concentrates on the remainder of the Barnstaple Staghound reports.

HUNTING
Staghunting by Barnstaple and North Devon Harriers
April 16th 1903

The Barnstaple and North Devon Harriers on Saturday met at Heddon Mills, Braunton. Lieut E Chichester, RN., (the son of Sir Edward Chichester, Bart), was in charge of the hounds, which were hunted by Mr W L Ashton. After drawing Pickwell Wood unsuccessfully, North Wood was tried and a stag was soon found. He went over Osborough Down, where the tufters were stopped and the pack laid on. The stag ran to Spreacombe Lodge, and turning to the left by Spreacombe and Pickwell Wood, went over the down at the back of Heddon Mills, and then down the stream as far as Buckland Mills, where he left the water, and turning to the right, went up over Incledon. Here he crossed the Georgeham road, and going down to Fairlinch, turned left-handed, crossing the Saunton road and Saunton Marshes, and into the Burrows. He ran the whole length of the Burrows, two miles where it was very difficult hunting. Rabbit holes were plentiful, and caused several empty saddles. making straight towards the hospital ship opposite Instow, the stag no doubt intended to cross the tidal river, but luckily some fishermen who happened to be on the spot with their boats prevented him doing so, and he then came straight back over the bank to Horsey Marsh. Going up the stream and across to Sir William Williams's duck-pond and Marsh Farm, he made his way in the tidal river straight up to Strand House, and then went by Ashford to Upcott, the residence of Mr E J Soares, MP, and on to Blackwell Mills, where he was lost among the trees. It was a most enjoyable run, lasting over five hours, the only check being one of 45 minutes' duration in the sand hills at Saunton.

NORTH DEVON HUNT COAT.

GUARANTEED WATERPROOF.
Stout Drab Twill .... 39/6.   Lighter Weight .... 29/6.

W. RICHARDS AND CO., OUTFITTERS AND TAILORS, JOY STREET, BARNSTAPLE.

Thought to be the Barnstaple Staghounds at Bratton Fleming. Photo courtesy of Edward Holroyd.

The Barnstaple Staghounds
Opening Meet
September 3rd 1903

The opening meet of the Barnstaple Staghounds was held at Youlston Old Park on Saturday in fair weather. There was a good attendance including Mr Edward G Chichester (Master), Mr W L Ashton (huntsman), Mr Morgan (whip), Lady Chichester, the Misses and Master Chichester (Youlston), Mr & Mrs C H Basset, Mrs Penn-Curzon, Mrs Olivery, Openshawe, the Misses Brown (Roborough), Capt & Mrs Johnson, Mr W E and Miss Arthur, Miss Buckingham, Mr E R Berry-Torr, Mr Comer Clarke, Mr Basil Fanshawe & son, Mr F W and Miss Taplin, Mr Tamlyn, Mr T W Smith, Mr J Stanbury, Mr Gillard, Mr F Gillard, the Misses German, Messrs W O Jenkins, T Ridd, J Berry, Camp, Southcombe, Chamings, W Pugsley, and A Thorn junr.

Hounds were kenneld in the Little Park. Tufters were drawn and taken to Mill Wood where the slot of a stag was seen. They drew Mill Wood blank, and afterwards went to Cox Wood where they got onto the heels of a stag, but could not hold the line across Cott Down. Tufters were next taken to Woolley Wood, where a hind was started. Hounds were whipped and three more hinds went away. The pack was unkenneled and laid onto a deer which ran to Kingdon Gardens and from thence to Ackland Wood where the hounds were stopped. It was unfortunate that a stag could not have been in the vicinity lately, but it presumably got into Arlington.

17th September 1903
Barnstaple Staghounds

These hounds met at Featherbrook on Thursday, in rough weather, under the Mastership of Mr C H Basset, in the absence of Mr E G Chichester. A stag was soon found in Stoneyard Wood, and after a little work by the tufters it took its line across Little Comford to Featherbrook, where the pack was laid on. The stag was viewed away to Featherbrook Court, Burland Cross, and the Ilfracombe road, where it ran down stream, pointing for Muddiford, with the hounds tight on its heals. It then turned right handed, recrossed the Ilfracombe road, over Billand Meadows, on to Huish, Stratford, pointing straight for Berrynarbour. It went near Berrydown Cross, to the left again, and then to the top of Berrynarbour Hill, swinging to the right to the back of Featherbrook and Combe Martin to Combe Martin Cross, on to the old quarries. It recrossed over the hills to

Bensrick Woods, and into the waters below, where the hounds had a check. However, they went on in the heavy downpour of rain, and, getting higher up in the cover, refound. After running a short distance the hounds were stopped on account of the rain and mist.

5th November 1903
Barnstaple Staghounds

The large field which attended Thursday's meet at Bratton Fleming were rewarded with an excellent run. Mr C H Basset acted as Master in the absence of Lieutenant Chichester. Those present included Messrs E J Soares, Stanbury, Litson, A E Arnold, E German, B Fanshawe, W L Ashton, Kent, Pugsley, Delbridge, W Crang, W Penhale, and W Smith, Mrs and Miss Arnold, Mrs Mathews, Miss Wyld and Mrs German.

A stag, which was harboured in Smithapark, was soon found with three couples of tufters, and after half an hour's sharp running around the cover, Mr Basset's horn was heard for the pack, which was laid on, on Mr Comer Clarke's ground opposite the station. The stag pointed down stream for Millwood, but soon retraced his steps back to Smithapark, on to Wistland Pound, turned to the left near Kentisbury, passed close to Easter Close Gate, on the Combe Martin road, through Cowley and Dene, down the valley to Hunter's Inn, and then crossed the road up over the covers. The field, which had had a gallop of 15 miles, now thought they were in for a moorland run, and were surprised when the stag jumped up in front of the pack after lying in the gorse. He pointed for Lynton in full view, then took a short turn, crossing the new road, and ran to sea.

"Gone to sea"

231

3rd December 1903
The Barnstaple Staghounds
A Kill

A large field assembled on Saturday at Bratton Cross, where the meet of the Barnstaple Staghounds took place in most unfavourable weather. Among those present were Miss Chichester (Youlston), Mr and Mrs Pearce (Watermouth), Messrs Comer Clarke, T W Smith, A J Gillard, G Litson, Tamlyn, W Williams, C Pearce, Lock, Lewis and E German. The pack was kennelled at Chelfham, and tufters were taken to Mill Wood, where three hinds were harboured. They were soon on foot, and went up under Long Timber, across the Cott Wood, into Woolley Wood, where, after half an hour's rattling about, the pack was strengthened by the addition of ten couples of hounds. One hind separated from the others, and, after running hard around Woolley Wood, across the Downs, and through Cott Wood, she came down the valley, where she took to water, being eventually killed just below Collar Bridge. This was the first hind killed for the season. News was then received that a deer had gone down the valley. Hounds were laid on in Coxleigh Wood, and ran through Kingdon Gardens, crossing the Lynton Railway and the river Yeo, up over to Ivy Lodge. It was there seen that the deer in front was a male, and after racing him down across Frankmarsh, into the water, hounds were taken off and away, and the deer went free.

Barnstaple Staghounds
January 21st 1904
Captured in River Yeo

These hounds met at Chelfham on Saturday in fine weather, under the field Master of Major Penn-Curzon. There was a good attendance, which included the misses Chichester, Buckingham, and Taplin, Mrs A E Arnold (on wheels), Mr and Mrs Speil, Messrs F Taplin, R Kent, A F Seldon, R Parminter, Tamlyn, A Lock, J Comer Clark, A E Dalling, R Pearce (Watersmouth), M Beresford, E J Gillard, H Richards, H Hitchcock, W Jones, A E Arnold, W L Ashton, German, T W Smith, Litson, Master Seldon and Morgan (whip). The hounds were kennelled at Loxhore, Wooley and Coxleigh Woods were drawn blank. The hounds were then taken to Smithapark, news arriving that a deer had been seen heading for Wistland Pound. The pack was soon laid on, and the scent being good, the hounds raced through Loxhore, Long Timber, over Deer Park, through Youlston Woods to Pitt Farm, turning right-handed over Roborough and the deer park to Long Timber, then to Chelfham, Sepscott, Snapper and Frankmarsh, where the quarry went to water. He swam under Pilton Bridge, Barnstaple; two boats were eventually put off in pursuit, in one being Messrs T W Smith and Litson, and in the other some fishermen. The fishermen reached the stag first and pulled him into the boat. He was immediately conveyed in a trap and driven to Westaway (Mr C H Bassett's) where he was placed in a loose box. Mr Smith and others groomed him well and dried him with straw. He was also given some gruel and a little whiskey, the treatment being so effectual as to compel Mr Smith to leave the box somewhat expeditiously. As he was very young, the stag was not killed but will be set at liberty. The hounds drew blank until this stag was found at 2 o'clock, but the run lasted over three hours and a good pace was maintained the whole time without a check.

© Terry
Gable

January 21st 1904

Mr Edward G Chichester of HMS Magnificent (son of Sir Edward Chichester, Bart, of Youlston Park, Barnstaple), who is Master of the Barnstaple Staghounds, has been called away from Youlston for a time on his Majesty's service. During his absence Sir Edward Chichester has consented to take the Deputy-Master, and Major Penn-Curzon will act as field master.

Barnstaple Staghounds January 28th 1904

These hounds met at Chelfham on Saturday, but the frosty weather accounted no doubt for the poor attendance. Smithapark was first drawn and two hinds were soon on foot, with the hounds close behind. One of them ran through Smithapark and Helewood, crossing the Loxhore Wood to Youlston Woods, Sepscott and Brightley, and took the water below Kingdon Gardens in Barnstaple Borough, where she was seen with her head just above water, with Hector and Gameboy watching her. The whole pack quickly gathered, and she proceeded again running the meadows across the Lynton railway, making her way near Frankmarsh, back over Gorwell and crossing the Bear Street road she ran to Sowden, Maidenford, Bales nurseries and Woolsley, crossing the bottom of Goodleigh to Northleigh, she ran back to Chelfham, going over the river Yeo into Coxleigh Woods and on to Millwood, running around by the wire fence and then back over Woolley Barton near Loxhore, pointing over the moor. Here she turned to the right, to Smithapark, running the water and into Helewood, from here the hind went onto Bratton Bridge and Collar Bridge, but it was thought by some that it was a fresh hind, and the hounds were taken back to Helewood, where the run hind was reported to have been last seen. This however turned out to be the one from whose track the hounds had been withdrawn, but darkness prevented any further hunting. It was afterwards ascertained that the hunted hind came on over Coxleigh and Roborough into Westaway, Barnstaple, where she stayed in the water for some time. Mr C H Basset and others made efforts to take her with a rope, but she went on again towards Tutshill. This hind proved the fastest four hours gallop that had been experienced in this district.

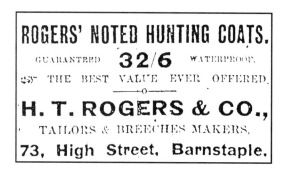

BSH Feb 4th 1904
Kill near town

Barnstaple Staghounds met at Blackmore Gate Station on Saturday, the field including Major Penn-Curzon, acting Field Master, Miss Penn-Curzon, Misses Wylde and Buckingham, Messrs W L Ashton, E German, A F Seldon, A E Arnold, G Litson, T W Smith, T Dallyn-Dallyn jnr, F Taplin, J Smyth, Master, A Lock and H Smyth and Morgan (whip). Litson, the head keeper to Mr Wylde, had harboured a fine stag at Heddons Mouth, and through the kindness of Mr Berry the pack were kennelled at Hunters Inn. Four couple of the tufters were taken into Hill Wood where in a few minutes a deer was disturbed. The tufters were stopped and the pack laid on. The deer headed for Colley Wood, Kentisbury, Church Hill, over Cott Down, through Mill Wood, Long Timber, Chelfham, Youlston, to the town near Messrs Miller Bros' lace factory, turning through the gates of the Miller Institute to the fields adjoining the cemetary, the deer was seen to great advantage as he took fence after fence, passing Zephyr Cottage heading for Frankmarsh, he was brought to bay amidst a scene of the greatest excitement, after a run lasting three hours. The stag was a famous one-horned deer, seven years old, and had provided good sport on several occasions. During their last three runs the Barnstaple Staghounds have run their quarry within the precincts of the borough, and close to the town on each occasion, one stag being killed, another taken alive at Pilton, while the third escaped owing to the darkness. So far this season the staghounds have killed on four occasions. One stag has been taken and one driven to sea at Heddons Mouth, while there is still two months hunting left.

Barnstaple Staghounds
February 25th 1904
Another kill in the Borough

These hounds met at Bratton Station on Saturday, those present were Major Penn-Curzon, acting field Master, misses Hurst and Buckingham. Messrs C H Basset, W L Ashton, Comer-Clarke, E German, A E Arnold, H Richards, C Pearce, A F Seldon, Fred Taplin, R Tamlyn, T Stanbury, H Hitchcock, J Burridge, F Lock, Messrs A Lock and Morgan (whip). Arriving at the meet, the fog was so dense that it was decided not to draw Smithapark Covers, where a deer had been harboured through the kindness of Mr Comer-Clarke. The pack was taken to Millwood, then to Long Timber, where a four-year-old hind was soon on foot and crossed the deerpark through Sepscott, Youlston and Coxleigh Woods taking water at Kingdon Gardens, and on to Pitt Farm in the borough of Barnstaple. Turning right-handed, it went over Roborough, Rawleigh, Maretop, crossing Westaway in view of Mr C H Basset. The hind returned again to the river Yeo, passing through Yeo Vale estate crossing the road and taking the wall into Pilton Park, Barnstaple. Here she was captured between the railings and the wall in the presence of a large number of towns-people and followers of the hunt. This is the second time a kill has been effected at Pilton this season.

March 24th 1904
An Extraordinary Run

Barnstaple Staghounds met at Heddon Mills on Saturday, when those present included Major Penn-Curzon (acting field master), Misses Chichester, Penn-Curzon, Hole, Mrs Till, Messrs W L Ashton, C H Basset, A F Seldon, E German, J Stanbury, C Pearce, A E Arnold, A Chichester, C Darbyshire and friend, R Lake, W Penhale, T Copp, R A Riddell, T W Smith, Baker, J Lock, Master A Lock, Chugg, H Hitchcock, B Moon, A J Gillard, J Litson, M H Toller, R Palmer, W Gill, and Morgan (whip). The harbourer stated that only one deer was in Spreacombe Covers, consequently the field master decided to draw with the pack, North Wood was a blank, but, on the hounds entering Pickwell Wood, two stags were soon on foot, which caused hounds to divide. One stag, breaking on the south side, crossed the Spreacombe road to Fox Hunters Inn. Turning to the right down stream under Ball Wood, over Fullabrook at a slow pace, and then headed for Burland, the deer ran the Ilfracombe road to Little Silver, taking to water at Muddiford. He pushed through Whitefield Wood, and Blakewell, pointing for Germans Down. The Master and huntsman, thinking the deer was bound for Arlington and put forward to prevent hounds entering, but, to their surprise, the deer turned right-handed through Woolley and Cott Woods to Long Timber, Chelfham, and Collar Bridge. Here the field met the other hunted deer, which broke from the north end of Pickwell Wood, and turning right-handed through Spreacombe and Knowle towards Braunton, crossed the river, railway, and road, leading for Ashwood. The hounds here ran him to Upcott, the seat of the member for the division, on to Bradiford, the property of Mr Basset, and across Roborough, meeting hounds and field at Collar Bridge. This being a fine five year old stag, the hounds ran him through Chelfham Valley to Cotts Wood, but returning again to water, the pack raced him to Bratton Cross, where he was taken after a three hours run. This accounts for six deer in six successive runs.

236

The Ring of Bells, Challacombe, where the Barnstaple Staghounds had regular meets. Today it is known as the Black Venus Inn. The Cheriton Otterhounds also met at this inn, as we can see from the following article from 1898 where three wagonettes left the Golden Lion in Barnstaple to attend the meet.

TO BREWERS, SPIRIT MERCHANTS, LICENSED VICTUALLERS & OTHERS.

TO be SOLD, by TENDER, that well-known old-established Fully-Licensed INN, known as the "RING OF BELLS" Challacombe, Devon, with about two acres of Meadow and Garden land adjoining.
For particulars apply to John Comer, Home Place, Challacombe, to whom Tenders are to be sent on or before February the 17th 1898.
Dated, Challacombe, Feb. 2nd, 1898.   [1509

June 2nd 1898
Mr Cheriton's Otter Hounds

This pack met on Saturday, for drawing the river Bray, at the "Ring of Bells", Challacombe. After having had a good hunt on the Yeo on Wednesday the 25th, but again meeting with disappointment through too much water in the river and getting the otter into an impregnable holt opposite Snapper and having to reluctantly give it up, hounds were sent on to Bratton to the White Hart Hotel to remain until Saturday morning, when William Leach (huntsman) and his smart son "Fred," acting as whip, took hounds on to the "Ring of Bells," Challacombe, to await the arrival of members and friends of the Cheriton Otter Hounds. Three waggonettes left the Golden Lion Hotel,

Barnstpale (Mr Roads) at 8.30, and started for the long hilly journey.

On arrival, they were met by a large gathering from all parts of the Exmoor district. After ten minutes interval, "Still they came" up, and the order was to carry on. A waggonette from Glen Thorne, containing a party, and including the Master of the Clifton Harriers (foot) with his brother, and many others, embracing from one-hundred-and-fifty to two-hundred from all parts of that very chilly district called "Challacombe," of stag, fox and hare, and last – but not lease – otter fame, and certainly the best bit of harrier country in North Devon. "Lampin," the water-bailiff, who loyally supports and preserves the otter for us, communicated with the Master that there were certain proofs of otter having been about and near Brayley Bridge during the early morning, so that orders were given to draw very slowly, and right well did William Leach do so. On coming to Brayford a slight halt was made for bread and cheese, and sparkling champagne cider and gingerade, at 1½d, at that little tee-to-tal hamlet. But followers had had a good walk and were thirsty, and, I fear, the natives found themselves a bit short after the followers of the Cheriton Otter Hounds had moved out of this comfortable little "stronghold". Going on, at about a quarter-of-a-mile above Brayford Weir hounds began to feather beautifully in the valley, viewed by the ladies and occupants of many traps, and I heard a voice from "one" more dependable than any other follower say, "That's right!" "Now we won't be long," and sure enough, in very few moments there was a grand crash of music. The river Bray, just at this point, comes a bit "mixed up," probably by an old mote having formed a miniature island and making a river a little buit diverging for a small part. Here the hounds found, and soon set her going, as she afterwards was proved to be. Mr Gottwaltz got a "tally" at once as she landed, and rightly pronounced the otter as a medium sized one. She soon got back to the river, and made straight for the weir, but was afraid to face an eager but good crowd, who had hurried on and got a little too forward. The Masters orders were at once respected, and all came back, and the otter took the first opportunity of going down, and got into a strong hover just under, when "Tiptings Bar" soon set her going into a powerful rush of water, and broke through a most competent lot of lower stickle watchers. Fortunately Mr Comer Clarke had viewed her under Newton Bridge, and then she appeared safe in the dreaded drains. however after an hour's endeavours, and Leaches idea of a "Waterwork," and with the bar at work took, the otter was bolted, and then for about two hours she tried all Leachs, Cunning, together with the hounds, amongst a lot of overhanging bushes and hovers, by swimming backwards and forwards until at last she tried to land and she was taken. it was a great hunt – three hours and ten minutes – and proved to be a bitch of fourteen pounds.

The Barnstaple Staghounds will meet on Tuesday January 20th 1902 at the Ring of Bells, Challacombe

---

10th March 1904

Lieut Edward G Chichester, Master of the Barnstaple Staghounds, son of Sir Edward Chichester, is home for a short time at Youlston. He was out with the staghounds on Saturday

---

Barnstaple Staghounds
April 7th 1904

On Monday these hounds met at Hunters Inn under the Mastership of Major Penn-Curzon. A large number of mounted and on wheels attending from the neighbourhood of North Devon. A photograph of the hunt was taken in front of the hotel. The deer had left the cover previously, but coming down under Westland two hinds were set on foot in the gorse. Followers had to gallop hard to keep up with them down the valley to Button Bridge near Bratton Station. Here one of them ascended up the hill at top speed on to Loxhore Cottage just in time, as the hounds were streaming down the meadows by Mill Wood, Long Timber, and opposite Chelfham, when she took to water. The huntsman, (Mr W L Ashton), having every confidence that she was going into the borough of Barnstaple, as so many others had done before, took the pack up the stream and followed as far as Collar Bridge, but the hind had given them the slip by going up the woods. They soon recovered the line over Youlston Wood. The pack soon got on the scent of both hinds again. One portion dividing and going up stream to Long Timber, and the other to Woolley Wood into Arlington when hounds were stopped. The remainder of the pack drove their quarry to Shirwell thence to the Warren, crossing the Kentisbury road and on to Churchill. Turning to the right this hind, too, entered Arlington Cover, which is forbidden ground, thus ending the day's sport.

Photograph taken in 1904 at the meet at the Hunters Inn

BSH April 21st 1904

The last meet for the season was on Saturday at Bratton, when there was a large field to meet the field-master Major Penn-Curzon. Mr W L Ashton, the huntsman, was present, the field including Misses Arthur (3), Miss Buckingham, Miss Tamlyn, Miss Hext, Messrs W E Arthur, Comer-Clarke, P Penhale, F Taplin, T Dallyn, J Robbins, J Lock and two sons, J Bater, Delbridge, Litson, T W Smith, W H Paltridge, George Bale and son, and R Kent. Mr Bowden's Covers at Knightacott were first drawn blank. We went back to Youlston Wood, but our deer had moved in the early part of the day. Afterwards a deer was seen standing on the top of a rock in Millwood. The pack being kennelled at the mill, a couple of tufters soon found a couple of deer and a stag. They ran to Coxleigh Wood and around Woolley. The pack was laid on the stag, which came through Long Timber and the old park to the stream at Chelfham, going up stream crossing by the Loxhore road, over Hillwood and Coombe valley, through Smithapark, on to Friendship, and straight for the moor at a very fast pace. Reaching Long Stone, the hounds were stopped for a few minutes by the Master to allow the field to get on terms. Again letting the hounds go, we travelled on to the Chains, Oare Oak and Dry Ride, Brendon road. Herds of deer could be seen on the moor, but evening drawing in, and all having had a brilliant run, the hounds were stopped, and we returned to the kennels at midnight.

240

May 12th 1904
Barnstaple Staghounds and Harriers
The Future of the Hunt

Rear Admiral Sir Edward Chichester, Bart., presided at an important meeting of the supporters of Barnstaple Staghounds at the Golden Lion Hotel on Tuesday afternoon, there being also present Rev. W W Arthur, Major Penn Curzon (the Field Master), Messrs W Penhale, W E Arthur, Comer Clarke, A German, Arundell Clarke, A W Chichester, A Heinemann, W L Ashton (Huntsman), T W Smith, W WIlliams, J Burridge, J Lock, R W Mairs, Catford, and W Bright.

The Chairman said that although he was a somewhat large landowner in the way of coverts, he was not a hunting man himself; but he took an interest in Barnstaple Staghounds, because he thought that if possible the pack should be kept in order to keep down the deer. Besides that, the hunting gave sport to the county, and he liked to see other people enjoying themselves. There could be no doubt that this district was one of the nicest little hunting districts in England, if there was not a "little spot" on the map. (Laughter.) But apart from that spot, from which they could keep the hounds out, they could have a little sport occasionally. He believed that Mr Ashton had had charge of the hounds and that they belonged to him; but hounds could not be kept for nothing, and proper arrangements would have to be made if the Hunt was to be continued. (Hear, hear.) As the landowner, he had for the past four years given up the Yeo valley to the staghounds: and he had not put any birds there for that reason whilst Mr Orlando Chichester, his next-door neighbour, had always allowed the hounds over his property. (Applause.) Next month he (Sir Edward) intended letting Youlston as next month he was going abroad, and he hardly expected that any incoming shooting tenant would care to have the coverts racketed by the hounds as they had been in the past. But he had some property at Bratton which was rather lucrative in the way of deer, Leworthy and Berry Wood, and if the hunt was to be carried on he should have great pleasure in allowing the Barnstaple Staghounds to hunt those woods, and all his Bratton

Rear Admiral Sir Edward Chichester Bart, who presided at the meeting of the supporters of the Barnstaple Staghounds

property. (Applause.) Mr Orlando Chichester, whilst agreeing that the deer ought to be kept down, thought the coverts were drawn too frequently. Like himself, he was only a gunner, and they felt that a little more consideration should be given the gunners. (Hear hear.) He thought the staghunters were too somewhat selfish in the way they left open the gates; on several occasions he had had to employ his keepers for the purpose of driving the bullocks out of his own coverts. He mentioned this, so that, if the hunt was to be continued, they might use their endeavours to keep the field up to the mark. (Hear hear.)

Writing from sea, Lieut E G Chichester, who had been acting as temporary Master to the hunt for some time, now placed his resignation in the hands of the Committee owing to his prolonged absence in the king's service. He expressed his sincerest thanks to all those gentlemen who had so kindly assisted him in endeavouring to further the sporting instinct, which did so much to create harmony, and the kindly feeling of interest existing between the landlord, tenant farmer and townsman. (Applause.) He referred in terms of warmest praise to Mr W L Ashton, without whom they would have no hunt. (Hear, hear.)

Subsequently, Major Penn Curzon moved a vote of thanks to Lieut Chichester for all he had done in keeping hunting going in the district when it was at a very low ebb. They all felt that but for Lieut Chichester the staghunting would undoubtedly have come to a standstill. – Mr Arnold seconded a hearty vote, which Sir Edward Chichester briefly acknowledged on behalf of his son.

The Secretary (Mr A E Arnold) reported that the hunt commenced the season at Youlston Old Park on August 29th and finished on April 16th. The staghounds were out on nearly forty days being only prevented from hunting on two occasions. They took five stags and five hinds, and took four stags and two hinds, which was, he thought, very satisfactory having regard to the adverse circumstances under which they laboured in respect of Arlington. (Hear, hear.) In regard to finance, subscriptions during the year had yielded £126 12s 6d, but they would want more money if the Hunt was to be continued. £13 of the £18 balance in hand would, he explained, be absorbed by further payments of course they were not a rich country, but to a certain extent divided, as on one side of the river were the Stevenstone hounds and there were also the Eggesford hounds.. Many farmers, who had suffered damage by the Hunt had withdrawn their claims, and in this way they had been able to pass on a much larger sum to the Huntsman than they could otherwise have done. (applause.) He did not believe the Hunt was ever more popular in the country than it was at the present. Wherever they went they had always been welcomed, specially so at the end of the season, so that things augured well for the continued success of the Hunt. The hounds were Mr Ashton's property last season; he bought the hounds at a time when there was a danger of their going out of the country and has had possession of the pack up to the present time.

On the motion of the Chairman, seconded by Mr W E Arthur, Major Penn-Curzon was unanimously elected the new Master, and, in returning thanks, expressed confidence that the present friction with the Devon and Somerset Hunt in regard to their respective districts might with a little tact be overcome. The Hunt had during the past season been run in a very slipshod manner, and it would have to be put on a business footing. With reference to the future of the hunt, Major Penn-Curzon said they were peculiarly situated. They did not belong to them, but they undoubtedly had one of the best huntsmen in the kingdom (Mr W L Ashton). The hounds were his property, and he had been paid £105, but that was nothing like what the hounds cost, and a very large part of that hunt came out of Mr Ashton's pocket. He would be glad to double his subscription, and if other members would do the same, they ought to be able to buy the pack. They would then be on a sound businesslike footing. Mr Ashton said if the committee would buy the pack he would be very pleased to sell the hounds and do everything for the benefit of the Barnstaple hunt.

On the motion of Mr Penhale, seconded by Mr Arthur, the following committee were elected. The Master (chairman) Sir Edward Chichester, Bart, Sir Bourchier Wrey, Bart, Messrs C H Basset, Arundell Clarke, Comer Clarke, W Penhale, G N Style, A E Arthur, B Fanshawe, E Wyld, A E Arnold, T W Smith, F Taplin, T Dalling, A F Seldon, A L Christie, E German, J Stanbury, J M Slade, W E Arthur, and Lieutenant E G Chichester.

Thanks were accorded the landlords and tenant farmers for allowing the hounds to run over their land, to the Huntsman (Mr Ashton), to Major Penn-Curzon (who had acted as Field Master), to Sir Edward Chichester, but for whose covers the hunting could not have been carried on, and to the Hon Sec (Mr A E Arnold). It was reported that Mr Arnold desired to retire and Mr Penhale, a former Secretary of the hunt, was suggested as his successor.

August 25th 1904
Appointment of Hon Secretary

A meeting of the committee of the Barnstaple Staghounds had been held at the Golden Lion Hotel under the chairmanship of the Master, Major Penn-Curzon. Among the others present were Messrs Arundell Clarke, A T Chichester, A F Seldon, C Pearce, A E Arnold, Wilde, E German, T W Smith, and W L Ashton. The meeting was held for the purpose of appointing an hon secretary in the place of Mr A E Arnold, resigned. The chairman spoke in complimentary terms of the efficient manner in which the late hon secretary had carried out his duties, and said he had pleasure in stating that Mr C Pearce of Oakleigh, Barnstaple, had in a sportsman like manner consented to act as hon secretary for the coming season. (Applause). He therefore proposed that Mr Pearce be elected, Mr A F Seldon seconded, and the motion was carried unanimously. Mr Pearce thanked the meeting for the honour, and promised to do his best to carry out the duties to the satisfaction of the hunt. He hoped too much would not be expected, but the interest of the hunt would always be considered by him. (Hear Hear.) The late secretary had been very generous in advising every subscriber by post of the meets. Mr Pearce would willingly do the same if the committee wished, but he thought it would be hardly necessary if the meets were advertised in the papers. After a little discussion, it was proposed, seconded and carried unanimously, that the secretary be not expected to advise per post of the meets, except in case of bye meets, or at his own discretion. Another meeting of the committee will be held in order to appoint a date for the opening meet. On the motion of Mr W E Arthur, seconded by Mr E German, a vote of thanks was accorded by the chairman. It is understood that the hounds have now been purchased from W L Ashton by the committee, a circumstance which will give a feeling of greater certainty as to the continuation of the hunt.

BSH September 1st 1904

The opening meet of the Barnstaple Staghounds, the Master of which is Major Penn-Curzon, will take place on Saturday September 3rd at Shirwell. In a letter which has been received, Mr R A Sanders, the Master of the Devon and Somerset Staghounds, has kindly offered the Challacombe Country for hind hunting after November 1st.

ESTABLISHED 1836.

PRIDEAUX & SON

(LATE GIBBINGS),

COACH BUILDERS,

BARNSTAPLE.

Several NEW & SECOND-HAND VICTORIAS GOVERNESS and SURREY CARS, LANDAUS, DOG CARTS, &c., FOR SALE. [132]

Hunting
Barnstaple Staghounds
Opening Meet
8th September 1904

The Barnstaple Staghounds opened their season on Saturday, when they met at Shirwell cross-roads, under the Mastership of Major Penn-Curzon. There were also present Mr Boyce Podmore, Master of the Cotswold Hounds, Master Bobby Podmore, Mr C Pearce, secretary of the Hunt, Mr W L Ashton (huntsman), Mr E German, and the Misses German, Mr A Incledon Webber, Mr Tom Chichester (whip), Miss Chichester, Mr and Mrs Bryant, Mr and Mrs A E Arnold, Mr and Mrs Wilson, Mr W E Arthur and Miss Arthur, Mr A J Gillard, Mrs Penn-Curzon and Miss Penn-Curzon, Mr Waldron, Mr R Kent, Mr G R Litson, Master Russell, Miss Buckingham, Misses Lethbridge, Mr J Gaydon, Miss Day, Mr W Smale, Mr F W Taplin and Miss Taplin, Mr W J Twigg, Capt and Mrs Johnson, Mr and Mrs Kirby (Youlston), Mr Powis, Mr and Mrs H W Woodall, Miss Dovell, Mr and Mrs D Smoldon, and Miss Smoldon, Mr Gillard &c.

The pack of twelve couples, first drew Smythapark, where several deer had been seen during the past few days.

At the hunt which followed, Master Podmore acted as first whip and Mr Tom Chichester as second whip. The tufters were first put into Coxleigh Wood, where they roused and chased a deer, which ran into Arlington, and the hounds were withdrawn A second deer was soon found in Cot Wood, and after a short but exciting run was killed at Woolley.

This is the first time in the history of the hunt that the hounds have belonged to a committee of the Hunt. Previously they were the property of Mr W L Ashton, of Barnstaple, who for some years has taken an active interest in the chase of the wild red deer in North Devon.

Hunting
22nd September 1904
Barnstaple Staghounds

A large company was present at the meet of these hounds at Spreacombe Park, Braunton, on Saturday. Spreacombe, formerly the residence of Mr Riddell, has recently been purchased by Mr J Style, a thoroughgoing sportsman, at whose cordial invitation the meet took place in the Spreacombe domains – amidst surroundings which look like giving some of the finest partridge and pheasant shooting in the neighbourhood. The followers of the hounds were most hospitably entertained by Mr and Mrs Style, and a large number of visitors to the district, many of whom afterwards rode with the hounds, were charmed with the unrivalled moorland and marine scenery obtainable from the precincts of the Park. The meet was attended by a much larger number in motor cars, traps, and on cycles than usual, whilst there were more riders present than for several seasons. Among those present were Major Curzon (Master), Mr W L Ashton (huntsman), Mr Arthur W Chichester (first whip), A West (second whip), Mr C Pearce (hon secretary), Mrs Penn-Curzon, Miss Lorna Curzon, Miss Riddell, Mrs Penhale, Miss Pitts-Tucker, Miss Clarke, Mr E J Soares, MP, Mr W Penhale, Mr Arundell Clarke, Mr Lyon Clarke, Mr E German, Mr A E Arnold, the Rev W H Hole, Mr A F Seldon, Mr W E Pitts-Tucker, and Sons, Mr R A Riddell, Mr E Incledon Webber, Mr B Fanshawe, Mr C Anderton, Mr S N Petter, Mr G Styles, Messrs J Stanbury, T W Smith, Copner, Cop, Palmer, J Berry, Martin, W Herniman, and Perryman. A large number of others attended in carriages on bicycles, and on foot. Mr Styles, a true sportsman and good preserver of game, who is now a large property owner in the district, having bought Spreacombe and Pickwell Barton, kindly provided refreshment at his residence. Coverts were drawn from Stoneyard to Fullabrook and back to Pickwell and Spreacombe. It appeared, however, that the deer had all shifted recently, and the day proved blank. It can hardly be regarded as being without profit, for in making the acquaintance of Mr Style, the hunt has discovered a valuable friend.

29th September 1904
Barnstaple Staghounds

The staghounds met at Chelfham yesterday. Mr C Pearce, of Oakleigh, took the Mastership, Major Penn-Curzon being absent through an accident. The hounds being taken to Smythapark it was drawn blank, as were also the surrounding covers. On returning homeward news was brought that a stag and hind were seen to enter Youlston Wood after the harbourer had passed in the morning. On trying the wood the hounds found them immediately. After running the length of the wood and crossing the old Park they took up the valley towards Loxhore Mills in the water. They crossed the Lynton road, over Smythapark, and ran into Mr Brooke's court yard, pointing straight to Bratton, when they unfortunately turned to the left and entered Arlington Covers in the midst of a very heavy thunderstorm, when the hounds were stopped. There was a good field at the meet.

October 7th 1904

Much disappointment was caused here and in the neighbourhood of Umberleigh on Wednesday when it became known that a meet of the Barnstaple Staghounds which had been advertised for that morning at Umberleigh bridge had been cancelled. As it was an unusual event for the hounds to meet in this district, one can imagine the large number which made their way to Umberleigh station, many of them losing time to do so. Others went in the neighbourhood of Chittlehamholt where it was known the stag had been lying for some time. On the previous day a message had been received from Sir John Amory's Staghounds to the effect that they considered the Umberleigh district to be theirs and when this was brought to their attention the meet was at once stopped some means should have been devised to have made it well known the day before.

Hunting
27th October 1904
Barnstaple Staghounds

Saturday's meet of the Barnstaple Staghounds at Chelfham was particularly well attended, among those riding out to support the Master (Major Penn-Curzon) being Mr E J Soares, MP. A deer was found in Bratton Wood and Mr Ashton very quickly had the pack laid on for the commencement of a very pretty run. The deer took the field along at a rattling pace to Wistlandpound, over Homer Common to Longstone, and turning to the left made for the moor across the chains in full view with the hounds well up. The Doone country was now entered, Badgeworthy water being passed, when the deer entered Mr Snow's Deer Park, Mr Snow kindly informed the hunt that the deer had joined a big herd, and accordingly the hounds were called off. The run, which was most exhilarating to the few who were in at the end, was right across the Exmoor forest, and lasted a little over three hours, some thirty miles being covered. A long ride back gave an opportunity to the field to discuss the various exciting incidents on the chase, and when Barnstaple was reached it was some hours after nightfall.

November 3rd 1904

The hounds met at Challacombe on Saturday, when besides the Master (Major Penn-Curzon), the huntsman (W L Ashton), and the whip (West), there were present Messrs C Pearce (hon secretary), W E Arthur, De Las Casas, W Crang, A E Arnold, Taplin, Dallyn (2), T W Smith, Robins, Tatterdill, &c.. The pack was taken on to Brendon Two Gates, leaving the tufters at Challacombe. In tufting the moors they found close to Mr Crang's. A stag, four hinds and a calf went away at a fast pace towards Mr Snow's Deer Park, the pack being laid on after Brendon Two Gates had been passed. There was great difficulty in getting a hind clear of the others, and after reaching Shepherd's Cot the hounds were called off. During the run, which was a fast one, there must have been quite 50 or 60 deer seen. The hounds returned to kennels at Barnstaple.. a distance of about 24 miles, just before nine o'clock.

Barnstaple Staghounds
10th November 1904

A large company assembled at Chelfham on Saturday to meet Major Penn-Curzon, the Master. A hind was harboured in Youlston Wood, but the tufters roused a stag in addition to the hind, and followed the former. The stag, however, jumped the wire fencing and got into Arlington. The tufters were taken back, and the whole pack was laid on to the hind. The scent had become very poor but the hounds went off in the direction of Smythapark and swept round the Yeo valley into Mill Wood and Cott, round Youlston Old Park, and up the valley again, through Mill Wood into Wolley Wood. Here a young male deer was aroused, and hunted near the mills under Mill Wood. He was captured in the mill leat and, as he was a young deer, he was lodged in the stables at the mills and after being cared for he will be liberated.

Hunting
Barnstaple Staghunting
An Exmoor Run
17th November 1904

These hounds met on Saturday at Challacombe, under the Mastership of Major Penn-Curzon who was accompanied by Mr R A Sanders, the Master of the Devon and Somerset Staghounds. Among the others present were Miss Arthur, Messrs C Pearce (hon secretary), De Las Cases, W Grang, T W Smith, Ross, Jones, Dallyn (3), Ridd, Taplin, &c. It was reported that a herd of deer were lying on the Chains, and on our arriving at Woodburrow the deer could be seen. The morning was clear and the air crisp, with the sun shining brightly. The huntsman laid on, and the herd of about a dozen made off over the Chains to Hoar Oak, Farley Water, Cheriton Ridge, and racing on to Badgeworthy Water, where there were three hinds and a stag in front of the hounds. The stag was settled on, and hounds were making it rather hot for him, when they were stopped a few minutes to recover wind and enable huntsmen to change horses. One of the hunted deer was then seen behind Badgeworthy Cot. The order was given to lay on, and hounds raced to Larkburrow, towards Hawkcombe Head, on to Lucott, near Porlock, where the deer was taken in the open field about half past 2 o'clock. Among those in at the death were Messrs Ashton, Smith, Sanders, Pearce, Taplin, Crang and De Las Casas. Unfortunately, the Master did not go further than the Deer Park, his horse having no doubt thrown a shoe, the moor being boggy. After the kill there was a short run, but the deer went into Porlock Park, and as there was a shooting party there, hounds were called off.

Barnstaple Staghounds at Umberleigh
November 19th 1904

These hounds met at Umberleigh on Tuesday. There was no find but there was an exciting incident at Yeotown, Kings Nympton. While Mr W H Hulland of Sampson was attempting to ride his horse across a narrow sheep bridge, the animal became frightened and slipped and fell, with its legs hanging on either side of the insecure structure. Eventually the horse was pushed off into the river, little injured by its peculiar mishap.

December 1st 1904

The accident to the hounds. It is feared that the four or five staghounds of the Barnstaple hunt which went over a high cliff at Combe Martin a few weeks ago in following a deer, will have to be destroyed. These disabled hounds were some of the best and fastest of the pack. They were to the front, close after the deer, and took what proved immediately to one hound to be a fatal leap of over 99 feet, which is the height of Combe Martin church tower. The loss of two or three couples more will be a serios one, considering the smallness of the pack. It is hoped that no time will be lost in supplying their places, as there is so much of the season left.

December 3rd 1904
Anthrax at Barnstaple
The Staghounds Affected
A Hound and a Pig Dead

Alarm was occasioned on Wednesday in certain circles in Barnstaple at the rumour that anthrax had broken out in the kennels of the Barnstaple Staghounds at Sowden. Nearly three weeks ago the hunt met at Challacombe and had a good run, in the course of which five hounds divided from the pack and were missed for a day or two. They were ultimately seen at Whitefield Barton, feeding on what was supposed to be the carcase of a cow. They returned to the kennels and have since taken part in other meets. On Wednesday morning however, three of the five spoken of and two others were noticed to be ill. The hon veterinary surgeon Mr W Penhale was immediately sent for, and it is stated on the authority of the superintendent of the borough police (Mr Eddy), that these hounds have been attacked by anthrax. One of the number died in a short time, and subsequently a pig which was in the same field as the kennels, and which had access to the offal has died. Mr Eddy telegraphed the circumstances of the outbreak to the board of Agriculture. He has taken all the usual precautions, such as ordering the immediate burial of the carcases in quick time. It is feared that the other hounds attacked will succumb. The whole five are valuable hounds and much regret is felt at the unfortunate circumstances. It will be remembered that a year or two ago anthrax was reported to be at the same kennels, but in that case it luckily turned out to be incorrect, the condition of the hounds being due to a fight having occured among them.

250

A meet of the Barnstaple Staghounds near the Hunters Inn, Heddons Mouth

December 29th 1904
BSH

A good following of Barnstaple Staghounds met at Chelfham on Thursday and in the absence of Major Penn-Curzon who is in London, Mr W E Arthur acted as Master. A hind and small deer were found in some gorse close to the railway above Bratton Station. Both came down the valley, followed by the pack, and at Youlston Wood turned to the right and ran through Long Timber and Cobb Down where the young deer made straight for the wire fence. Hounds were with difficulty kept back, and after some delay laid on to the hind at Woolley. After skirting the Warren, the hind ran close to Youlston House, crossed the road at Plaistow, and came back over Sloley, across Mr Acland's farm to the Shirwell road, where the hounds were stopped as time was getting short. It was a slow hunt, owing to the delay occasioned by calling the pack away from the young deer after which the hounds were a long way behind.

We now come to 1904-5 when Peter Ormrod returned to become Master of the Exmoor Foxhounds and hunt with his staghounds on the moor

15th September 1904
The Exmoor Foxhounds

A wet unpleasant day on Thursday was the cause of a small field meeting at Oare Ford. Captain Ormrod with 191/2 couples of hounds was soon busy and one or two cubs were soon on foot at Daddy Combe. After a short run one of the cubs went to ground at Lilly Combe and was dug out. The hounds drew for several hours without success.

Mr Peter Ormrod's Staghounds

We hear that Mr Peter Ormrod's staghounds are coming down the first week in October and will commence work at the beginning of November, Mr Sanders, Master of the Devon and Somerset Staghounds having given Mr Ormrod permission to hunt this country. Kennels have been erected near Oare House and are completed with the exception of the floors. Mr Ormrod is bringing down about 35 to 40 couple of fine staghounds.

29th September 1904

Capt and Mrs Ormrod of Oare House, Brendon, are paying a visit to their home at Wyresdale Hall, Lancashire, at the end of the week. Capt Ormrod will be shooting next week over the Wyresdale estate, which affords varied and splendid sport, the bag being always a very heavy one.

January 12th 1905
Barnstaple Staghounds
An Extraordinary Run – Hunting in Boats

The members of the Barnstaple Staghounds had an exciting and extraordinary experience during a run on Tuesday. The meet was at Spreacombe, and there was a good attendance, including Major Penn-Curzon (Master) and Mr W L Ashton (Hunting Master). The stag which had been found near Spreacombe ran by devious windings to Braunton Great Field. He took to the river, which was at low tide, and swam across to the Westward Ho! Pebble ridge. A boat was quickly obtained, and, leaving their horses with their friends, and accompanied by the hounds, the Master, with Messrs W L Ashton, E J Soares, MP, Incledon Webber, and W Arthur, was ferried across and continued the hunt on foot. The hounds at once picked up the scent, and a novel and interesting spectacle was afforded the remainder of the hunt who from the lighthouse watched the hounds coursing up over Northam Burrows in full view of the stag, which eventually swam across the Torridge to the Instow side. Boats were again requisitioned, and the exciting chase continued, but without result.

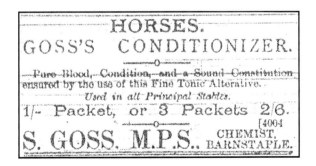

Barnstaple Staghounds
12th January 1905

By invitation, Barnstaple Staghounds on Saturday met at Woody Bay, Major Penn-Curzon, the Master, being accompanied by an excellent field. A hind was found in Sir Henry Carew's covers at Woolhanger, and at once facing the moor, crossed Farleigh Water and Oare Oak. Hounds were far ahead of the field, the pace being so great that one could scarcely live with the pack. Still keeping up the pace, the hind reached Brendon two Gates, where several herd of deer were seen running. The leading hounds, however, stuck to their hind, racing on by Badgeworthy Water to the Deer Park. Here hounds became mixed with the Devon and Somerset pack, and matters were very much involved. More than one deer was seen, but eventually the Barnstaple pack caught a hind at Cloud, which was killed by Sidney Tucker, the Devon and Somerset huntsman, who had become separated from his pack, and an interesting day ended.

Throughout this book we have seen that Wistlandpound was a regular run with the Barnstaple Staghounds. Today this area is well known to us not through hunting, but because of the reservoir seen here. © Richard Lethbridge

A 1905 advert for the Wistlandpound slate quarry.

A report from the *North Devon Journal* referring to the Barnstaple Staghounds.
March 2nd 1905

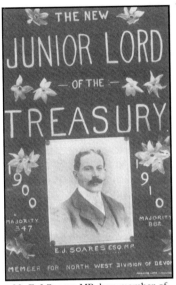

Mr E J Soares MP, hon member of the Barnstaple Division and a regular follower of the Barnstaple Staghounds.
Courtesy of Tom Bartlett's postcard collection

The *Herald* has shown such bad taste, and has been so palpably unfair, in its criticisms of the hon member for the Barnstaple Division, that one ought not to have been surprised at the meanness to which it descended last Thursday. In a note relating to the Charity Ball at Barnstaple it had the following: "Mr Soares and Mr Horne were prevented by other engagements from being present, but they supported the function by the purchase of tickets. It was generally understood that the member for Barnstaple had to hurry up to London to take part in a division on Mr Redmond's amendment to the Address. As a matter of fact, either he or his double is said to have been proceeding to the meet of the Barnstaple Staghounds before nine o'clock the morning after the ball, and if he reached London in time for the division after Tuesday's run he must have travelled at thunderbolt speed." The inference which the writer intended should be drawn is obvious. The story as to Mr Soares going hunting the morning after the ball is absolutely untrue, as the least inquiry would have shown. As a matter of fact, Mr Soares, accompanied by Mrs and Miss Soares, left Barnstaple for London by the 10.5 am train on Monday, February 20th, the day on which the Charity Ball was held, and he has since then remained in London attending to his Parliamentary duties.

April 13th 1905
Barnstaple Staghounds
The pack to be sold

Meeting at Bratton Fleming on Saturday, for the last time this season, under the Mastership of Major Penn-Curzon. Seven hinds were reported in Millwood, and two couple of tufters soon put two of them on the move up the valley to Cottwood, then across Wooley to Warren, and on to Germansdown. Here however, they turned right-handed and ran towards the forbidden cover, and the tufters had to be called off. Again retracing our steps to the valley, we found the Master waiting with the pack, having a couple of hinds under his eye in Long Timber. The pack was then laid on with the hope of having a gallop down the valley, but they turned right-handed back to the higher end of Long Timber, on to Woolley Cott. In jumping a wire fence one of them became hung up, but was liberated by a passer-by only to run into the Arlington Covers. The other one went down the valley, through Millwood and Long Timber, crossing Shirwell Old Park on to Sepscott, Coxleigh and Brightly Cott down, where she laid up in the gorge until the field came on her. Again jumping up into view, she turned back over the same ground, leaving the covers on her right and crossing the old park, coming to the water above Bratton Cross. Here going down the stream below Chelfham, she crossed the main road and went to Goodleigh, Eastacott, around Tree Beach House, below Gunn, over Birch, and down to Hackett and Taddiport Cover. Here she ran upstream, and went through Stoodleigh, straight to the Bray. The hounds had to be stopped for fear of disturbing fresh deer, and a most enjoyable day brought the season to an end. The run was probably the last for these staghounds, for in consequence of the fact that the country is so confined, the pack is to be sold. Deer, however, still appear to be plentiful, judging by the last day the pack was out. The pack of harriers will still be kept.

April 20th 1905, Barnstaple

On Saturday at Chelfham, a very good field met the Master, Major Penn-Curzon. Deer were reported to be harboured in Smithapark and Mr W L Ashton, with the tufters, very quickly roused two stags which went up the valley as if for the moor. At Huntacott however, they were blanched by the whip, and retracing their steps got back to Smithapark, where the pack was laid on. Both stags were brought down under Loxhore Cott on to Millwood, under Long Timber, and across Youlston Old Park to Sepscott, pointing straight down the valley. Blanched again by some ladies at Collar Bridge, they took to the water at Bratton Bridge, going upstream and again through Long Timber and over Shirwell Old Park to Sepscott, where the deer separated. The strongest and best, who by his subsequent tricks proved to have been oft hunted, turned to the right, crossing the Shirwell road and going down over Bradlicott, and Heartpiece to Blackford Mills, and then turning upstream under Putner, ran the water through the meadows to Sloley, making the pace very hot at times. The hounds all the way were moving easily, but at a great rate. Crossing the Ilfracombe road, the stag went through the nurseries to Blakewell, crossed Tutshill and then went in front of Mr Soares' residence, Upcott, on to Ashford, passing with a few miles of Barnstaple town. Turning right-handed, the stag crossed Springfield, close to the late Sir Wm Williams' kennels, and went through Mainstone, under Luscot to Ashwood. Turned by two men, he came back from close to Ash Farm through Ashwood, crossing the Braunton and Barnstaple road, under Heanton Punchardon. There he took to the stream and ran under West Ashford, where he took a gateway in full view of the field, off again, but evidently feeling his long run, he got under Lower Luscott, where he was taken about 6.30 in the evening, the run having lasted since 12 o'clock and ending about four miles from Barnstaple.

May 4th 1905

The Barnstaple Staghounds are likely to be given up says *The Field* after a short existence dating from 1901 in which year they were established to keep down the Exmoor deer, which had become exceedingly numerous. At first the pack was under the joint Mastership of Captain Ewing Paterson and Mr Arundell Clarke but in 1903 a change took place and Major Penn-Curzon assumed command. In his interesting book staghunting with the Devon and Somerset Staghounds, Mr Philip Evered significantly remarked three years ago.

"At Barnstaple there is hardly room for the maintenance of a sufficiently large herd to stand regular hunting from season to season, and the lie of the land hardly admits of many days being given by invitation to a pack on the western border of the moor itself."

October 5th 1905
Barnstaple Staghounds
A Kill in the Sea

A small party including Mr W L Ashton (acting Master), Miss Amy Pitts-Tucker, Miss Soares, Messrs Soares (MP), W E Arthur, J Berry, D Smalldon, and W Herniman, met by invitation at Upcott for the purpose of finding and hunting a fine stag which had been seen on the Upcott estate from some days past. The stag, a heavy animal, was harboured in Upcott Covers, and was soon found by the tufters. After a round or two in the covers, the stag broke and he went in the direction of Mr Tarr's mills at Wrafton, then close to Mr Isacc's machinery works, crossed the railway line at Braunton by the gates, passing straight over Braunton great field, the marshes, and the huge sandhills where there was a good deal of twisting about, and from there to Saunton Sands where he was viewed by the hounds and went to sea. A boat went off and the stag was captured and dispatched, and afterwards drawn to shore and carted to Upcott. The deer was cut up and subsequently distributed by the direction of Mr Soares. It is reported that there are several deer in the Barnstaple district and a hope has been expressed that staghunting will not be allowed to drop, for both staghounds and harriers will have no difficulty in obtaining sport.

On the shore line, watching the stag at sea

Barnstaple Staghounds, January 1906

The meet at Bratton yesterday brought out a very good field, many ladies being present. The hounds were put in at Smythapark Wood where five hinds were turned out, two making away down the valley towards Barnstaple. After a fast run of 3 1/2 hours, a fine hind was taken at Loxhore.

Barnstaple Staghounds, March 8th 1906
A Fast Run

The followers of the Barnstaple Staghounds had a most enjoyable run on the occasion of the meet at Bratton Fleming. Two hinds and a calf were found in Thorne. The tufters ran them swiftly down to Smithapark, where they turned to the right for Loxhore Cott. Hence the pack was laid on, and made straight for the Warren, thence turning left-handed to Ford Mill Woods and Shirwell Park. At this point one hind and the calf turned towards Chelfham and headed for Goodleigh. The other hind, which the pack continued to pursue went on to Sepscott, Collar Bridge, and into the river Yeo near Pitt Farm. She crossed over Pitt and Smokey Lane, leapt some high banks, and, passing the front of Mr Seldon's house at Roborugh, crossed the Shirwell road. She continued to the right by Mr Ackland's farm into Shirwell Park. Then, turning yet again to the right, she crossed the Shirwell road at the top of the village, made across Mr Dayman's and Mr Western's, onto the Old Park, and back to Ford Mill Wood and Woolley. She took the water near Cott Down, and entered the Arlington refuge, hounds had then to be whipped off. The distance covered was about 20 miles. there was no check and the pace throughout was exceedingly fast.

An advert from 1906, perhaps about the time when people were thinking about selling their carriages and going hunting in a car.

October 22nd 1908, Barnstaple Staghounds

Mr W L Ashton of Barnstaple, taking advantage of the fact that a few couples of the old Barnstaple Staghounds were available, arranged a meet for yesterday at Chelfham, a large number of sportsmen attending. It had been reported that deer were plentiful in the locality and with Mr Ashton in charge, a hind was soon started in the Youlston Covers. The quarry made for Bratton, but soon returned through Youlston Wood to Sepscott. It took to the water just below Shirwell Mill, with hounds pressing it hard. With hounds close in attendance, the quarry crossed the railway line at Chelfham, and made its way to Kingdon Gardens, taking the water several times. The deer ran through Raleigh, and on reaching Pilton Bridge, leaped the parapet into the river Yeo. The advent of the deer caused great excitement in this part of the borough and a large crowd followed the field. The stag made its way behind Fair-View Terrace to Pottington, and it was reported to Mr Ashton that it had crossed the river Taw. Mr Ashton and others proceeded to Anchor Wood, but were unable to find any trace of the deer. They returned to Pottington, and it was subsequently found that the quarry had followed the water to Ashford, information being received that the deer was in a field at Ashford with some cattle. The hounds resumed the hunt, and shortly afterwards the deer was taken in a field belonging to Mr Fisher, the exciting hunt extended over four hours.

December 31st 1908 Barnstaple Staghounds

The Barnstaple Staghounds had a splendid run on Saturday, when there was a large field to meet the new Master B Chester at Chelfham. By the generosity of Mr Brass of Chelfham Bridge, the company was entertained at breakfast, and advantage was taken of the occasion by Mr A F Seldon to propose the health of the new Master which was received with rounds of cheering. Mr Chester acknowledged the complement and attributed the acquaintance with the hounds to Mr W L Ashton of Barnstaple, who, in turn, they also cheered for his good sportsmanship. Mr H Waldron proposed, and M Squire seconded a vote of thanks to Mr Brass for his hospitality. The compliment was acknowledged amid cheers. The tufters drew Shirwell Covers blank, although deer had been there recently. They then went on to Smithapark and there noble deer were found. The Master came up with the pack and soon there was a burst of music. The hounds ran towards Barnstaple where the deer took to water and went on to Coxleigh and took to water again here owing to darkness the hounds were stopped.

Barnstaple Staghounds
January 10th 1909

This hunt was discontinued a few years back owing to the hindrance to hunting caused by certain estates being closed to all packs. Of late, however, stirred by complaints as to damage done by deer, several local sportsmen, prominent amongst them being W L Ashton, of Barnstaple, one of the keenest followers of Nimrod of the district, the hunt has been re-established on a smaller scale, Mr B Chester being the new Master, while Mr Ashton fulfils the duties of hon huntsman. On Wednesday the new hunt enjoyed a splendid run. About half past two the tufters started a fine stag in Lock's Wood. Crossing to Cottdown and Millwood they were reinforced by the pack, which the Master had been holding in readiness. In bringing them up the Master got what might have been a very nasty spill, his horse falling upon his leg. However, though considerably bruised, he was able to finish the run. Sinking the valley, the stag ran to Collar Bridge, where he entered the water and ran down the stream to Snapper. Determinedly breaking through a cordon of riders who tried to induce him to keep down, he ascended the steep wood, and afforded the Master and Mr Brass, of Chelfham, a nice private gallop over Brightleycott Down. Crossing Sepscott Lane he picked up the rest of the field and took them to Long Timber, soiled at Shirwell Mill, then crossing the main road ran via Lower Loxhore, Specott Barton, and Bratton valley to Combe and Smithapark. It was now dark, and though we could hear hounds running him well down the river again, we were compelled to call off, regretting the find had not taken place an hour earlier, when we should doubtless have killed. – "LUPUS," in the *Western Morning News*.

January 14th 1909
Barnstaple Staghounds
New Master

Mr B Chester, a new comer to North Devon, who has taken up residence at Fremington, has undertaken the Mastership of the Barnstaple Staghounds. Hunting has commenced under the new regime and on January 15th, Mr Chester will entertain the farmers of the district at dinner at the Golden Lion Hotel, Barnstaple. Mr Chester is a man of extensive experience. He first hunted in Kent; at the age of 18 he owned his own pack of harriers. He was a school fellow of the late Mr W V Benfield, one time Master of the Barnstaple and North Devon Harriers. Later he spent seven years at various German universities, and he subsequently took up dog-breeding and exhibiting as a hobby, his fancy being bulldogs with which he won many prizes. He has judged this breed of dog frequently at home and abroad, and he entirely ran a London bulldog show for many years. He is a life hon member of the Principal Bulldog Club. Mr Chester has interested himself in the breeding of both dogs and cats, winning over 300 prizes. Now, however, he only has, at Fremington, a cocker spaniel and probably the only Mexican hairless dog in England. Besides these, he keeps a brace of wolves, a special hobby of his being the care of pet wolves. He had hunted in Devon, Cornwall, Kent and Scotland, and also chased the wild boar in Germany. He had baited the bear with dogs in the old English style. Mr Chester had found time to contribute a good deal of sporting news to the papers, and he has been on the staff of the leading kennel organs of England and Austria. He still contributes to the same over the nom de plume of 'Lupis' or the initials of his former exhibiting name 'HCB'. It is interesting to note that no less than eleven dogs from his former kennels have been chosen to illustrate their respective breeds in Messrs Cassells recently published new book of the dog.

Those followers of the Barnstaple Staghounds who allowed the mist and rain to keep them at home on Wednesday lost a very good run. At 2.30 the tufters started a fine stag in Locks Wood. The Master B Chester was holding the pack in readiness close at hand, and in bringing them up experienced what might have been a very nasty spill, his horse falling with him and rolling on his leg within six feet of a place where, curiously enough, a hunt member had a somewhat similar accident a week ago. Luckily, beyond a few bruises, no damage was done. The stag ran over Long Timber and Youlston, down the valley to Collar Bridge, and then downstream to Snapper. Here he turned up the wood and, boldly breaking through a cordon of riders, ran over Coxleigh and back into the wood to Kingdon Gardens. Again breasting the hill, he afforded the Master and Mr Brass a nice private gallop over Brightley Cottdown to Coxleigh. Picking up the field as he crossed Sepscott lane, he took them by Newbarns back to Long Timber, soiled at Shirwell Mill, then crossed lower Loxhore and Sepscott Barton, and headed upwards to Bratton Mill, and thence round to Coombe Wood and Smithapark. The hounds were tight behind, but the light was beginning to fail, and nothing more could be done.

Barnstaple Staghounds
January 15th 1909

At the invitation of the new Master of the Barnstaple Staghounds (Mr B Chester) on Friday evening, a large company of farmers over whose land the Hunt runs, met for dinner at the King's Arms hotel, Barnstaple. The Master occupied the chair. Among those present were Messrs W L Ashton (the hon huntsman), G Lidstone, W Hoskings, M Squire, T W Smith, W M Burridge, M W Dickinson, C L Brass, T Dalling, L W Ashton, W Parker, W Marquis, and many others.

Mr Smith proposed "The health of the Master," which was accorded musical honours.

Mr Chester, in responding, thanked them very much, and said he would do all he could for the Hunt. As he had been a hunting man all his life, it stood to reason that anything in connection with hunting had always been a source of great pleasure to him. They would have to pull together, and he hoped they would all do what they could to help him. (Hear, hear.) In particular, those who followed the Hunt must take care not to trespass on forbidden land. For that reason he did not advertise his meets. If he found anyone entering covers he would take the hounds straight home. (Hear hear.)

"The health of the Hon Huntsman (Mr Ashton)" was given by the Master, who said that Mr Ashton had the true interest of sport at heart, and he asked them to drink his health with all possible honours. (Applause.) – Mr Ashton suitably replied.

The chorus of "John Peel" was lustily sung, and other toasts and songs followed.

Mr M Squire, in proposing "The Landowners and Farmers" coupled with it the names of Mr Comer Clark and Mr Tom Dalling. Mr Squire referred to the obligation of the Hunt to the farmers of the neighbourhood, who were a very sporting lot.

The toast of "The Kennelman" was proposed by Mr Lidstone, Mr Williams replying.

March 18th 1909
Barnstaple Staghounds
A Kill at Combe Martin

Combe Martin was alive with excitement on Saturday, when a deer was taken in the middle of the town. It has, all this season, been most difficult to get deer away from the coverts. On this occasion, however, as hounds were being walked along the road from one covert to another, old Rustic and Guardsman suddenly threw up their heads, and the next minute, breaking through the hedge, they put up a straight running deer, which had been lying like a rabbit in a gorse bush a few feet from the road. Owing to the impossibility of crossing the "forbidden ground", the field experienced difficulty in getting away with the flying pack, but after making a long detour caught up with the tail hounds and enjoyed a very pretty run with good hound work from the find at Loxhore, via Churchill, Shortacombe, Berry Down, Sterridge and Berrynarbor.

The hunted deer was seen by several spectators in the Athletic Club Grounds, making its way from the Saltwood rifle range towards Eastacotts, just above the Rectory Wood, clearing gates and fences in splendid style. Crossing the Glebe Lands, it halted for a few minutes and began quietly feeding in the middle of a flock of sheep, not far distant from where Mr W Wyborn, the occupier, was at work. The barking of his dog evidently startled the deer for it immediately made tracks for the Combe Martin Valley, crossing the Rectory Allotments and Mr Arthur Norman's garden, to reach the main stream that runs almost parallel to the lengthy street. The three leading hounds were close to it, however. Down the stream, which was nowhere hardly knee-deep, past Baker's workshop, the Old George and Dragon Inn garden, and the school playgrounds, the deer hurried onwards until it came to the bridge close by the residence of Dr Mannings, where it was caught. Mr Ernest Norman, a butcher, who lives close by, came up and promptly administered the coup de grace. By this time there were almost a couple of score of excited spectators near the scene, few of whom had had an opportunity of seeing a wild deer before. The "field" arrived about ten minutes afterwards, and included Messrs B Chester (Master), W L Ashton, Stanbury, Seldon, Squires, Gillard, Master Gillard, Burridge, and "Uncle Litson," the much respected veteran Exmoor sportsman. Owing to the impossibility of crossing certain grounds on the way, the field were unable to keep up with the flying pack, and were compelled to make a long detour from the find near Loxhore to Berrydown, Sterridge, and Berrynarbour, and thence on to Combe Martin. The huntsmen subsequently dined at the King's Arms Hotel.

October 28th 1909
BSH

A novelty in the High Bickington district was provided yesterday when the Barnstaple Staghounds met at Week Cross, although the weather was wet and stormy there was a large field. As there are no deer in the locality, a carted stag provided the days sport, the stag being released on Azes moor. The tufters ran the quarry to Wadlands, where after 20 minutes' grace had been allowed, the rest of the pack were laid on. Hounds followed the course to Burrington moor, where the stag turned to the left and made straight for Burrington. it soon, however, turned sharply to the left and reached the Taw near Portsmouth Arms, closely followed by the hounds. The deer took to the water and proceeded downstream, being taken and killed near Umberleigh. The enjoyable run lasted 2 1/2 hours.

August 19th 1910
Barnstaple Staghounds

This meet will be carried on during the forthcoming season by the same executive as last year, ie Messrs B Chester (Yelland, Master), W L Ashton (Barnstaple, Hon Huntsman), and W L Ashton and Barrett (hon secretaries). At the request of certain landowners steps are being taken which will, it is confidently expected, result in an increased number of deer being taken. As the executive carry on the hunt without requiring a guarantee fund, it is hoped that sportsmen will subscribe liberally and early towards expenses incurred. Non-subscribers will be "capped" at each meet they attend.

November 25th 1909
BSH

The pack again enjoyed a very good run on Saturday, when the meet was at Bratton Cross. Several coverts were drawn blank, but on the tufters entering Woolley Wood, signs of deer were at once evident. From Cottdown the field could view a herd of six, led by a noble stag, move slowly towards Smythapark then, frightened by a sheepdog, they returned while four, within two gunshots of Loxhore, lay and sunned themselves in a field. Yet, though so near, they were unattainable owing to the conditions which prevail in that locality. Not until about 2 o'clock did the welcome tidings arrive that a hind had crossed the water near the Arlington smithy. By the time hounds were brought all the way round Corkscrew she was nearly an hour ahead. But the pack took up the line with a grand burst and then it was away over a rough country with some stiff boundary fences and trappy banks. The line was through East Down past the mill towards Berrydown Cross, at which time the line was almost identical with that taken by the Combe Martin deer last season. Hopes were entertained of a similar happy ending. From here she raced through Berry Bowden, Willscott Cleave, crossed the

Watermouth to Kaypitts and doubled up and down the water. Some of the pack slipped away silently, and reports next morning said they ran their deer to sea near Ilfracombe pier. The rest remained with the field and failing to hit the line, stopped about half a mile from Ilfracombe where with a failing light, it became necessary to call off. There were only present at the finish the Master, the hon huntsman, Messrs Williams, Webber (Braunton), T W Smith, J Stanbury, and one other.

The Barnstaple Staghounds meet at Heddon Mill, 1909.
Note the caption which says "Barum Staghounds"
(Barum being the old name for Barnstaple)

March 3rd 1910
BSH

Barnstaple Staghounds enjoyed a clinking good run in the Braunton district on Saturday, through the kindness of Mr F Cole and Mr G Style, and the interest taken by keepers Martin and Hannaford. Unhappily the Heddon Mills meet has twice been blank this season, so that on the third occasion there was a small hunt. The pack was thrown on near Foxhunters Inn, and a deer soon rose in front of them. The run lasted for over four hours and there was no check exceeding five minutes. The deer was constantly in view, and it is estimated the distance covered was bout 35 miles, the quarry was taken in Mr R Irvin's cottage garden in South Street, Braunton, in the presence of a crowd of onlookers.

CHAPTER 13

THE MINEHEAD STAGHOUNDS (MR RIDLER'S)
IN THE BARNSTAPLE COUNTRY

Throughout 1910 and into early 1911, the *North Devon Journal* ran articles on the Minehead Staghounds. The Baily's Hunting Directory of the time gives no mention of them at all, but further research in the *West Somerset Free Press* reveal that the Minehead Staghounds were a draft pack from the Devon and Somerset Staghounds. On account of the damage being done by the enormous herds of deer in the district, Captain A S Adkins, Master of the Devon and Somerset Staghounds found it necessary to temporarily send a draft pack to Mr J W Ridler of Minehead who, under Captain Adkins' directions, had consented to hunt them. Between 1910 and 1911 they were referred to in the West Somerset Free Press under different headings: "Mr J W Ridler's draft of staghounds"; "A draft of the Devon and Somerset Staghounds"; "The Minehead Staghounds"; "The Minehead draft staghounds"; "Mr Ridler's Staghounds". There follows an account of a meeting to discuss plans on the introduction of Mr Ridler and his staghounds in the Barnstaple district, at this stage it seems that regular hunting by the Barnstaple Staghounds had ceased. Also following are accounts of the Minehead Staghounds who visited and hunted the Barnstaple district as well as their own between 1910 and 1911.

—— STAGHUNTING. ——
—o—
A PUBLIC MEETING
Will be held in the
GUILDHALL BARNSTAPLE,
TO-MORROW, FRIDAY, OCTOBER 28TH,
To consider the question of Hunting the Deer in the Barnstaple Country this Season. Chair to be taken at 4 p.m. [8297]

267

The Minehead Staghounds hunted by J W Ridler.
Photograph courtesy of Alan Stapleton.

HUNTING APPOINTMENTS.

DEVON AND SOMERSET STAGHOUNDS.
Saturday, October 29...... ......Larkbarrow
At 10.45 a.m.

MINEHEAD STAGHOUNDS.
Saturday, October 22 .... Bratton Fleming
Wednesday, October 26 Cheltham
Saturday, October 29 . ..... Bratton Fleming
At 10.30 a.m.

EXMOOR FOXHOUNDS.
Saturday, October 22...... .... Warmsmead
Tuesday, October 25 .. .. Shallowford
Friday October 28 . . Landacre Bridge
At 11 a.m.

DULVERTON FOXHOUNDS.
Friday October 21 ... . Combe
At 10 a.m.

STEVENSTONE HOUNDS.
Thursday, October 20 . Cranford Cross
Monday, October 24 . .. . Meeth
At 10 a.m.
Thursday, October 27 . Port Bridge
At 9 a.m.

SOUTHMOLTON HARRIERS. ·
Friday October 21 . Garland Cross
Tuesday, October 25. Broadmoor Cross, Warkleigh
Friday, October 28. . Sandyway
At 11 a.m.

INSTOW BEAGLES.
Saturday, October 22 . ..... Newton Tracey
Wednesday, October 26 Mullacott Cross
At 11 a.m.

Hunting appointments in 1910, including the Minehead Staghounds hunting in the Barnstaple district

269

Staghunting in the Barnstaple district.
Meeting at Barnstaple, October 28th 1910

A public meeting was held at Barnstaple Guildhall on Friday afternoon to consider the question of hunting the deer in the Barnstaple country this season. Mr E R Berry Torr, secretary of the Instow Beagles, was voted to the chair on the proposition of Mr A E Ardold JP, seconded by Mr G Litson. There was a very large attendance, including Messrs E J Soares MP, B Chester (late Master of the Barnstaple Staghounds), J Webber Ridler (Master of the Minehead Staghounds), T W Smith, C L Brass, Congdon, J Stanbury, M Squire, D Smaldon, G Litson, C Withecombe, A E Arnold, J Baker, A J Gillard, Watts, H Saxon, G Pitts-Tucker, Openshaw, W L Ashton, T Symons, Pugsley, W Burridge, T S Watkinson, J Trump, M Ffoulkes, W Richards junr, T Dallyn, G Prodger, A A Seldon, and H H Hamling.

The Chairman said he did not expect to have to preside, but was happy to know that they were anxious to see sport carried on in a regular and legitimate way. The Instow Beagles had the support of every landowner and farmer over the country which was hunted, and he should like to see the same with regard to staghunting in the Barnstaple district. They had, of course, to consider the opinions of those who might differ from them. There were some, no doubt, who did not see eye to eye with them. He asked them to bear with those people, and to treat their feelings with respect and in a sportsmanlike manner.

Mr Ridler with his Minehead Staghounds had been invited by the Devon and Somerset Staghounds to hunt the Barnstaple country in the coming season and arrangements for this were then discussed.

First, they had to see how far the country was capable of being hunted and it was suggested that Mr Ridler should hunt the country to the end of December. If they managed to keep out of Arlington, if sufficient interest were taken in the pack, and if everything went on satisfactorily, they might call at other meeting. They all appreciated what hunting did for a neighbourhood, and if everything went on satisfactorily to Christmas then he thought they might consider the matter on a more permanent basis. For the present they must look on the whole thing as temporary.

Mr T W Smith believed that they would get very good sport without entering the Arlington coverts. He moved that they hunt the country until December next.

Mr Pugsley, of Shirwell, seconded, and spoke of the increasing number of deer. He hoped if Mr Ridler went on with the hunt the farmers would give him every support. Hunting was a good thing for them all. The farmers would supply oats and if they bred good hunters they could sell them. He strongly objected to having the deer killed in anything but a legitimate sportsmanlike manner. Nothing was so bad as shooting them, for the deer only escaped to linger in pain and die. He strongly urged on the followers of the hunt the necessity of respecting the rules of hunting by closing the gates and refraining from damage. There was no reason why there should not be splendid hunting in the Barnstaple country.

The motion was carried unanimously.

Mr Soares stated that Mr Ridler had got leave to hunt all this side of the Lynton and Barnstaple Railway. He proposed that Mr Stanbury be the secretary and Treasurer of the hunt, at least till Christmas, and that he be asked to receive subscriptions. This was seconded by Mr T Dallyn, and carried unanimously.

Mr Soares said in regard to the expenditure incurred in maintaining the hunt, Mr Ridler had mentioned a very reasonable sum, and if there was any craving for sport the sum of money he asked ought to be found.

On the motion of Mr Arnold, seconded by Mr Soares, a vote of thanks was given to the Chairman for presiding.

The Chairman in his reply, reminded them that their thanks were greatly due to Sir Edward Chichester and Mr Comer Clarke for the support they gave the hunt in preserving the deer.

The Minehead Staghounds March 5th 1910
(in the Barnstaple District)

The hunt enjoyed on Saturday the best day probably known on this side of the country, shortly after the pack was thrown in near Foxhunters Inn a deer rose in front of them, and ran at great pace across the Willingcott road, behind Spreacombe House to Pickwell, then, hard pushed, back to Willingcott Farm, and through Buttercombe Wood. At the lower end this deer broke cover and soiled, and then went over Buckland Down to the Braunton fisheries. Hounds were close, and the line now ran over Nethercott, North Buckland, through Spreacombe Cover and Pickwell towards Woolacombe where it was thought she had gone to sea, but close to the water hounds turned to the right through Roadway, and at Eastacott our quarry lay down in full view of the field, but hounds were soon there and back went the chase over Roadway and through Pickwell Covers to Heddon Mills. Showers of sleet and icy rain made scent so bad that hounds had to puzzle it out at a walking pace on the plough, but across Nethercott and through Buckland Wood matters improved. Above Braunton the deer soiled, crossed the railway, then turned, and beat up and down stream several times, three times coming to the bridge near the New Inn. But hounds were close up all the time, and the quarry was taken in a cottage garden a hundred yards from the New Inn in the presence of a large number of the population of Braunton. The run, at which the Master was out for the first time since his illness, occupied just over 4 hours, part of the country being pretty stiff. There was no check exceeding five minutes, the deer was constantly in view, and those familiar with the country estimated the distance covered at between 30 and 35 miles.

April 10th 1910 Minehead Staghounds

A complimentary dinner will be given at the Plume of Feathers Hotel, Minehead on Monday April 18th by tradesmen and others interested in Minehead to all stewards, farmers and keepers who have so kindly supported and helped to make the necessary draft of staghounds, hunted by Mr J W Ridler and maintained by the inhabitants of Minehead, so successful. If any stewards, farmers or keepers should not have received a personal invitation, the committee trust that they will accept this as a cordial invitation and hope to be honoured with their company. Captain A S Adkins, Master of the Devon and Somerset Staghounds, has kindly consented to attend. Visitors and others are cordially invited and the committee trust that every tradesman of Minehead will be present, dinner at 7pm sharp.

Captain AS Adkins who was Master of the Devon and Somerset Staghounds in 1910, and who attended the dinner given by the Minehead Staghounds at the Plume of Feathers, Minehead.

6th October 1910
Mr Ridler's Staghounds

Mr J Ridler, whose staghounds were so much appreciated in the Minehead district last season, (and for the continuation of which hunt, we understand, a numerously-signed petition of owners and occupiers has been presented,) has been hunting the Barnstaple district during the past week, but luck has not turned his way. on Tuesday scent was very bad, and little could be done, though it improved towards evening, when darkness saved the quarry. On Thursday the meet was at Chelfham, when scent was worse, and, though Longtimber held two stags, hounds could not run a yard. The Master unfortunately hurt his back, which prevented him from attending the meet at Bratton on Saturday, when a local sportsman, aided by the whip, took charge of the pack. Smythapark was drawn blank, and it was unfortunately not until late in the afternoon that a five year old deer quitted Woolley wood, and, crossing Cott, entered the Warren. Then, running across the park, it went through Sepscott and crossed the valley near Kingdon Gardens, passing close to Ivy Lodge, being then only five minutes in front of the hounds, despite poor scent. Here the first delay occurred, owing to the field and hounds being turned by barbed wire. Through Derby the line went, and here a hind was said to be also afoot. A further delay was caused by locked gates at Pitt, the key of which could not be found at once, so that as the field passed along the Ilfracombe road the deer was half an hour ahead. Through Putnor, hounds held the line, but night was fast closing in, and though the deer was reported to be done to a turn and hardly able to cross his banks, he saved himself in pitch darkness in the stream near Muddiford. Half an hour more daylight and he would have certainly been killed.

The large attendance at the meet, including Messrs Comer Clarke, Fanshawe, De Las Casas, Stanbury, Litson, Chester (Late Master of the Barnstaple Staghounds), Northcote, Parminter, Gorrings, and several ladies, as well as motors and carriages, amply demonstrated how the district suffers from the lack of a properly organised hunt. At the request of the sports-men of the district, Mr J Ridler has kindly consented to stay a few more days in the Barnstaple district.

Wednesday's fixture was at Collar, about three miles out of Barnstaple, where Mr Gorrings kindly entertained a fair field, which turned up to meet the Master, who, everyone was glad to see, had recovered from last week's spill. Wooley Wood produced a deer which however turned back into Arlington. The necessary was found in Millwood, and made down the valley at a good pace.

He was soon in the wood and retraced his steps but only for a short distance when he soiled just under Mr Parker's farm and was taken.

October 15th 1910
Mr Ridler's Staghounds

Mr Ridler's Staghounds on Saturday had a splendid run from Bratton Fleming with over sixteen miles without a check, when hounds were stopped owing to having changed to a fresh deer. The time was one hour and fifty minutes and only three of the field – Messrs Stanbury, Chester and Richards – besides the hunt officials, were in at the finish. The veteran staghunter Mr Gabriel Litson experienced a nasty fall, his horse blundering at a bank and injuring his rider's knee. But with great pluck he remounted and nearly finished the run.

October 22nd 1910
Mr Ridler's Staghounds

The Minehead Staghounds had a splendid day on Tuesday when the meet was at Chelfham. Mr H Flatman of Minehead had come down to harbour, and reported a fine stag in Wooley Wood. At 11.30 this noble stag crossed Cott and ran down Longtimber through Youlston wood, then turned up the Bratton Valley, through Hill Wood and Smythapark wood to Button bridge, next turning to the right to Wistland Pound, then left handed to Burdick and Kentisbury Ford and East Down rectory, back over Garmansdown to the Warren at Shirwell, Loxhore Cott, then down the water to Kingdon Gardens, about three miles from Barnstaple. Here he proved himself a good old warrior, charging several of the hounds, and giving the late Master of the Barnstaple Staghounds (Mr B Chester) who helped to take him, an anxious moment, when it looked as if he would be pinned against a tree when finally brought to book at 3.50, at Kingdon Gardens where the kill took place. He proved to be a stag of great age, with enormous slots and his head was a remarkable one, showing on the one side, brow, bay and tray with three on top. The width from point to point was 30 inches. Good judges estimated him to be twelve or fourteen years of age. Among those at the kill were Mr E J Soares (MP), Miss Soares, Mr J W Ridler (Master) and his brother Mr T K Ridler, Messrs G Litson (Barnstaple), T W Smith, S L Hancock (Fremington), B Chester, late Master of the Barnstaple Staghounds (Fremington), Prodger (Bratton), Yendell (Spreycott), W Richards, Pugsley, Northcott, D Smolden (Barnstaple), H Flatman and Morris (Minehead) and Mrs and Miss Smolden.

October 29th 1910
Mr Ridler's Staghounds kill at Barnstaple

Mr Ridler's staghounds from Minehead met at Chelfham on Wednesday. Cott was drawn, and news was brought that three deer were going on by Longtimber. The tufters were laid on, and went on to Shirwell Old Park, through the cover and on to Sepscott. The pack was laid on in Sepscott Lane, and the stag ran to Coxleigh Covers, then to Kingdon Gardens, and after retracing his steps, came down the stream to Frankmarsh, in the borough of Barnstaple where he was dispatched. A portion of the pack got on the line of another good deer at Coxleigh and ran to Muddiford, the quarry however being lost in Kinnacott Courtyard.

December 10th 1910
Mr Ridler's Staghounds meet at Chelfham

These hounds met at Chelfham on Saturday. Unfortunately the Master and huntsman Mr J W Ridler could not attend and the horn was carried by Mr T W Smith, his brother-in-law. Owing to the hounds being brought down by the Great Western Railway, they were a little late at the meet. The tufters were drawn out and taken to Woolley Wood, Shirwell, which was drawn blank, as was also Cott Down Wood. Soon afterwards, in Woolley Warren, hounds roused a couple of hinds and ran them very fast across Little Park, Shirwell Park, to New Barns Wood, and then to Coxleigh Wood, where the two deer divided and took to the water. The pack was laid on and ran the bigger of the two up through

Coxleigh Wood and part of Coxleigh Farm, crossing Sepscott lane and farm into the wood, through the New Barns Wood and Youlston Wood, when the deer again took to water below Black Pool Bridge. She continued in the water to above Shirwell Mill, and then went over Mill Farm, and ran into a herd of about 10 deer. The herd dispersed and hounds were stopped. It being 3 o'clock, the hounds were brought back to the new kennels at Ivy Lodge, all returning except two.

29th December 1910
Grand day with the Minehead Staghounds

The Minehead Staghounds met at Chelfham on Bank Holiday and had quite a red-letter day. The large company was entertained by that good sportsman Mr C L Brass with refreshments. At 10.30 Tom Tame, with whip, brought to Chelfham 19 couples quite fit and looking well. Among those at the meet were Mr E J Soares (MP) and Miss Soares, Messrs De Las Casas, A F Seldon, A A Seldon, B Fanshawe, Kent, Ashford, B Pitts-Tucker, R Tamlyn, W Richards, R Stanbury (hon sec), G Litson, A J Gillard and son, Burridge, F Ratcliffe, F Hancock, W L Ashton, W Ashton junr, E Chamings, H Rawle, Pugsley, Master D Petter, Northcote, Chanter and Son, Perkins, Prideaux, Miss Squire, and a host of others. There was quite a regiment of bicycles and people on foot. The sport was quite suitable for a Bank Holiday, deer were often viewed, causing great excitement among those in the turnpike road. The horn was again carried by Mr T W Smith.

A deer was found in Sepscott Wood at 12.15, and was followed by the tufters through Youlston Wood. The quarry turned back over the park, and he was found running through Newbarn's Wood to Coxleigh. Here the deer, which was an old one, found a substitute in a younger animal, which the greater part of the pack followed, 3 1/2 couple of the leading hounds and some of the riders stuck to their deer, but most of the field went with the pack, which ran back over Newbarns and Sepscott Wood, Youlston and the Parks. Being headed at Longtimber, the deer had to retreat back over the Wood and

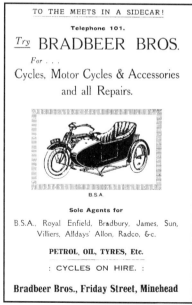

Park to Kingdon Gardens; it was evidently a woodland deer. He was killed at 3 o'clock at Bratton Cross, and just then Mr Parker, of South Molton, ran up shouting that the big deer was soiling in the river just below. Of course it was not long before the hunstman came with the hounds. This deer had taken a much better line, running to Kingdon Gardens, down stream to Frankmarsh, to the Cemetery, by Crookman's Corner and Maidenford, taking a right hand turn and running just above the Great Western Station, back over Gorwell to Mr John Lee's farm, up stream to Coxleigh Wood and farm to Sepscott Wood and Newbarns, Youlston, and on to Chelfham. Here he took the stream and ran up to where he was met by the pack. The hounds then ran him through Youlston Wood, to Longtimber, Little Park, to Hillwood, up over Mr Western's farm to Cottdown Wood Down. Arriving here the huntsman tried hard to keep him from Arlington, but in vain. In coming over the cover fence, he nearly jumped on Mr De Las Casas' horse, and consequently managed to get into Arlington just in the nick of time to save his life. This ended a most enjoyable day's sport, and one that will be remembered for a very long time.

January 21st 1911
Mr Ridler's Staghounds

Tom Tame brought up seventeen couples of hounds at the meet at Bratton on Saturday, the whole pack looking very fit. The morning was frosty, and there was some little delay in starting. Tufters were started in Mr Comer Clarke's Covers at Smythapark. A deer was started, but it ran in the wrong direction, and a fresh start was made at Youlston, which with Millwood and Longtimber, was drawn blank. A relay of tufters were taken out at 1 o'clock and the Warren was being tried when news came that a deer was seen in Woolley Wood. As Mr Orlando Chichester was shooting in this wood, Mr T W Smith who was carrying the horn, decided not to follow the sign. A deer was ultimately found in Millwood at 3.15 and the pack was laid on in the fields above the Rookery. She crossed the main road and the river and took a straight line for Youlston wood, and then, turning right handed, hounds hunted their deer through Newbarns, Sepscott into Coxleigh wood, and, at a clinking pace, brought the deer to water below Kingdon Gardens. At Raleigh she was headed by some people on foot, and she consequently turned back over the marshes to Kingdon Gardens again. A few hounds were observed running her at great pace through the bottom of Coxleigh Wood, Sepscott, and Newbarns. But the pace was too great for the hind, and she went to the right, and back through the covers to Coxleigh wood again. Here she was viewed by Mr Stanbury, with a few hounds. At this point it was found that some part of the pack was running another deer, and, darkness setting in, it became necessary to collect the hounds. This was done, leaving three of the pack running the deer for Brightly Cott Farm by moonlight. Had we found a little earlier, we should, without doubt have accounted for our deer. Among those out were Miss Soares and a lady friend, messrs Fanshawe, Docking, Northcote, Burridge, McMenamin, A De las Casas, Gillard, Down, J & W Pugsley, A Seldon, Chamings, W Richards, Brooks, Crang, Perkins, Miss Squire, Master Bowden, Mr J Litson and Mr Stanbury (hon sec and treasurer).

March 16th 1911
Mr J W Ridler's Staghounds in Barnstaple district.
A Red Letter Day

The Minehead Staghounds met at Loxhore Cott on Saturday, and had quite a red-letter day. At the outset there was news of an outlying stag in the parish of Eastdown, and at a quarter to eleven, hounds were moved away in the vicinity of the deer, which was found in less than half an hour running over Garman Down and Woolley Wood, where a substitute was found in a bigger deer which crossed over to Smythapark wood, where the pack was laid on. The stag turned up the valley first, but soon changed his mind, and came down stream to Bratton Cross, then went up through Youlston Wood and over the park to Newbarns Wood, Sepscott Wood and Farm, crossing the road and over Coxleigh Farm to Raleigh Wood. He ran down to water, leaving it some way above Mr John Lee's and going up over his farm to Roborough. When on the top he came down by the quarry, and crossed the main road to Blakewell Mill, through Tuts Hill Wood, going straight up to the top making for Upcott, but turned right-handed into the lane that leads up to the lodge, where hounds were foiled for a few minutes with sheep. Crossing the road over the field towards Guinaford, and turning left under Lee House, Marwood, the quarry went down the valley to White Hall, then left-handed to Mainstone, not going far in this direction. He ran right-handed to Luscott Barton and on to Beer Charter, to the southern boundary of Halsinger Down, where he made a sharp left-hand turn to Boode, then running through the Winsham valley, over North Winsham to Stoneybridge level-crossing, where he doubled back to Lower Winsham. He then crossed the Ilfracombe railway to Incledon Wood, through Incledon Farm, crossing the Georgeham road above Darracott when he turned left-handed to Lobbythorne Style, running down into Lobb to East Saunton, then ascending the hill to the top of Saunton Down. Here several of the horses began to show signs of having had enough, many keeping to the coast road, this proving lucky. The deer continued its course over the north side into Croyde Brake, where it lay up for a few minutes. Re-found, he made straight for the sea, where he was met by a lot of riders who came along the coast road, the deer then setting his head for Croyde. This was a very exciting moment, as if he had crossed the road he would have gone to sea, with the tide running up strong. He went on to the back of the village to South Hale Farm, towards Darracott, where he turned sharp back for Croyde village, at the lower end of which he made into the orchard, where he stood at bay for the first time, then broke away and took to the road and ran through the village in full view of the inhabitants, crossing and re-crossing the road and stream for some little time. The quarry was killed by Mr T W Smith. The animal was one of the gamest stags ever hunted. The run, too, was one of the longest known, being 4 3/4 hours from find to finish, and extending over nine parishes – Eastdown, Arlington, Loxhore, Bratton Fleming, Shirwell, Barnstaple, Marwood, Braunton and Georgeham, the estimated distance being from 32 to 34 miles – a record for a stag with two on top both sides. Several gentlemen who were playing golf at Saunton entered their motors, following to Croyde to see the finish. The horn was carried by Mr De Las Casas, who was in at the end with Messrs T W Smith, Stanbury (Hon Sec), A F Seldon, Down, Northcott junr, Isaac, Lock, Alford, Jones, Perryman, Lee, Litson, Collings and the Whip, several others having pulled up.

Correspondent (*Chain Snaffle*)

This concludes the reports of the Minehead Staghounds' hunts in the Barnstaple district throughout 1910 and the early part of 1911.

We can see how the district was suffering from the lack of a properly organised hunt at this stage and that the slow demise and break up of staghunting in the Barnstaple district was imminent but for the Minehead Staghounds who extended the existence of the hunt for a few extra years. After 1911 there was no more mention of the Barnstaple Staghounds, so we can safely say this was the end of staghunting in the Barnstaple district. There was also no more mention of the Barnstaple and North Devon Harriers.

Three years later, in 1914, we see how the deer were suffering, through being shot and maimed, without a pack of staghounds.

21st February 1914
Shooting Red Deer near Barnstaple

The *North Devon Journal* says:
A novelty in the annals of sport in North Devon was provided on Wednesday, when an organised red deer 'drive' took place in the Chelfham district. The explanation is supplied by the fact that owing to the cessation of stag hunting in the Yeo Valley due to the closing of the Arlington coverts to the hunt, red deer have become very plentiful, with the result that complaint it made of the extent of the damage done by the deer. Wednesday's drive excited widespread interest, and there was a large gathering of farmers and others, many being provided with guns. Over 30 deer were roused and two were shot. It is understood that arrangements are being made for a visit of the Devon and Somerset Staghounds to the district.

An advert from 1926:

History of the Devon & Somerset Staghounds
by
William Scarth Dixon
(Author of "The Sport of Kings", (etc)
23 ILLUSTRATIONS
ONE SHILLING
From Barnes, Bookseller, Barnstaple and Sydney Harpers & Sons, 27 High Street Barnstaple

---

28th February 1914
Red deer near Barnstaple

Owing to the objection in some quarters to the hunting of the red deer, they have, of late years, become more plentiful in the neighbourhood of Barnstaple, and have done considerable damage to farmers crops, so much so that there have been many what the writers considers unsportsmanlike methods adopted to catch the deer with rope and wire snares, and some of these noble animals have been found partly strangled possibly where they have been yoked for hours or even days, and it is said that a farmer who tried these experiments had his bull caught in the snare prepared for the deer. There have also been many deer shot at, some of which have no doubt been maimed for life, while quite recently a drive was arranged, some persons on horses, and others, with dogs and guns, and report has it that although many shots were fired, only two deer were killed. But what about the remainder fired at, for it is only fair to surmise that some of the shots, though not sufficient to kill outright, took effect. Surely these methods for reducing the number of these fine animals are to be much deplored, at the same time, it is evident that some steps will have to be taken to scatter them and cause them to return to their native land, the forest of Exmoor. The only sportsmanlike means are staghounds, and it is a pity that the landowners do not approach the Master and the committee of the Devon and Somerset Staghounds for the purpose.

A FRIEND OF THE DEER.

281

CHAPTER 14

THE NORTH WEST DEVON DRAGHOUNDS

T he last pack of hounds to hunt in the Barnstaple district, were the North West Devon Draghunt, they met in the town and had their functions there. This hunt was in existence between 1934 and 1939. They appear to have alternately hunted the drag and the fox. There follows some of their runs.

4th October 1934
North West Devon Drag Hounds

Lovers of sport and pastime will be glad to know that the North Devon Drag Hunt is thriving apace under the energetic Mastership of Lieut-Col R Longstaff, DSO, JP. Already eight couple of hounds are being trained by Mr AJ Hopkins, who is giving his services as huntsman. They are being kennelled close to Twitchen, Mortehoe, in excellent accommodation arranged by the Master. Judging by the support given by the majority of landowner farmers and prospective members, an excellent season is assured. It is now many years since the district had a pack of hounds, and they will provide a popular novelty for many who have never seen them at work, and a grand sport and pastime for participants in the chase.

It is hoped to hold the opening meet at Twitchen, Mortehoe, on Saturday, October 20th, and dates and times of future meets will appear under hunting appointments in the this paper.

8th November 1934

NW DEVON DRAG HUNT (2PM)

Sat Nov 10th	Combe Martin
Wed Nov 14th	North Walk, Barnstaple
(bye meet)	
Sat Nov 17th	Croyde Bridge
Sat Nov 24th	West Down Village

NORTH-WEST DEVON DRAG HOUNDS

By the kind permission of Sir William Williams, Bart, hounds met at Upcott, Barnstaple, last Saturday, under ideal weather conditions. It was a truly picturesque and memorable scene, for it is now more than 25 years since a hunt met there. Owing to the absence of the Master, Mr Harry Prideaux acted in that capacity.

There was the very large field – nearly fifty riders – and many others had assembled to see the meet, including Mr James Paton, an ex-Master of Hounds.

THE RUN

Hounds were put into the Pinctum behind Upcott, and went quickly up the line which took them through the back drive across the road to Tutshill, and down through Blakewell Mill to Blakewell, carrying a good head. With hardly a check they turned into the Blakewell Copse and carried the line to Broomhill and on into the Ilfracombe Barnstaple road, and thence over the hill to Sloley, where they were at fault. They were then cast on the other side of the valley, and hunted very prettily up to North Hill.

Here they were lifted and taken on through Shirwell Village to Shirwell Old Park. They were very soon running again, and with Benzine leading gave the field a splendid gallop across the park into Newbarn Wood. Turning right handed they hunted on into Sepscott Wood, through Sepscott Farm, and Coxleigh Barton into Smoky-lane and out into the field below Trayne, to end a very fast and glorious hunt.

We all sympathise with Mr C W Lee over his regrettable accident, and wish this thoroughly good sportsman a speedy recovery

"DRAGMAN"

3rd December 1934
NW Devon Drag Hunt: Shirwell Meet

With the prospect of hunting a fox, Saturday's meet was at Shirwell. The weather was fine and mild, and there was the large field of nearly fifty, which included many farmers whose land we had passed over while out with the drag.

Hounds were put in at the higher end of Newbarn Wood, but drew without any success. It was not until drawing up the cleave to Mr May's piggeries that they put up their quarry. A fine strong fox had been lying very tight in the bracken, and hounds and most of the field were after him before he broke away to run over the park. Unfortunately he was headed and turning down to the stream he crossed and ran into the lower end of Newbarn Woods, hounds hard on his brush. With plenty of music they hunted him through Sepscott Wood to the road just above Collar Bridge, where again he was headed as he was making his way for Coxleigh. By doubling back through the top of the wood, he was lucky enough to put up another fox, which split the pack. Hounds had to be collected after this, and Mr Hopkins took them on to where a very light coloured fox had been viewed. However, scent was cold, and it was some time before he was roused lower down in the cover. After running him for some minutes other foxes split the pack again, and after drawing up to Newbarn Farm hounds were called off.

I think everyone will agree that we had a good day's sport, and we were exceedingly unlucky not to kill. It must be remembered that the foxes in these covers had not been disturbed this year before, and that this was one of our first ventures in hunting them. It is not too much to expect that we shall do better next time.

Spectators had a good view of the day's sport, and besides seeing many foxes, saw two hinds making off towards Coxleigh. Our thanks are due to Mr C H May, Mr Friend, Mr John Tucker, and Mr Codde for so good a day.

DRAGMAN

Preliminary Notice.

North-West Devon Drag Hounds
MOUNTED GYMKHANA

Organised by the Combe Martin and District Supporters, will be held on

AUGUST BANK HOLIDAY

in a Field on the main Ilfracombe Road kindly lent by F. J. Richards, Esq'

PLEASE KEEP THIS DATE OPEN

Further particulars later.   45

21st February 1935
NW Devon Drag Hunt

Hounds met at Pilton Bridge, Barnstaple, on Saturday, and in spite of a wet and blustering day, a good crowd attended. Among a field numbering some twenty-five riders we were pleased to see that good sportsman Mr C W Lee back in the saddle again.

THE RUN

After casting in front of Pilton House, Mr Hopkins soon had his hounds running, and crossing the Higher Raleigh road they ran to Westaway Corner without a check. Turning down Smokey-lane, they hunted a somewhat catchy scent over the high ground to Brightley-cott, and dropped down to the Shirwell road, where

285

they circled the meadows on the left-hand side of the road before making away for Hartpiece and North Hill and thence to Abscott. Wheeling left-handed, they showed us a very pretty bit of hunting down the Slowly Valley and on through the cover to Blakewell. Turning in to Blakewell Mills, they ran with a good head skirting Tutshill to Pippacott, where we ran into a smart shower. This slowed down the hunting as hounds worked a line through the Lee Woods to Marwood.

From a hunting point of view I think that this was one of the best runs we have had. The pace was never very fast, but it was very enjoyable to be able to sit back and watch hounds hunting out the line away in the distance, rather than riding hard a-top of them.

Congratulations are due to Miss Lorna Penhale and Mr Symons for planning so good a run. I understand that Miss Penhale is starting a riding school in Barnstaple. Good luck to her.

DRAGMAN

24th October 1935
North West Devon Drag Hunt
Barnstaple Dinner to Farmer Friends
Mayor and Hunting

The North-West Devon Drag Hunt held a dinner in the Bell Hotel, Barnstaple, on Friday evening, presided over by Lieut-Col R Longstaff, DSO, JP, MDH, at which invitations were extended to farmers who had permitted the hunt over their land. The gathering included Mr B G Lampard-Vachell (prospective National Conservative candidate). During the evening songs were sung by Messrs A J Jeffrey, A S Jones and R Woodward. The accompanists were Dr F H Hollingshead and Miss McGuire, the latter for Mr Jones's songs.

After the serving of an excellent dinner and the honouring of the loyal toast the Major of Barnstaple (Councillor Charles F Dart) proposed "The North-West Devon Drag Hunt," and spoke appreciatively of the hunts' friendship with the farmers. Some people, he said, contended that hunting should cease, and they argued it was cruel. There was also the argument that hunting was the real life-blood of this district, and assisted in the breeding of good horses and keeping men engaged in looking after the hounds. In his opinion, however, drag hunting only was not cruel. It seemed a pity that the stag should be harassed to death, but he did not wish to express any opinion on that subject. He remembered attending one of the drag hunt meets, when he found 50 or 60 horses there, and he knew that this would never have been possible without the generosity and kindness of the farmers.

The chairman, responding, explained that the drag hunt had been in existence barely a year, and he thought that the members of the committee had worked extremely well, as had also the huntsman, Mr Hopkins. Until last year he (the chairman) had never been out hunting in this country since the South African War, so really he was absolutely new to it. However, he thought he had helped to make the season fairly successful. (Applause.) If it had not been a success he did not think there would have been so many happy faces present. He expressed a desire to see more farmers participating in the hunt. The roads, he said, were not fit for horse traffic, and this he supposed was one of the reasons why so many people did not keep horses. If the farmers were as good to the drag hunt this year as they had been during the past season, no-one could wish for more. (Applause.) In conclusion he extended a hearty invitation to the farmers to attend the celebration of the first birthday of the drag hunt at his residence at Mortehoe.

Mr Michael Slade in submitting "The Guests", said that hunting in this country could go on only by the courtesy of the landowners and farmers. He explained that the majority of damage was done through ignorance, and however observant were the master and secretary they could not see everything. The farmers had, though, been very helpful. Adverting to the Mayor of Barnstaple's remarks, he was bound to say that hunting was not very cruel. Staghunting he would not, however, say anything about. Lately the horse trade had not been too good, but he thought it was now on the up grade. In conclusion he said he did not think that hunting would do any harm, but if there were any bad cases of damage help could always be obtained from Lieut-Col Longstaff.

Mr William Dunn JP, CC, in acknowledging, thanked Mr Slade for his kind words and the sympathetic way in which he had proposed the toast. It was good of Lieut-Col Longstaff, and the committee, he continued, to provide farmers and landowners with a dinner, for he could assure them it was a God send. (Laughter.) He was pleased to hear that the farmers were considered good sportsmen, and generous in every way. The drag hunt, he thought, was a very good organisation, for the young people learnt to ride, which was excellent exercise. He had been used to people riding over his farm, and he was certain that the farmers would continue to assist the hunt in the provision of good sport. (Applause.)

In proposing the toast of "Absent Friends – The Ladies," Mr Reginald Petter remarked that the ladies had played a very important part in the success of the hunt, and in this connection thanks were due to Misses Longstaff and Reed, who had so ably whipped in the pack during the season, to Mrs J C Dixey and Miss Lorna Penhale for their splendid work on the committee and sub-committee, to the ladies of Combe Martin and Woolacombe Gymkhanas, and likewise to Mrs T Dunn and Miss Dunn, who were very good riders to follow.

At the close the chairman moved a vote of thanks to the sub-committee who organised the dinner, and also to the artists. The vote was cordially endorsed.

NORTH WEST DEVON HUNT

Farmers' Dinner

TO BE HELD AT

THE BELL HOTEL, BARNSTAPLE

ON

FRIDAY, October 15th

1937 at 7 o'clock.

Tickets 2/6, can be obtained from Members of the Hunt, or R M. Petter, Lloyds Bank Ltd., Fox's Branch, Barnstaple

1001

8th April 1937
North Devon Drag Hunt

The North West Devon Drag Hunt held very successful hunter trials at Bradiford, Barnstaple, yesterday, when there was a good entry and a fairly good attendance. Mrs Charles Chichester presented the prizes as follows:

Horses the property of subscribers of the NW Devon Draghounds and for farmers residing in the country: , 1, Lieut-Col R Longstaff's Valkyrie; 2, Mr A J Hopkins' Sergeant-Major; 3, and special farmer's prize, Mr A S Fry's Joey. Also ran: Mr G S Chugg's Little Man, Mr F R Fry's Becky Sharp, Col Longstaff's Pat, Mr C W Lee's Miss Judy, Miss E Longstaff's Pendragon, Mr T Charley's Whizz Bang, and Mr A J Hopkins' Danny Boy.

Open: 1, Mr F T Heal's Tommy; 2, Mr J Hill's Irish Lad; 3, Lady Ann Walpole's Nancy. Also ran: Mr C John's Charlie, Col Longstaff's Pat, Mr A J Hopkins' Sergeant-Major and Danny Boy, Miss E Turner's Gipsy and Julie, Mrs A Thurston's Nonsuch, Mr J Hill's Irish Lad, Miss E Longstaff's Pendragon, Col Longstaff's Valkyrie, Lady Ann Palpole's Nancy, Mr F R Fry's Becky Sharp, Mr Charles Chichester's Skipjack, and Mr F T Heal's Tommy.

Horses owned by members of the hunt and ridden by a lady follower: 1, Col Longstaff's Valkyrie; 2, Mr C W Lee's Miss July; 3, Miss E Longstaff's Pendragon. Also ran: Col Longstaff's Pat and Valkyrie, Mr A J Hopkins' Danny Boy and Sergeant Major. Mr G S Chugg's Little Man, Mr A S Fry's Joey, and Mr C W Lee's Miss Judy.

Teams of two horses, open: 1, Mr T T Heal's Tommy and Mr H Hill's Irish Lad; 2, Mr A J Hopkins' Sergeant major and Danny Boy. Also ran: Lady Ann Walpole's Nancy and Mr C Johns' Charlie, Col Longstaff's Valkyrie and Pat, Miss E Longstaff's Pendragon, Mr A S Fry's Joey, Mr F R Fry's Becky Sharp and Mr G S Chugg's Little Man.

31st March 1938
North-West Devon Hunt
Supporter's Meeting: Extension of Territory Possible

North West Devon Hunt is to continue. This was decided at a meeting of supporters of the Hunt in Fremington House, on Tuesday night, presided over by Mr Charles Chichester (Hall). Hunting over the Barnstaple side of the Stevenstone country has recently been undertaken.

Lieut-Col R Longstaff JP, who some four years ago took on the Mastership of the Drag Hunt started in North Devon, explained that he had since been approached by the Master of the Stevenstone Hunt and had taken over part of that country in order to keep fox hunting going there. He intimated, however, that without a guarantee it would be impossible to carry on. It was for the supporters of the Hunt to decide whether they could form a committee to be responsible for raising £200 a year, which was the minimum on which kennels and hounds could be kept. If that were done he was prepared to carry on as Master, and he thought it would be possible to negotiate with the Stevenstone Hunt for an extension of territory.

After much discussion it was agreed to raise the minimum subscription, and it was considered possible, with gymkhanas and other events, to get the necessary guarantee. A committee was appointed. Lieut-Col Longstaff then intimated his willingness to carry on, and was heartily thanked.

Oare Deer Park
from The Red Deer of Exmoor by Archibald Hamilton pub. Horace Cox 1907

CHAPTER 15

THE BARNSTAPLE AND NORTH DEVON
BADGER CLUB

Apart from having a pack of staghounds, a pack of harriers, and a pack of otterhounds, Barnstaple also had a Badger Club known as the Barnstaple and North Devon Badger Club. Here are just a few articles showing the sport they had.

January 8th 1914
Barnstaple and North Devon Badger Club

The outcome of a recent representative meeting at Barnstaple, which a number of local gentlemen attended, was the formation of the Barnstaple and North Devon Badger Club. Amongst the objects of the club are: (1) The hunting of the country in a regular and systematic manner; (2) the preserving of badgers by discouraging promiscuous digging during breeding seasons; and (3) the breeding and training of working terriers. The Club has already received substantial support. The financial side is also on a sound basis. Mr Arthur B Heinemann, founder of the Devon and Somerset Badger Club, has given the Club his strong support and goodwill. The Hon Secretary is Mr W L Barrett, the Master Mr H J F Stewart, and the Deputy Master Mr W A Collins.

The opening meet took place on Boxing Day, and a large field witnessed two fine badgers taken out. A number of meets have been arranged to the end of January, when badgers will be left for the breeding season (until about the beginning of May).

Barnstaple and North Devon Badger Club
5th February 1914

This Club provided fine sport at two meets at Clovelly last week, three badgers aggregating 85lbs being taken. One of the badgers was a sow, and the breeding season being at hand it was despatched to and liberated in another district. A local sporting gentleman, at whose invitation the meets were held at Clovelly, kindly provided lunch and refreshments for the field. The Club held its last meet for the season on Monday last, a large party assembling at Kipscomb Wood to meet the deputy-Master and party from Barnstaple. Two badgers (23lbs and 30lbs) were taken. During the month in which the hunt was held 12 badgers were found; 9 were captured, 2 bolted, and one was left owing to the darkness.

April 16th 1914
Badger Club Dig

A bye meet of the Barnstaple and North Devon Badger Club took place at Combe Martin on Monday. Hentridge Woods were drawn, and a badger soon found by "Ilfracombe Spot," who stayed under for three hours, during which time a couple of diggers were obtained and the pipe containing the badger and terrier dug down to. "Ilfracombe Gipsy" was used to draw the badger, which was tailed and bagged, and proved 25lbs weight. Several terriers were tried, including "Ilfracombe Nell," "Teaser," and Mr Southcombe's dog (which entered well and behaved quite like an old hand at the game). The Club met at the kind invitation of Mr Charley of Hanstridge, a keen supporter of the Hunt. The opening meet of the Club will take place in a week or so's time. – "BROCK."

May 14th 1914
Barnstaple and North Devon Badger Club

The opening meet of the Barnstaple and North Devon Badger Club took place at Chittlehampton on Wednesday. A few bye-meets had previously been arranged and good sport always shown, and it was with confidence that a fairly large field turned out to meet the Master and party from Barnstaple.

Several earths were tried, but "brock" was not found until after 3 o'clock in the afternoon. The field were partaking of a late lunch while the Master with "Ilfracombe Gipsy" and "Vic" were still trying fresh earths. A tally ho! and a few notes on the horn soon brought the field to a small earth in an adjoining wood where "Ilfracombe Gipsy" had just found her badger. Afterwards several terriers were put to ground, some local ones entering in first-class style.

"Ilfracombe Spot", "Teaser", "Turk" and "Nell" and "Barum Rags", "Gipsy" and "Tartar" all went under; the latter terrier is from the ilfracombe kennel, and should be a splendid dog to draw, being full of pluck. He is now owned by the Deputy Master, who nearly parted with him last week, but after his performance at this hunt it is anticipated he will be loth to part with such a game terrier. "Barum Spot" was given very little opportunity to draw, the badger being allowed to walk out only to be tailed and bagged. On the balance "Brock" scaled 26½lbs. Messrs Fred Day and Rather and several gentlemen from South Molton were out together with Messrs Hulland and Madge, of Georgenympton, Mr Vickery and party from Chittlehampton. The field numbered in all about 60. –"Brock."

April 24th 1924
Blue Fox at Chelfham

Mr A Ash of the Angel Hotel, Barnstaple, participated in a Badger hunt with four or five working terriers on Good Friday on the land at Chelfham Barton. Two badgers – weighing respectively 20lbs and 32lbs - were taken from the same holt, in which was also discovered the lair of a fox. Mr Ash captured a beautiful young blue fox, a rare find in North Devon. Unfortunately it was killed by an instrument while the digging opertions were in progress. Although quite young the animal had a lovely coat and the promise of an exceptionally fine brush. The animal is to be preserved. Other members of the family were left undisturbed. A third badger scaled 24lbs. On Monday Mr Ash accounted for two more badgers at Mr Turner's, Dean, Goodleigh, one being 35lbs and the other 29½lbs. One often hears of the moon being made of green cheese, but not of a blue fox on Bank holiday Monday.

The Barnstaple and North Devon Badger Club outside the Fortescue Hotel, Mortehoe.
26th December 1923
5th from right is the hon Secretary Mr W L Barrett, and 9th from right is Mr H Stewart, the Master

So ends the short yet remarkable story of the Barnstaple Staghounds, one that lay dormant for so many years until discovered recently through old copies of the *North Devon Journal*. I felt that here was a story which deserved to be told and this motivated me to put pen to paper, as I did in my book on the Tiverton Staghounds. I hope you have enjoyed this one as much.

I wrote this history partly as a tribute to the Huntsmen and Masters who hunted with the Barnstaple Staghounds. However it is also a tribute to the reporters of the time who have left us with much valuable information on this pack and enable us to build such a clear picture of the hunt.

Throughout this book, some great hunts have been relived, and some hardened Barnstaple stags have been 'hunted' for the first time in 94 years.

Richard Lethbridge MBE